RHETORICAL ECONOMIES OF WHITENESS

RHETORICAL ECONOMIES OF WHITENESS

EXPLORING THE INTERSECTIONS OF POWER, PRIVILEGE, AND RACE

Edited by Robert Asen
and Casey Ryan Kelly

THE OHIO STATE UNIVERSITY PRESS
COLUMBUS

Copyright © 2024 by The Ohio State University.
All rights reserved.

Library of Congress Cataloging-in-Publication Data
Names: Asen, Robert, 1968– editor. | Kelly, Casey Ryan, 1979– editor.
Title: Rhetorical economies of whiteness : exploring the intersections of power, privilege, and race / edited by Robert Asen and Casey Ryan Kelly.
Description: Columbus : The Ohio State University Press, [2024] | Includes bibliographical references and index. | Summary: "An edited collection that examines the interactions of rhetoric, economy, and whiteness to illuminate how economic and racial structures and practices in the United States perpetuate social inequalities and frustrate efforts to enact alternatives. Essays take up issues of housing, education, judicial appointments, politics, entertainment, and culture to critique how whiteness resecures its social position in economic contexts"—Provided by publisher.
Identifiers: LCCN 2024022623 | ISBN 9780814215784 (hardback) | ISBN 0814215785 (hardback) | ISBN 9780814283806 (ebook) | ISBN 0814283802 (ebook)
Subjects: LCSH: White people—Race identity—United States. | Racism—United States. | Race awareness—United States. | Power (Social sciences)—United States. | Race—Social aspects—United States. | Rhetoric—Social aspects.
Classification: LCC HT1575 .R44 2024 | DDC 305.809/073—dc23/eng/20240805
LC record available at https://lccn.loc.gov/2024022623

Other identifiers: ISBN 9780814259320 (paperback) | ISBN 0814259324 (paperback)

Cover design by Brad Norr
Text design by Juliet Williams
Type set in Adobe Minion Pro

CONTENTS

INTRODUCTION	Economizing Whiteness, Rhetoricizing Economy: Investigating Discourses of Whiteness and the Production of Racial and Economic Inequality ROBERT ASEN AND CASEY RYAN KELLY	1
CHAPTER 1	"The Cause Is the Consequence": Biden's Nomination of Justice Ketanji Brown Jackson and the Right to Include CORINNE MITSUYE SUGINO AND CHARLES ATHANASOPOULOS	29
CHAPTER 2	Racially Restrictive Covenants and the Spatialization of Race: Whiteness as Property and the Rhetorics of Whiteness DEREK G. HANDLEY AND ANNE BONDS	52
CHAPTER 3	Gradations of Self-Reflexivity: Reckoning with Racial Privilege in Progressive White Parents' School Choice Discourse KELLY JENSEN	75
CHAPTER 4	Rhetorical Economies of Whiteness through Citizenship Excess in Higher Education GODFRIED ASANTE, PAULAMI BANERJEE, ADEDOYIN OGUNFEYIMI, AND STACEY K. SOWARDS	98
CHAPTER 5	The *Master* Narrative: A Black Nihilistic Reading of Misogynoir, H(a)unting, and US Higher Education RICO SELF	122
CHAPTER 6	Jeremy Lin and the Global Rhetorical Economy of Whiteness LINSAY M. CRAMER	145

CHAPTER 7	Parasitic Movement in the Public Sphere	
	GEORGE (GUY) F. McHENDRY JR. AND KYLE R. LARSON	168
CHAPTER 8	Cisnormativity as Rhetorical Obstruction: The Silencing Effects of White and Cisgender Innocence	
	V. JO HSU	193
AFTERWORD	The Endgame of Whiteness	
	THOMAS K. NAKAYAMA	218

List of Contributors	225
Index	229

INTRODUCTION

Economizing Whiteness, Rhetoricizing Economy

Investigating Discourses of Whiteness and the Production of Racial and Economic Inequality

ROBERT ASEN AND CASEY RYAN KELLY

Carrying lengthy, polysemous, and often contentious histories, the three key concepts in our volume's title—rhetoric, economy, and whiteness—function forcefully in our current era as mediators of human interaction, builders of institutions, objects of ideological conflict, sites of struggle, crafters of common cause, and sources of division. From antiquity onward, practitioners and scholars of rhetoric often have felt a burden of justification, defending the legitimacy of their efforts against characterizations of rhetoric as a "knack" and the deceptive opposite of reality. Recurring scholarly debates address the function and scope of rhetoric, whether it resides narrowly in the statements of civic leaders or circulates expansively in the constitution of our shared worlds. From a classical conception as the management of the household, and a subordinate relation to the exalted stature of the polis, economy has gained prominence as a shaper of societies and director of nations.[1] Contemporary political leaders pledge themselves to economic growth and its attendant rewards, while business leaders and entrepreneurs present themselves as heroic innovators and stewards of prosperity. As a marker of identity, claim of superiority, and exercise of privilege, whiteness has served European and

---

1. On the growth of the household and its invocation in neoliberal policy rhetoric, see Megan Foley, "From Infantile Citizens to Infantile Institutions: The Metaphoric Transformation of Political Economy in the 2008 Housing Market Crisis," *Quarterly Journal of Speech* 98, no. 4 (2012): 386–410.

Western imperialist visions and societal hierarchies by distinguishing its qualities from the supposedly inferior knowledges, cultures, and societies of people deemed not white.[2] On this basis, whiteness justifies exploitation, conquest, marginalization, exclusion, and recurring violence; it deploys symbolic and material resources to advance the interests of people identified as white.

In this volume, we bring together rhetoric, economy, and whiteness in a contemporary US and Western context conditioned by neoliberal regimes of governance and white supremacy to illuminate how hegemonic economic and racial structures and practices in the United States perpetuate social inequalities that shape participation in public life and frustrate efforts to enact more just alternatives. Seeking to refashion society and human relationships, as Wendy Brown suggests, "neoliberal rationality disseminates the *model of the market* to all domains and activities—even where money is not at issue— and configures human beings exhaustively as market actors, always, only, and everywhere as *homo oeconomicus*."[3] Affecting people, places, and possibilities, neoliberalism implicitly and explicitly modifies the meaning of economy to promote market economies and to discredit other potential economic and political alternatives. Neoliberalism idealizes market economies as sites for realizing human agency, individual freedom, and sovereign choice. Neoliberal champions in politics, culture, and society represent markets as generating innovation and excellence, justly rewarding economic winners and punishing losers. In her foundational scholarship on whiteness, Cheryl Harris critiques this tendency to regard "the 'market value' of the individual as the just and true assessment."[4]

As these processes have unfolded, public advocacy for white supremacy has gained prominence in the United States, Europe, and elsewhere in recent

---

2. On rhetoric, whiteness, imperialism, and colonialism, see, e.g., Patricia Davis, Brandon Inabinet, Christina L. Moss, and Carolyn B. Walcott, "Decolonizing Regions," *Rhetoric & Public Affairs* 24, nos. 1–2 (2021): 349–64; William Mpofu, "DeColonising Rhetoric [of Modernity] in the Age of Alternative Facts," *African Journal of Rhetoric* 10, no. 1 (2018): 65–88; Tiara R. Na'Puti, "From Guåhan and Back: Navigating a 'Both/Neither' Analytic for Rhetorical Field Methods," in *Text + Field: Innovations in Rhetorical Method*, ed. Sara L. McKinnon, Robert Asen, Karma R. Chávez, and Robert Glenn Howard (University Park: Pennsylvania State University Press, 2016), 56–71; and Catalina M. de Onís, *Energy Islands: Metaphors of Power, Extractivism, and Justice in Puerto Rico* (Berkeley: University of California Press, 2021).

3. Wendy Brown, *Undoing the Demos: Neoliberalism's Stealth Revolution* (New York: Zone Books, 2015), 31.

4. Cheryl I. Harris, "Whiteness as Property," *Harvard Law Review* 106, no. 8 (1993): 1778. Harris does not reference neoliberalism explicitly, which is not surprising since scholarship on the topic had not yet proliferated at the time her article was published.

years.⁵ Moreover, its contemporary force circulates widely through what Eduardo Bonilla-Silva terms "color-blind racism," through which "whites rationalize minorities' contemporary status as the product of market dynamics, naturally occurring phenomena, and blacks' imputed cultural limitations."⁶ Discourses of colorblindness support ostensibly neutral norms and practices that sustain an unequal racial and, as Bonilla-Silva's reference to "market" indicates, economic status quo. These discourses abstract individual agency and social standing from contexts and histories; they deny and deflect from structural forces shaping society to insist upon individualist explanations and assessments that legitimate existing institutions and arrangements. As Stuart Hall observes, neoliberalism depoliticizes structural inequality and bolsters market logics promoting collective resignation to racist, classist, and sexist arrangements wrought by capitalist accumulation.⁷

Rhetorical scholars have investigated the mutually reinforcing qualities, dynamics, and implications of neoliberalism and whiteness. For instance, in an analysis of the discourse of intellectual property law, Anjali Vats demonstrates how legal and political institutions effectively render intellectual property as a kind of white property that may be extended to nonwhite others conditionally and in specific situations. Vats argues that these processes depict white people as generators of knowledge to whom nonwhite others must demonstrate fidelity and deference. In one case, Vats considers how US public debates and legal cases about music sampling normalize "white practices of knowledge making as central to expertise and thus property ownership."⁸ On this basis, the use of sampling techniques by primarily Black hip-hop artists constitutes theft of white property. In this discourse, rather than expressing creativity, artists using sampling engage in the facile copying of another's imaginative work. Addressing the larger stakes of her analysis, Vats writes that "race and economics are intertwined in ways that guarantee the valuation of *particular* kinds of ideas with *particular* kinds of owners." To redress this situation, Vats calls for scholars to ask questions that may answer "fundamental

---

5. Mark Davis, "The Online Anti-Public Sphere," *European Journal of Cultural Studies* 24, no. 1 (2020): 143–59; and Kyle R. Larson and George F. McHendry Jr., "Parasitic Publics," *Rhetoric Society Quarterly* 49, no. 5 (2019): 517–41.

6. Eduardo Bonilla-Silva, *Racism without Racists: Color-Blind Racism and the Persistence of Racial Inequality in the United States* (Lanham, MD: Rowman & Littlefield, 2010), 2.

7. Stuart Hall, "The Neo-Liberal Revolution," *Cultural Studies* 25, no. 6 (2011): 705–28.

8. Anjali Vats, *The Color of Creatorship: Intellectual Property, Race, and the Making of Americans* (Stanford, CA: Stanford University Press, 2020), 69. On whiteness, knowledge, and ownership, see also Vincent N. Pham, "Truth as White Property: Solidifying White Epistemology and Owning Racial Knowledge," *Communication and Critical/Cultural Studies* 20, no. 2 (2023): 288–305.

and pressing questions about race and capitalism."⁹ By attending to rhetorical economies of whiteness, we may consider how issues of exchange, resources, and value inform public discourse and engagement.

Across rhetorical scholarship on neoliberalism and whiteness, conceptual and thematic resonances indicate the mutually informative relationship of race and economy. Scholars in both areas have explored how these discourses situate the individual as the primary social actor and how commitments to individualism protect racial and economic privilege. As discourses of color-blindness promote an individualist perspective to deny racial privilege and discrimination, colorblind discourses promote market economic practices by insisting that differences in identity and social positioning do not affect individual success, and that discriminatory actors only disadvantage themselves by rejecting opportunities for exchange.¹⁰ Public discourses on neoliberalism and whiteness both place individuals in competitive environments characterized by zero-sum relationships that represent gains for one actor as losses for another, as evidenced in anti-immigrant discourses that ascribe economic and cultural dangers to migrants and the prospects of changing societal demographics.¹¹ More broadly, privilege itself intimates zero-sum relationships as the advantages afforded to one individual operate exclusively to produce disadvantages for others.¹²

As powerful social forces, discourses of neoliberalism and whiteness employ ahistoricism and decontextualization to justify current racial and economic structures and practices and to disqualify critiques.¹³ If colorblind norms and practices treat all individuals the same, then no individual suffers because of their differences. If market economies present all individuals with

---

9. Vats, *Color of Creatorship*, 207–8. See also Lisa A. Flores, "Choosing to Consume: Race, Education, and the School Voucher Debate," in *The Motherhood Business: Consumption, Communication, and Privilege*, ed. Anne Teresa Demo, Jennifer L. Borda, and Charlotte Kroløkke (Tuscaloosa: University of Alabama Press, 2015), 243–65.

10. Thomas K. Nakayama and Robert L. Krizek, "Whiteness: A Strategic Rhetoric," *Quarterly Journal of Speech* 81, no. 3 (1995): 291–309; Rebecca Dingo, "Linking Transnational Logics: A Feminist Rhetorical Analysis of Public Policy Networks," *College English* 70, no. 5 (2008): 490–505.

11. J. David Cisneros, "A Nation of Immigrants and a Nation of Laws: Race, Multiculturalism, and Neoliberal Exception in Barack Obama's Immigration Discourse," *Communication, Culture & Critique* 8, no. 3 (2015): 356–75.

12. As Ersula Ore renders this dynamic starkly, "The mattering of black life remains predicated upon a possessive investment in whiteness and the maintenance of a white worldview." Ersula J. Ore, "Black Death and the Limits of the Utopian Gesture," in *The Conceit of Context: Resituating Domains in Rhetorical Studies*, ed. Charles E. Morris III and Kendall R. Phillips (New York: Peter Lang, 2020), 104.

13. Raka Shome, "Outing Whiteness," *Critical Studies in Media Communication* 17, no. 3 (2000): 366–71.

the same opportunities for success and failure, then individuals succeed and fail primarily through their own initiative and aptitude. Along these lines, on the topic of education policy, Laura Hernández explains that neoliberal advocates' adoption of a colorblind ideology individualizes racism and pathologizes students of color. This approach benefits white students by "leaving institutionalized forms of racism that disproportionately benefit them intact while discursively and structurally erasing them as a dominant group."[14] In education and elsewhere, this approach attributes unequal outcomes to the dynamics of meritorious competition.[15] For these reasons, both neoliberalism and whiteness cast inequality as a necessary virtue. White supremacy manifests in both vicious forms, through ongoing brutality and violence, and supposedly benign forms, as, for example, when white advocates assert a benevolent desire to uplift nonwhite groups and expect gratitude and deference in return.[16] Scholars such as Jodi Melamed and Roopali Mukherjee argue that neoliberal actors often employ benevolent expressions of multicultural uplift to fold markets—the very seat of whiteness and structural racism—into antiracist projects.[17]

Discourses of neoliberalism and whiteness work together to sustain racial and economic inequalities and to disqualify structural critiques and appeals for alternatives. Exploring how neoliberal and conservative advocates try to reconcile their insistence that the nation has reached an era of full civic equality amid ongoing inequalities among Black and white Americans, Kimberlé Crenshaw discerns the continuing influence of the racial and market logics of the infamous Supreme Court *Plessy v. Ferguson* decision, which affirmed the constitutionality of "separate but equal" segregation laws. Crenshaw argues that *Plessy* and its contemporary counterparts, such as court decisions that reject affirmative action policies by asserting a colorblind Constitution, propagate a binary opposition of nominal, public equality with substantive, private

---

14. Laura E. Hernández, "Complicating the Rhetoric: How Racial Construction Confounds Market-Based Reformers' Civil Rights Invocations," *Education Policy Analysis Archives* 24, no. 103 (2016): 9.

15. Jo Littler identifies the language of meritocracy as "a key ideological term in the reproduction of neoliberal culture." Jo Littler, *Against Meritocracy: Culture, Power and Myths of Mobility* (New York: Routledge, 2017), 2.

16. Matthew Houdek, "Racial Sedimentation and the Common Sense of Racialized Violence: The Case of Black Church Burnings," *Quarterly Journal of Speech* 104, no. 3 (2018): 279–306; Casey Ryan Kelly, "Donald J. Trump and the Rhetoric of White Ambivalence," *Rhetoric & Public Affairs* 23, no. 2 (2020): 195–223; Jenna N. Hanchey, "All of Us Phantasmic Saviors," *Communication and Critical/Cultural Studies* 15, no. 2 (2018): 144–60.

17. Jodi Melamed, *Represent and Destroy: Rationalizing Violence in the New Racial Capitalism* (Minneapolis: University of Minnesota Press, 2011); Roopali Mukherjee, "Antiracism Limited: A Pre-History of Post-Race," *Cultural Studies* 30, no. 1 (2016): 47–77.

inequalities. This logic treats substantive inequality as the purview of the market. As Crenshaw explains: "In this market the state cannot interfere to redistribute racial value. Such redistribution is an illegitimate end that would upset the natural outcomes of the market." To achieve equality, Black people "would have to get in there (in the market) and work for it."[18] Addressing references to postracialism common to discourses of neoliberalism and whiteness, Kent Ono argues that these references reproduce "the age-old mythology of American exceptionalism under capitalism."[19] Yet legitimating tales of equal opportunities for individual advancement in meritocratic markets depends upon strategies of ahistoricism and decontextualization to occlude structural inequalities.

Engaging rhetoric, economy, and whiteness, this volume raises critical issues for rhetorical scholarship as well as research in related fields such as cultural studies, media studies, and more. As researchers have long identified correlations between economic and racial inequality, rhetorical scholars may illuminate the dynamics of these interactions.[20] Further, by exploring these relationships, we may avoid binary framings of scholarship that promote partial understandings of inequality. In this spirit, Dreama Moon and Lisa Flores call for an intersectional study of whiteness that recognizes how "oppressive systems tend to be linked within relations of domination and subordination," such that "singling out only one aspect produces skewed visions of relations of power."[21] Rhetorical scholarship on neoliberalism and whiteness has considered varied practices and societal realms, including politics, social media, popular culture, and more.[22] Across these realms, we may explore the sym-

---

18. Kimberlé Williams Crenshaw, "Color Blindness, History, and the Law," in *The House That Race Built*, ed. Wahneema Lubiano (New York: Vintage, 1998), 283.

19. Kent A. Ono, "Postracism: A Theory of the 'Post'- as Political Strategy," *Journal of Communication Inquiry* 34, no. 3 (2010): 228.

20. Bonilla-Silva, *Racism without Racists*, 44–52.

21. Dreama Moon and Lisa A. Flores, "Antiracism and the Abolition of Whiteness: Rhetorical Strategies of Domination among 'Race Traitors,'" *Communication Studies* 51, no. 2 (2000): 109.

22. Scholarship on popular culture and race illustrates how even inclusive representations of people of color still promote whiteness and racial neoliberalism by featuring narratives in which racially marginalized individuals transcend structural racism and class inequality through hard work, self-reliance, and working within the parameters of white meritocracy. See Jeffery L. Bineham, "How the Blind Side Blinds Us: Postracism and the American Dream," *Southern Communication Journal* 80, no. 3 (2015): 230–45; Suzanne M. Enck and Megan E. Morrissey, "If Orange Is the New Black, I Must Be Color Blind: Comic Framings of Post-Racism in the Prison-Industrial Complex," *Critical Studies in Media Communication* 32, no. 5 (2015): 303–17; Herman Gray, *Watching Race: Television and the Struggle for Blackness* (Minneapolis: University of Minnesota Press, 2004); and Rachel Alicia Griffin, "Problematic Representations of Strategic Whiteness and 'Post-Racial' Pedagogy: A Critical Intercultural Reading of *The Help*," *Journal of International & Intercultural Communication* 8, no. 2 (2015): 147–66.

bolic and material advantages and disadvantages that rhetorical economies of whiteness maintain and promote. By further engaging these two robust areas of scholarship, we may produce new insights on hegemonic public discourses and potentially emancipatory alternatives. In the remainder of this introduction, we amplify our critical perspective and discuss its implications for rhetoric and communication. Then, we preview our contributors' chapters.

Rhetorical Economies as Exchange, Resources, and Value

As an all-encompassing term to denote a sphere of autonomous activity separate from society, culture, or politics, "the economy" is somewhat misleading. As humanities scholarship organized under the banner of "cultural economy" illustrates, economies are infused into all modes of social relations as much as what is considered "economic" is discursive, that is to say the economic is a symbolic assemblage of tropes, signifiers, and cultural symbols that coordinate value and facilitate relations of use and exchange.[23] For example, the cultural value assigned to merit or meritocracy within Western philosophies of individualism drives policy and economic decision-making to suggest that upward mobility must be "earned" by hard work regardless of structural economic disadvantages that disproportionately affect people of color.[24] Put another way, the cultural, the rhetorical, and the economic are not independent fields within a social totality. As Lawrence Grossberg observes, "The project of a cultural studies of economies entails finding ways of studying the contextual construction and specification of economies and the economic. We have to understand the economies as completely integrated into the social totality even as we recognize their distinctive mode of existence as standing somehow apart from that social totality."[25] Thus, we find it fruitful to advance the chiasmatic statement that rhetoric is economical and the economic is rhetorical. This argument avoids reducing all social totalities to political economy (economic reductionism) but without, at the same time, folding all economic activity into the realm of the symbolic.

To say that rhetoric is economical is to observe how language is itself a system for the exchange, substitution, distribution, and circulation of signs that accord to use and exchange value. In Krista Ratcliff's words,

---

23. Paul du Gay and Michael Pryke, *Cultural Economy: Cultural Analysis and Commercial Life* (Thousand Oaks, CA: Sage, 2001).

24. Joquina M. Reed and Ashley Noel Mack, "Act Right White: Displacing Meritocracy and Recentering Intimacy," *Departures in Critical Qualitative Research* 8, no. 4 (2019): 94–99.

25. Lawrence Grossberg, *Cultural Studies in the Future Tense* (Durham, NC: Duke University Press, 2010), 102.

persuasion-as-identification is a site where "conscious and unconscious rhetorical exchanges transpire."[26] In the language of neoliberalism, terms like freedom, merit, and self-reliance are value terms that circulate widely and increase the worth of particular forms of economic activity for which they stand in place.[27] Rhetoric garners investments, buy-ins, valuations, and wagers from publics in the process of meaning-making and the construction of durable social formations. Likewise, to say that economics is rhetorical is to observe that the economic activity that occurs throughout the social totality functions through actors' ability to deploy symbols that facilitate exchange and create the impression of value. For example, self-reliance and merit are valuable signifiers because they naturalize the free market and sustain the economic investments of those who profit from that economic system. As the authors in this volume demonstrate, rhetoric defends and builds adherence to systems of exchange that reinforce structural, racial, and economic inequality.

Consider the strong connections between housing property values and the cultural values attached to particular types of homes. According to the Brookings Institute, homes owned by Black and Latino residents are consistently appraised at 23 percent less than comparable white homes. In 2022, Baltimore residents Nathan Connolly and Shani Mott "whitewashed" their home and raised their appraisal by $300,000.[28] Here, the economy of homeownership is premised on cultural fantasies of whiteness and anti-Blackness: homes and neighborhoods marked by whiteness are arbitrarily associated with abstract concepts like cleanliness, good upkeep, community, and safety. Black homes and neighborhoods are constructed as disorderly, crime-ridden, unhealthy, and dangerous.[29] This example illustrates the entwining of cultural and economic value where the cultural value of whiteness is affirmed by the marketplace and arbitrarily overinflates commodities with economic value.

Economics is also rhetorical insofar as systems of exchange and value require argumentative justification, particularly where alternatives threaten stakeholder interests. For instance, rhetorical scholars such as James Arnt

---

26. Krista Ratcliffe, *Rhetorical Listening: Identification, Gender, Whiteness* (Carbondale: Southern Illinois University Press, 2005), 49.

27. See William Davies, "What Is 'Neo' about Neoliberalism?," in *Liberalism in Neoliberal Times: Dimensions, Contradictions, Limits*, ed. Alejandro Abraham-Hamanoiel, Des Freeman, Gholam Khiabany, Kate Nash, and Julian Petley (London: Goldsmiths Press, 2017), 13–22; and Stuart Hall, "The Neoliberal Revolution," *Soundings* no. 48 (2011): 9–27.

28. Jonathan Rothwell and Andre M. Perry, "Biased Appraisals and the Devaluation of Housing in Black Neighborhoods," Brookings Institution, November 17, 2021, https://www.brookings.edu/research/biased-appraisals-and-the-devaluation-of-housing-in-black-neighborhoods/.

29. Keeanga-Yamahtta Taylor, *Race for Profit: How Banks and the Real Estate Industry Undermined Black Homeownership* (Chapel Hill: University of North Carolina Press, 2019).

Aune, Michael Lee, and Paul Johnson have observed that the Cold War political right helped naturalize the ideological presupposition that there are no viable alternatives to market-based capitalism, and in doing so they were able to successfully dismantle the robust social safety net that had facilitated an uncommon period of general prosperity in the immediate postwar period.[30] The rise of so-called "capitalist realism" is the cumulative effect of incessant chatter from well-funded libertarian think tanks and conservative politicians about the supremacy of free markets—a remarkable feat given that free markets neither exist nor are efficacious at producing the collective good on their own.[31] As discourses of neoliberalism and whiteness work together, this assertion of a "capitalist realism" invokes, in the words of Derrick Bell, a "racial realism."[32] In both cases, this realism does not refer to a naturally occurring state of affairs that resists human intervention. Instead, these realisms reflect the unwillingness of people who benefit from the status quo to acknowledge the possibility of alternatives. Capitalist realism operates as a command for people to comport themselves with market logics. Racial realism refers to Bell's skepticism that white people will cede their power and privilege to facilitate full racial equality. Offering evidence for his prognosis, Bell cites the interaction of racial and economic inequalities: "The reality is that blacks still suffer a disproportionately higher rate of poverty, joblessness, and insufficient health care than other ethnic populations in the United States."[33] In these situations, discourses of neoliberalism and whiteness engage in reification: the disparities that Bell identifies may cause human pain and suffering, but these disparities supposedly are unavoidable.

This volume is located at the intersection of economic rhetorics, the economics of rhetoric, and the rhetorical construction of whiteness. How do rhetorics of whiteness reproduce relations of economic exploitation? How do rhetorics of economics necessarily reproduce white privilege and implicitly center white identity? The authors in this volume suggest that one cannot adequately address the former without attending to the latter. Consider,

---

30. James Arnt Aune, *Selling the Free Market: The Rhetoric of Economic Correctness* (New York: Guilford Press, 2002); Paul Elliott Johnson, *I, the People: The Rhetoric of Conservative Populism in the United States* (Tuscaloosa: University of Alabama Press, 2021); and Michael J. Lee, *Creating Conservatism: Postwar Words That Made an American Movement* (East Lansing: Michigan State University Press, 2014).

31. Mark Fisher, *Capitalist Realism: Is There No Alternative?* (Winchester, UK: John Hunt Publishing, 2009).

32. Derrick Bell, "Racial Realism," *Connecticut Law Review* 24, no. 2 (1992): 363–79.

33. Bell, "Racial Realism," 377. On racial progress narratives and postracialism, see Ian F. Haney López, "Is the 'Post' in Post-Racial the 'Blind' in Colorblind?," *Cardozo Law Review* 32, no. 3 (2011): 807–31.

for example, Cedric Robinson's theory of racial capitalism to illustrate this point. Robinson contests the notion that capitalism was a modernizing force that homogenized and produced the universal European proletarian subject.[34] Instead, he suggests that the history of capitalism is concomitant with a project of racialization. The enclosure movement that ended feudalism; the colonial plundering of Africa, Asia, and the Americas; and the practice of slavery produced racialized subjects as the object of labor and class subjugation. For Robinson "racial capitalism" names the development of a system of economic exchange premised on relations of exploitation that amplified regional and phenotypical differences into racial ones.[35] Hence, Euro-American conceptions of private property necessarily excluded indigenous people and people of color from its legal and philosophical frameworks of personhood.[36] The theory of racial capitalism articulates how whiteness—as a dominant genre of colorless universal personhood—is embedded in all modes of economic exchange, production, and value. Rather than understanding race and capitalism as separate but parallel and mutually reinforcing modes of exploitation, Robinson urges us to attend to the economic as racial and the racial as economic.

A rhetorical economy of whiteness emphasizes the embeddedness of the racial and the economic but also the degree to which symbolic constructions of negative difference are foundational to both. Thus, we offer three overlapping definitions of rhetorical economies to highlight the variety of contributions offered by the authors in this book: resource, value, and medium of exchange. As a resource, whiteness can be marshaled as a privilege that offers access to a bevy of material and immaterial resources—from access to property and public accommodations to implicit ethos and presumption in nearly all social, personal, and professional interactions. When attached to particular objects and ideals, whiteness can implicitly and arbitrarily enhance something's value, such as a home or the desirability of a job candidate in an all-white workplace. Conversely, the racial legacy of whiteness as property establishes white subjects as agentive economic actors in a marketplace but reduces people of color to fungible commodities or material resources to be exploited in labor and commodity markets.[37]

Both of these economical forms of whiteness are underwritten by a third term, or a system of *exchange*. Whiteness, then, can be understood as both a

---

34. Cedric J. Robinson, *Black Marxism: The Making of the Black Radical Tradition*, 2nd edition (Chapel Hill: University of North Carolina Press, 2005).
35. Melamed, *Represent and Destroy*.
36. See Harris, "Whiteness as Property."
37. Anthony Paul Farley, "Toward a General Theory of Antiblackness," in *Antiblackness*, ed. Moon-Kie Jung and João H. Costa Vargas (Durham, NC: Duke University Press, 2021).

material and symbolic commodity but also as a kind of raw material shaped and given value by the forces of production, distribution, trade, and circulation. As use value, whiteness affords individuals who code or identify as white access to other material (housing, jobs, wages, health care, property) and immaterial resources (social support, mobility, networks, prestige, ethos, etc.). As George Lipsitz explains, whiteness is like an economic "investment" that matures and accrues value in the form of privileges of mobility, access, social standing, and safety.[38] The use value of whiteness is located in the social, cultural, and financial opportunities it affords. Whiteness also has exchange value but not necessarily because it is a commodity that one can trade. Indeed, as Harris notes, whiteness is nontransferable property, as holders of a property right in whiteness cannot grant this right to others.[39] But whiteness is something that gives *identities* value by virtue of their proximity to an idealized concept of colorless humanity, much in the same way that hard currencies and natural resources "back" paper or digital currencies or immaterial financial assets (something akin to the gold standard or collateral for an investment or loan). Though it is arbitrary in terms of use, much in the same way that gold or diamonds have commercial applications but are primarily valued for their immaterial or cultural qualities, whiteness is most valuable in terms of exchange. There is no practical usage for whiteness outside of its cultural meanings in a society organized around white supremacy. White identities only accrue use-value because of the social resources we invest in those identities. Drawing from W. E. B. Du Bois, historian David Roediger argues that the "wages of whiteness" were the petty social and economic privileges afforded to white workers during Reconstruction in lieu of other more direct forms of compensation, thus cultivating white worker's investments in maintaining racial hierarchies and disrupting interracial worker solidarity.[40]

This definition of rhetorical economies also emphasizes exchange as a form of substitution. For example, when an individual gives money for another good or service both parties likely agree that each has relative or equal value. In this exchange, money stands in the place of something else, substituting for the good/service that parties may seek or provide. In this way, all economies are metaphorical. Whiteness can be thought of as economic in the sense that it

---

38. George Lipsitz, *The Possessive Investment in Whiteness: How White People Profit from Identity Politics*, revised and expanded edition (Philadelphia: Temple University Press, 2009).

39. Harris, "Whiteness as Property," 1731–34. Harris writes that the nontransferability of whiteness "may be more indicative of its perceived enhanced value" (1734).

40. David R. Roediger, *The Wages of Whiteness: Race and the Making of the American Working Class* (New York: Verso, 1999); see also W. E. B. Du Bois, *Black Reconstruction in America, 1860–1880* (New York: Free Press, 1998).

stands in place of something else; namely, the assumed metonymic connection between whiteness and humanness and, as Paul Gilroy and others remind us, between whiteness and the nation-state.[41] Whiteness is economic because it is part of a terminological and conceptual exchange, where whiteness stands in for a host of other associations of value in the rhetoric of humanism and possessive individualism. In a rhetorical economy, symbols or signifiers can be traded, exchanged, and bought/sold. In semiotics, subjects must "labor" and "invest" in the arbitrary and accidental connections between signifiers. For example, Christian Lundberg argues for an "economic" approach to trope, insofar as tropes differentiate, connect, and assemble signifiers into chains of equivalence.[42] Tropes also garner investments in chains of signification. The labor of trope—of belaboring that signifiers have durable meanings—is what enchants signifiers with meaning, in which subjects invest to anchor themselves to reality. Assertions of whiteness as universal humanness rely on tropological economies because habitual reiterations of this association cement ostensibly meaningless connections between signifiers so that they can stand in the place of one another.

For this reason, rhetorical scholars, including some of the authors featured in this volume, theorize the concept of "affective economies," which denotes the exchange of emotions, investments, felt intensities, and a range of bodily affects circulated through rhetorical practices. By affect, we mean ineffable and prediscursive or nonrepresentational bodily sensations that are imperfectly translated into language, or named, as emotions.[43] Sara Ahmed observes that affects are garnered and exchanged through discourse, creating felt attachments to ideas (and ideologies) as well as investments in the connection between signifiers that might escape our conscious registers. Publicly powerful feelings like hate and love act economically as they "circulate between signifiers in relationships of difference and displacement."[44] Put another way, hate and love participate in an affective economy in which

---

41. Paul Gilroy, *Against Race: Imagining Political Culture beyond the Color Line* (Cambridge, MA: Harvard University Press, 2000). See also Lisa A. Flores, *Deportable and Disposable: Public Rhetoric and the Making of the Illegal Immigrant* (University Park: Pennsylvania State University Press, 2020).

42. Christian Lundberg, *Lacan in Public: Psychoanalysis and the Science of Rhetoric* (Tuscaloosa: University Alabama Press, 2012).

43. See Melissa Gregg and Gregory J. Seigworth, eds., *The Affect Theory Reader* (Durham, NC: Duke University Press Books, 2010); Jenny Rice, "The New 'New': Making a Case for Critical Affect Studies," *Quarterly Journal of Speech* 94, no. 2 (2008): 200–212; and Erin J. Rand, "'What One Voice Can Do': Civic Pedagogy and Choric Collectivity at Camp Courage," *Text and Performance Quarterly* 34, no. 1 (2014): 28–51.

44. Sara Ahmed, *Cultural Politics of Emotion* (Edinburgh, SCT: Edinburgh University Press, 2014), 44.

signifiers of sameness and difference circulate across a social field and become attached to racialized bodies. For Hall, because signifiers accrue meaning by virtue of their difference from other signifiers, racial economies of difference give meaning and value to whiteness by virtue of its constructed opposition to Blackness.[45] In the context of white supremacy, we might understand hate and love as attachments mobilized by signifiers that belabor arbitrary associations and attribute qualities to particular bodies through a racialized standard of value, such as contrasting associations of whiteness with humanity and Blackness with abjection and animality.[46]

Racist tropes must be repeated incessantly to belabor arbitrary connections precisely because no signifier's meaning is ever guaranteed in advance. And because racial difference has no metaphysical, ontological, or biological meaning guaranteed in advance of its utterance, quotidian investments in racial difference are cemented at the level of affect more so than at the level of rational argument (with perhaps the exception of overt white supremacy rather than the everyday discursive practices of whiteness). In an affective economy, then, "emotions *do things,* and they align individuals with communities—or bodily space with social space—through the very intensity of their attachments."[47] Rhetoric, then, is a medium of affective exchange through which felt intensities (many of which far surpass even conscious commitment or rational self-interest) become attached to particular social groups—with the effect of binding in-groups and differentiating threatening out-groups. Rhetoricians have turned to the concept of "affective economy" to explain, among other things, the circulation of animus, resentment, and enmity that currently animate US political culture. Eric King Watts has deployed the concept of affective economy to illustrate how race and whiteness have become embroiled in the politics of "post-truth," where suspicion has been "weaponized and charged with hostility" toward government agencies and policies that threaten white population's hegemony over the social field.[48] Conspiracy theories and contrived facts, he argues, are less evidence of rational reality-based commitments than they are a mobilization of hostility that prepares dominant publics for "tribal warfare" against perceived incursions into the white body politic.[49]

---

45. Stuart Hall, "The Spectacle of the Other," in *Representation: Cultural Representations and Signifying Practices* (Thousand Oaks, CA: Sage, 1997), 234.

46. On race and representation, see Stuart Hall, *Selected Writings on Race and Difference,* ed. Paul Gilroy and Ruth Wilson Gilmore (Durham, NC: Duke University Press, 2021), 246–56.

47. Sara Ahmed, "Affective Economies," *Social Text* 22, no. 2 (2004): 119.

48. Eric King Watts, "'Zombies Are Real': Fantasies, Conspiracies, and the Post-Truth Wars," *Philosophy & Rhetoric* 51, no. 4 (2018): 441–70.

49. Watts, "Zombies," 444.

Others have mobilized the concept in similar ways. Paul Johnson argues that the theories of possessive individualism that animate conservative populism run on an affective economy of anti-Blackness.[50] By this, he means that conservative populism's conception of personhood—rooted in unbridled individualism without social responsibility—equates whiteness and masculinity (synonymous with self-possession and property ownership) with fully actualized political selfhood. By contrast, restrained freedom and collectivity, particularly in terms of property and economic activity, are equated with slavery, which is virtually synonymous with Blackness. He explains that "less widely acknowledged and yet no less important is modern conservatism's reliance on a racist theory of personhood, one that equates autonomous selfhood, power, and property ownership with whiteness while associating vulnerability, immiseration, and abjection with Blackness."[51] In sum, an affective economy is a discursive system in which racialized bodily affects such as fear, fascination, and arousal are exchanged, managed, and attached to objects and signifiers with which there is no inherent connection.[52]

The authors in this book approach rhetorical economies in either one or all three of the definitions we have offered herein. Whiteness names the process by which society accumulates, conserves, and distributes scarce resources; accords value to particular objects and signifiers; and facilitates the production and trade in both symbols and material goods. Our title modifies *economy* with *rhetoric,* which suggests that we are foregrounding notions and practices of rhetoric and communication in our thinking about exchange, resources/scarcity, and value. This suggests both thinking of exchange, scarcity, and value as communication practices as well as thinking about communication as constituting, justifying, promoting, and critiquing existing practices of exchange, scarcity, and value. Rhetoric and communication also may articulate not-yet-existing alternatives, reframe existing practices in idealized ways, and more. Neoliberals, for instance, speak an idealized language of individual action that does not adequately characterize existing economies, but their individualism does a lot of work in disciplining people to act as individuals who must bear the full responsibility for their actions, even as human action is situated in networks of human interdependence and structural forces that condition our action. Alternatively, we may consider rhetorical economies that seek to resist

---

50. Johnson, *I, the People.*

51. Johnson, *I, the People,* 8. Similarly, Calvin Warren argues that Blackness operates as a vehicle or vessel (property) in a white symbolic economy. Calvin L. Warren, *Ontological Terror: Blackness, Nihilism, and Emancipation* (Durham, NC: Duke University Press Books, 2018).

52. See Frank B. Wilderson III, *Red, White and Black: Cinema and the Structure of U.S. Antagonisms* (Durham, NC: Duke University Press, 2010).

neoliberal logics by envisioning exchange, scarcity, and value through communal practices that exhibit solidarity.

Implications for Scholarship in Rhetoric and Communication

Across this volume, contributors' explorations of economies of whiteness illuminate their cases and hold larger lessons for scholarship in rhetoric and communication, as well as cross-disciplinary scholarship on media, culture, politics, and more. In this section, we address how a focus on rhetorical economies may illuminate connections, resonances, and potential reconsiderations of major scholarly issues. In doing so, we do not wish to suggest that all of our contributors address each of these issues nor that they address these issues to the same degree and in the same manner. Rather, we offer our discussion in this section both as a heuristic for considering potential implications of our contributors' essays and for reflecting on potential contributions of this approach in bringing together rhetorical scholarship on whiteness and neoliberalism. We discuss issues of agency, identity, and public.

Agency

The opportunities and constraints of rhetorical agency regularly serve as points of scholarly discussion and debate. Articulating a rhetorical approach to agency, Karlyn Kohrs Campbell writes that "agency is communal, social, cooperative, and participatory and, simultaneously, constituted and constrained by the material and symbolic elements of context and culture."[53] Campbell's emphasis on the collaborative and engaged aspects of agency resonates with rhetorical scholarship's attribution of a constitutive force to the web of human relationships within which rhetors operate. Attention to constraints, too, has informed rhetorical understandings of agency as contextualized in particular situations, cultures, histories, and collectives. Watts articulates these dynamics in terms of the related concept of voice: "Rather than conceptualize 'voice' as strictly a possession of the subject or an effect of the linguistic, I posit the concept of 'voice' as a relational phenomenon occurring

---

53. Karlyn Kohrs Campbell, "Agency: Promiscuous and Protean," *Communication and Critical/Cultural Studies* 2, no. 1 (2005): 3.

in discourse."[54] Approached relationally, voice carries significant ethical and affective potentiality. Indeed, as Gloria Ladson-Billings explains, critical race scholars have emphasized voice as a means of communicating "the experience and realities of the oppressed, a first step in understanding the complexities of racism" and identifying paths for redress.[55] Ladson-Billings connects voice with storytelling as a mode of expressing voice that may resonate with dominant and marginalized publics. For predominantly white dominant publics, stories may convey the harms of racism through compelling testimony. For Black publics, "storytelling has been a kind of medicine to heal the wounds of pain caused by racial oppression."[56] By considering the hegemonic force of rhetorical economies of whiteness, scholars may identify and extend alternative, creative, and resistive modes of agency.

Indeed, champions of neoliberalism and colorblindness often view relationships in transactional terms as narrow, one-dimensional exchanges undertaken to achieve a predetermined end. Insisting on the autonomy of the individual who interacts with others, these advocates assert that only individuals as individuals may develop a sense of their personhood, articulate their needs and interests, foster their development, and fully realize their potential. To cede one's sovereignty by acknowledging an intersubjective aspect to agency would be to disavow the very freedom that distinguishes one's humanity. In this way, the individual ideology orienting this exchange presents an antirhetorical view. Agency in economic exchange positions the individual as "anterior to politics," resistant to transformative public engagement, and possessing a freedom that stands "beyond deliberation."[57] Even in situations where white people and white-dominated institutions claim an explicit interest in attending to difference in the name of diversity, as Sarah Mayorga-Gallo explains, this interest may appear as "intertwined with neoliberal instrumentality." As such, diversity appears as a commodity that aligns with existing inequalities, as "one more good available in the marketplace, rather than a set of practices necessary to combat structural racism and white supremacy."[58]

---

54. Eric King Watts, "'Voice' and 'Voicelessness' in Rhetorical Studies," *Quarterly Journal of Speech* 87, no. 2 (2001): 180.

55. Gloria Ladson-Billings, "Just What Is Critical Race Theory and What's It Doing in a Nice Field Like Education?," *Qualitative Studies in Education* 11, no. 1 (1998): 14. Ladson-Billings has been a leading figure in introducing critical race theory to education scholars.

56. Ladson-Billings, "Just What Is Critical Race Theory," 14.

57. Johnson, *I the People*, 3.

58. Sarah Mayorga-Gallo, "The White-Centering Logic of Diversity Ideology," *American Behavioral Scientist* 63, no. 13 (2019): 1800. On neoliberal multiculturalism, see Jodi Melamed, "The Spirit of Neoliberalism: From Racial Liberalism to Neoliberal Multiculturalism," *Social Text* 24, no. 4 (2006): 13–20.

In more avowedly supremacist terms, some online white nationalists have embraced the convergence of economic exchange and whiteness by lauding a so-called "achievement society." These white nationalists do not question "the commodification of the self but [regard themselves] to have been priced incorrectly."[59] In this way, their supremacist visions seek to enlist market valuation and validation.

Practicing agency signals resources that rhetors may possess, invoke, and employ as they interact with others to fulfill their interests. Resources of time, energy, effort, finances, and more may bolster some rhetor's agency while constraining others. On public education funding, Ladson-Billings explains that the intersections of racially segregated housing and economic stratification mean that poorer students of color typically attend underresourced schools while their white counterparts regularly attend generously funded schools. In this cycle of inequity, "without suffering a single act of personal racism, most African Americans suffer the consequence of systemic and structural racism."[60] Their capacity for agency confronts serious constraints, in Campbell's terms, that most white students avoid. On housing, Crystal Colombini argues that the individual promoted by neoliberal discourse and policy may exert their independence so long as they comport their actions with market norms that promote a view of human motivation as operating through "the incessant calculation of rational self-interest."[61] And yet, when some homeowners in the late 2000s US housing crisis found themselves owing more money on their mortgages than their homes' market value, they encountered moral suasion from various economists and media commentators to resist strategically defaulting on their loans. These admonitions discounted how homeowners lacked the resources necessary to weather the ups and downs of market activity. Further, the economic moralists urging faithfulness from homeowners, including financial executives and prominent government officials, often benefited from resources that ordinary homeowners lacked.

To value something is to discriminate among multiple actors, objects, ideas, and more. Valuing in an economic sense, certainly in a market economy sense, invokes inequalities in processes (as represented through differential access to resources) and outcomes. We may value agency differently by ascribing to some actors greater influence, reach, significance, and relevance. Economic valuing foregrounds these judgments and scales them upward

---

59. Alan Finlayson, "Neoliberalism, the Alt-Right and the Intellectual Dark Web," *Theory, Culture & Society* 38, no. 6 (2021): 182.

60. Ladson-Billings, "Just What Is Critical Race Theory," 20.

61. Crystal Broch Colombini, "Energeia, Kinesis, and the Neoliberal Rhetoric of Strategic Default," *Advances in the History of Rhetoric* 21, no. 2 (2018): 182.

through networks of exchange and the allocation of resources. In her discussion of whiteness as property, Cheryl Harris addresses the question of agency as she maintains that holders of a property right in whiteness can expect societal institutions, norms, and rules to bolster and protect their actions from encroachment or interference by others.[62] We see these dynamics at play in Vats's analysis of legal and popular debates over the propriety of music sampling; judges issued legal decisions that protected the owners of white music against the unauthorized and supposedly unethical pilfering from artists of color. And yet, as rhetorical concepts like *topoi* suggest, aesthetic creativity and innovation have long involved the imaginative remixing and repurposing of cultural artifacts, themes, and touchstones.[63]

Identity

For neoliberal theorists and other proponents of colorblind discourses, identities should not matter in economic exchange. For direct exchanges, when potential partners are familiar with each other, self-interest supposedly outweighs concerns about the identities of potential exchange partners. If one individual offers another individual a good or service at an agreeable price, then this consideration should facilitate an agreement. In their book *Capitalism and Freedom*, Milton and Rose Friedman assert that "there is an economic incentive in a free market to separate economic efficiency from other characteristics of the individual."[64] They explain that economic actors who rely on these other characteristics, such as race or sex, only place themselves at a disadvantage. By choosing an inferior or more expensive good or service, these discriminators limit their range of choices and impose upon themselves higher costs. Thus, according to the Friedmans, nondiscriminators will tend to drive discriminators out of markets: "The man who exercises discrimination pays a price for doing so."[65] Scaling up from specific, direct exchanges to broader markets, the Friedmans claim that anonymity protects participants from discrimination: "When you buy your pencil or your daily bread, you don't know whether the pencil was made or the wheat was grown by a white

---

62. Harris, "Whiteness as Property," 1778.
63. James Jasinski, "Topics/Topoi," in *Sourcebook on Rhetoric: Key Concepts in Contemporary Rhetorical Studies* (Thousand Oaks, CA: Sage, 2001), 578–82.
64. Milton Friedman and Rose Friedman, *Capitalism and Freedom* (Chicago: University of Chicago Press, 1962), 109.
65. Friedman and Friedman, *Capitalism*, 110.

man or a black man."⁶⁶ Along these lines, anonymity ostensibly dissociates communicator and message.⁶⁷

These assertions about economic efficiency and impersonal interactions invoke a kind of invisible hand of race and racism that suggests that individuals may promote a greater good by distinguishing their interests from the identity of an exchange partner. Indeed, the Friedmans frame their discussion of anonymity with reference to Smith, whom they interpret as economizing the substance of human interactions, since markets permit cooperation with minimal investment as individuals may exchange without needing to "speak to one another or like one another." As this quote indicates, economic safeguards against discrimination operate negatively as passive inducements that effectively circumscribe individuals' relationships with each other. Presumably, the possibility for discrimination diminishes as the dynamics of human interactions flatten in alignment with a uniform economic basis. This system "enables people to cooperate peacefully in one phase of their life while each goes about his business in respect of everything else."⁶⁸ In going about one's business, disregarding identity signals a wider withdrawal from active engagement with others, intimating that efforts to learn about different backgrounds, experiences, and cultures serve as distractions from—if not impediments to—successful exchange.

This perspective demonstrates the power of abstraction that detaches individuals from contexts, structures, and collective norms and practices that betray the limits of a colorblind framework. As a corrective, critical race theorists regularly remind readers of the structuring influences of race and racial inequalities in the United States.⁶⁹ Kimberlé Crenshaw presents a compelling example of these dynamics of identity in her foundational discussion of intersectionality. Crenshaw offers her readers two statements about race and identity: "I am Black" and "I am a person who happens to be Black."⁷⁰ The first statement asserts the importance of race to identity and identity to interactions, including economic exchanges. The second statement strives toward a colorblind universal that makes race incidental to identity. If someone happens to be Black, then their Blackness does not warrant an accounting in interactions with others. To be sure, Crenshaw supports the orientation toward

---

66. Milton Friedman and Rose Friedman, *Free to Choose* (New York: Harcourt, 1980), 13.

67. Robert Asen, "Knowledge, Communication, and Anti-Critical Publicity: The Friedmans' Market Public," *Communication Theory* 31, no. 2 (2021): 177.

68. Friedman and Friedman, *Free to Choose*, 13.

69. Gloria Ladson-Billings and William F. Tate IV, "Toward a Critical Race Theory of Education," *Teachers College Record* 97, no. 1 (1995): 48.

70. Kimberlé Crenshaw, "Mapping the Margins: Intersectionality, Identity Politics, and Violence against Women of Color," *Stanford Law Review* 43, no. 6 (1991): 1297.

identity expressed in the first statement, but she also seeks to understand the intersections of race and gender, which requires attending to "intersecting patterns of sexism and racism."[71] Crenshaw offers the concrete example of staffers at rape crisis centers seeking to work with women of color. She explains the marginalized position of Black and Brown women in US society requires crisis centers to target these women with specific communication outreach campaigns. However, the added cost of this outreach often places counselors at these centers in conflict with their funding agencies, "which allocate funds according to standards of need that are largely white and middle-class." Such uniform standards, ostensibly colorblind in making counseling services available to women without regard to race, "ignore the fact that different needs often demand different priorities in terms of resource allocation."[72] By connecting identity and resources, Crenshaw illuminates how different aspects of rhetorical economies together produce and sustain racial inequalities.

As the case of rape crisis centers demonstrates, attention to identity—and comparative lack of attention to specific identities—informs the distribution of resources in connection with disparate economic values ascribed socially to different identities. In conditions of white hegemony, whiteness orients resource distribution for individuals and among individuals. For individuals, whiteness provides some individuals with proprietary access, standing, and use of various materials and goods. As white people may expect to send their children to well-funded public schools, they also may carry an expectation of institutional responsiveness that motivates efforts to fight for their children's needs and interests. Even among self-identified progressive white parents, concentrations of whiteness in school demographics may signal educational desirability apart from curricular and pedagogical concerns.[73] White people may draw on historical advantages to amass intergenerational wealth and social capital. Among individuals, the distribution of resources ensures disparities shaped by identities. Black children are more likely than white children to attend highly segregated and high-poverty schools.[74] White people benefit from racial inequalities on matters of employment and income, occu-

---

71. Crenshaw, "Mapping the Margins," 1243.

72. Crenshaw, "Mapping the Margins," 1250.

73. Allison Roda and Amy Stuart Wells, "School Choice Policies and Racial Segregation: Where White Parents' Good Intentions, Anxiety, and Privilege Collide," *American Journal of Education* 119, no. 2 (2013): 261–93.

74. Emma García, "Schools Are Still Segregated, and Black Children Are Paying a Price," Economic Policy Institute, February 12, 2020, https://epi.org/185814; and Stephen Menendian, Samir Gambhir, and Arthur Gailes, *The Roots of Structural Racism Project: Twenty-First Century Racial Residential Segregation in the United States*, June 30, 2021, https://belonging.berkeley.edu/roots-structural-racism.

pational status, family wealth, and numerous other areas.[75] Harris writes that across US history, whiteness has operated as a "consolation prize": "it does not mean that all whites will win, but simply that they will not lose."[76] In this spirit, the prize of whiteness constitutes status and social position, which ensures access to and enjoyment of greater resources than nonwhites by virtue of their identities. White identities thus function as a kind of economic asset. White people can draw on the value of their identities, protect the worth of their identities, invest and plan for financial gains in their identities, and leverage their identities to obtain additional assets.

Public

Discourses of neoliberalism and white supremacy articulate a view of relationships among people and publics as given, not warranting further reflection or investigation, and based on clear and apparent qualities. For neoliberal relationships within and across publics, self-interest and a transactional dynamic obviate any need to learn about diverse others. Indeed, insofar as self-interests are known only to the individuals that hold them, efforts to generate wider knowledge represent naivete or, worse, inclinations toward domination. In *The Road to Serfdom*, F. A. Hayek argued that social planners based their actions on a false idea of knowledge, namely, that a small group of people could accurately and appropriately understand the needs and interests of wider publics. Any effort to do so, which collective action entailed, rested on a false foundation that usurps individual freedom.[77] Drawing inspiration from Hayek, the Friedmans stated this dictum succinctly: "Humility is the distinguishing virtue of the believer in freedom; arrogance, of the paternalist [i.e., the social reformer]."[78]

Discourses of white supremacy approach the dynamics of public relationships differently, but end with the same judgment that differences among individuals do not warrant reflection and learning. In these discourses, strong in-group/out-group binaries posit essential differences among races that make bridge building ineffective and irrelevant. In these discourses, individuals may know all they need to know by heeding the lessons of biology in putatively constituting race. Threats of contamination appear as more salient concerns

---

75. Bonilla-Silva, *Racism without Racists*, 44–50.
76. Harris, "Whiteness as Property," 1758.
77. F. A. Hayek, *The Road to Serfdom*, definitive edition (1944; Chicago: University of Chicago Press, 2007), 102.
78. Friedman and Friedman, *Capitalism*, 188.

in these discourses than understanding differences in background and culture. Lamiyah Bahrainwala analyzes this fear of contamination in Donald Trump's rebuke of immigrants to the United States from the Caribbean and Africa as emanating from "shithole" countries.[79] Bahrainwala argues that Trump's foul language participated in an established tradition of associating immigrants of color with disease, filth, and poor hygiene. Further, Bahrainwala explains that this discourse, which included similar rebukes by Trump, justified militarized interventions in immigration—building walls, banning and surveilling immigrants—that sought to control the actions of immigrants while protecting the purity and safety of the white homeland.

Whether they seek to learn from others and/or minimize the scope and extent of their interactions, participants in publics bring a range of resources to these encounters: access, opportunities, material goods, experiences and education, orientations and goals, and dispositions. Indeed, as Trump's crass and racist rebuke of immigrants of color exemplifies, these resources both signal and facilitate affective charges across interactions. To denigrate an immigrant's country of origin reveals more about the person lobbing the insult than their target. The insult reveals emotions of disgust and fear, anxiety about one's own standing as imperiled by another's presence.[80] The public distribution and recognition of these varying resources intimates the outlines of larger economic structures. As relations of power shape interactions within and across publics, the amount and intensity of energy directed toward moods and feelings express the capacity of publics to demand attention from others, an attention economy, if you will, that itself facilitates the distribution of resources. For example, in the aftermath of Trump's 2016 election, intrepid reporters and media commentators ventured out among rural and working-class white people to understand their pain. While people of varying backgrounds and identities undoubtedly have suffered under the strictures of neoliberalism, this media spotlight compared favorably to the comparative neglect of pain felt by people of color, both in the current moment and in previous eras. Indeed, this media focus on white pain functioned to diminish and excuse expressions of racism from Trump and his supporters.[81]

Publics may value different things, and they may value other publics and find themselves valued by other publics positively and negatively in varying amounts. Under conditions of white supremacy and neoliberalism, whiteness

---

79. Lamiyah Bahrainwala, "Shithole Rhetorics," *Journal of International and Intercultural Communication* 14, no. 3 (2021): 187–89.

80. See Lynn Clarke, "The Public and Its Affective Problems," *Philosophy and Rhetoric* 45, no. 4 (2012): 376–405.

81. Casey Ryan Kelly, "White Pain," *Quarterly Journal of Speech* 107, no. 2 (2021): 209–33.

itself may serve as the measure of public value, the standard against which publics may be judged.[82] Indeed, a significant theme of public sphere scholarship consists of exploring people's efforts to struggle against these value hierarchies, combat the exclusions of dominant white publics, and assert the value of Black interests, identities, and agency across publics and counterpublics.[83] Sarah Jackson and Daniel Kreiss have introduced the concept of "defensive publics" to characterize the engagement of hegemonic publics seeking to deflect, disempower, and disqualify challenges to "white supremacy, imperialism, and other forms of social domination." In this vein, they see contemporary publics promoting and/or excusing inequalities "as aligned with historically dominant orders that continue to shape the nature of power and publics."[84] Resonating with what we have argued in this introduction, they call for greater efforts to engage the contexts and histories of public engagement to resist the abstracting strategies of dominant publics that seek to deny the structuring roles of racial and economic inequalities.

Engaging Rhetorical Economies of Whiteness

Our ordering of the contributions to this volume recognizes cross-cutting themes that we have arranged informally as two thematic groupings to organize the first and second "halves" of this volume. The first four chapters of this volume address issues of public policy—judicial appointments, housing, and education—that illuminate the operation of rhetorical economies at local, national, and international levels. These chapters illuminate dynamics of inclusion and exclusion perpetrated by institutional actors across these levels. For instance, judicial decisions by the US Supreme Court and lower courts have endorsed and enabled laws and policies that historically have implicitly and explicitly promoted residential and educational segregation. Even as they have gained formal entry to various institutional settings, people of color have

---

82. Nakayama and Krizek, "Whiteness."
83. See, e.g., Shardé M. Davis, "The Aftermath of #BlackGirlsRock vs. #WhiteGirlsRock: Considering the DisRespectability of a Black Women's Counterpublic," *Women's Studies in Communication* 41, no. 3 (2018): 269–90; Sarah J. Jackson and Brooke Foucault Welles, "Hijacking #myNYPD: Social Media Dissent and Networked Counterpublics," *Journal of Communication* 65, no. 6 (2015): 932–52; and Eric King Watts, "Pragmatist Publicity: W. E. B. DuBois and the New Negro Movement," in *Public Modalities: Rhetoric, Media, Culture, and the Shape of Public Life*, ed. Daniel C. Brouwer and Robert Asen (Tuscaloosa: University of Alabama Press, 2010), 33–59.
84. Sarah J. Jackson and Daniel Kreiss, "Recentering Power: Conceptualizing Counterpublics and Defensive Publics," *Communication Theory* 33, no. 2–3 (2023) 107.

encountered specifically stipulated conditions of participation variously constraining their opportunities and actions in legal, residential, and educational realms.

Our four remaining chapters attend to rhetorical economies of whiteness in the intersections of politics, news and entertainment media, and culture. As these chapters investigate various media practices, from narrative films to global entertainment to reactionary advocacy and punditry, they demonstrate how political and social culture may circulate norms and practices that reinforce and legitimate hegemonic discourses on race and economics. Focusing on media raises important questions of discursive production and reception. Contributors ask how producers of discourse in entertainment, politics, and academia consider the societal meanings and implications of their work as well as the degree to which they may challenge prevailing views on race and economics. Regarding reception, contributors ask how the audiences for these discourses may treat their experiences as opportunities for self-reflection and critique and/or may deepen their commitments to hegemonic structures, particularly among white audiences.

Across the volume, explorations of institutions and policies, media, and cultures work together to illuminate the reach and power of discourses of whiteness in sustaining racial and economic inequalities. Toward this end, contributors employ multiple and varied methods that illustrate different ways that scholars may study intersections of race and economics across and within societies. Some contributors adopt methods of textual and discourse analysis to analyze prominent political and media statements and practices, while others draw upon archival approaches, ethnographic interviewing, and focus groups to elucidate more localized discourses and practices. Still others weave together personal narratives and storytelling with more conventional scholarly frameworks to reveal the connections between our experiences as individuals and the professional and public worlds we inhabit. All of the contributors have made thoughtful methodological decisions to answer the questions guiding their studies.

Focusing on the public discourses surrounding President Joe Biden's nomination of Supreme Court Justice Ketanji Brown Jackson, Corinne Sugino and Charles Athanasopoulos explore how economies of whiteness co-opt and deploy difference to fortify existing institutions and manage social tensions. Building on Cheryl Harris's explication of the force of exclusion in securing whiteness as property, Sugino and Athanasopoulos articulate a "right to include" that permits the participation of people of color in predominantly white institutions under specific conditions to project affirming images of diversity. Sugino and Athanasopoulos examine how some political and media figures used Justice Jackson's nomination to sow division among minority groups, particularly African Americans and Asian Americans, thus reinforcing whiteness as a supposedly neutral standard against which others may be judged. Moreover, they explicate how some advocates associated Justice Jackson's nomination with a teleological arc of progress across the history of the United States.

While Supreme Court nominations directly implicate national institutions by shaping jurisprudence for the federal judiciary, other policies directly impact the everyday capacities of individuals and families. Investigating the influence of rhetorical economies of whiteness on the fundamental issue of where someone may live, Derek Handley and Anne Bonds analyze the language of racially restrictive residential covenants that proliferated across the Milwaukee metropolitan area in the twentieth century. These covenants, which emerged as a form of "private zoning," prohibited the occupancy or ownership of houses, in the words of an early covenant, "by any person other than of white race." Drawing on Cheryl Harris's concept of whiteness as property, Handley and Bonds argue that these covenants materialized the legal recognition and protection of white privilege. Further, they maintain that the covenants also reveal the utility of reversing Harris's terms to consider how property itself has been construed as a quality of whiteness. Analyzing the language of the covenants, Handley and Bonds focus on their use of legalese, their designation of Black people as domestic servants of white property, and their dehumanization of Black people.

Sustaining a local focus on rhetorical economies at an interpersonal level, Kelly Jensen draws from ethnographic interviews and focus groups that she conducted with self-identified progressive, socioeconomically advantaged white parents to investigate their decision-making on schooling choices for their children. In studying the discourses of these parents, Jensen demonstrates that rhetorical economies of whiteness are not bounded by political ideologies or party memberships. Further, by considering how these parents articulate progressive values while also capitalizing on their white privilege in varying degrees, Jensen elucidates the tensions and conflicts that white people may encounter and potentially reflect upon as they deploy the resources and values of their identities for themselves and their children. Identifying varying degrees of reflexivity among her subjects about white privilege, Jensen foregrounds three themes of white identity formation in her analysis: ambiguous articulation of white identity, sense of ease and comfort in school settings, and perceptions of relationships with other white people.

From K–12 to postsecondary education, US colleges and universities often claim a global outlook and community as part of their stated missions, holding that they educate and employ people from across the globe and promote understanding across cultures. However, as Godfried Asante, Paulami Banerjee, Adedoyin Ogunfeyimi, and Stacey Sowards argue, these celebratory claims often encounter the grinding protocols of educational and governmental bureaucracies. Colleges and universities may look to international students as sources of revenue, a motive that belies claims to community and understanding. Moreover, as these authors argue, for students and faculty alike, the US system of higher education is predicated on the status of legal US citizenship, which creates hardships and burdens for noncitizens. Reflecting on their own experiences, the authors reveal how rhetorical economies structured at institutional levels may be experienced acutely, and perhaps traumatically, by people seeking to understand how protocols of value and exchange may affect their everyday lives and aspirations.

Leading our second grouping of chapters, Rico Self analyzes the psychological horror film *Master*, which featured Black women in the roles of writer, director, and lead actors. Articulating the everyday qualities of racism, Self considers the important issue of representation in the film's depictions of three Black women—an administrator, a faculty member, and an undergraduate student—trying to survive daily struggles, slights, and cruelties at an elite, primarily white university in the Northeast. Dealing with hauntings and horrors of prior university residents as well as the obliviousness and hostility of their contemporary colleagues, these women experience the challenges of trying to maintain one's humanity as a person of color in a white institution. This fictional account offers valuable lessons for understanding interactions in the halls, offices, classrooms, and dorms of real-life universities. Often tokenized as evidence of an institution's inclusivity, Black faculty, students, and administrators find their institutions populated with people and practices that sustain the power of white privilege.

Investigating rhetorical economies of whiteness relating to the US National Basketball Association (NBA), where highly paid and mostly Black professional athletes play on teams owned by uber wealthy and mostly white businessmen, Linsay Cramer illuminates the tensions of these exchanges as personified in one figure, NBA veteran Jeremy Lin. As the first Taiwanese American to play in the NBA, Lin used his celebrity to build bridges among Asian American and Black communities before, during, and after the emergence of the COVID-19 pandemic to rally Asian American and Pacific Islander American groups experiencing increasing levels of discrimination and hate. Lin also pursued commercial endorsements in the US and Asia that required him to downplay his Taiwanese heritage. In these ways, the economic value of Lin's identity depended on its mutability to accommodate the economic exigences of the mostly white businessmen who controlled the league and sought to sustain cordial relations with China as they expanded their global brand.

Exploring discourses in right-wing media ecosystems that trade on feelings of fear, anxiety, guilt, and more, Guy McHendry and Kyle Larson apply their concept of "parasitic publics," which they define as reactionary discursive spaces that affectively engage in the creation and circulation of demagogic rhetorics, to contemporary public attacks on "critical race theory." These attacks create their own demagogic versions of critical race theory to warn against threats to white publics and privilege by a growing awareness and discussion of the ongoing influence of structural racism in perpetuating societal inequality and injustice. As people protested the brutal murder of George Floyd and other African Americans by police officers and voiced critiques of structural racism more widely, participants in parasitic publics co-opted the phrase "critical race theory" as a useful straw figure for projecting their fears of a changing, increasingly diverse society and rallying white people around an alternative rhetorical economy.

In their chapter, Jo Hsu engages virulent contemporary public discourses targeting trans people, especially trans people of color, and tells their story of trying to circulate counterdiscourses in news media. Hsu argues compellingly that these anti-trans discourses uphold binary identity categories that limit people's reproductive freedom and bodily autonomy, while serving as a site of convergence for aligned racist and ableist discourses. Seeking to disrupt dominant modes of knowledge, Hsu invokes storytelling as a critical tool to foreground the knowledges of writers of color. Describing their approach as writing a "braided essay," Hsu interweaves the theoretical reflection and critical analysis of a traditional scholarly essay with their own personal reflections. In particular, Hsu recounts their experiences working with news editors and university administrators as they composed and revised multiple drafts of a brief news article to expose connections among transphobia and other harmful public discourses. However, across a series of exchanges, Hsu realized that their interlocutors ultimately appeared unwilling to support such a critique.

In the afterword, Thomas Nakayama reflects on contemporary challenges to whiteness that offer possibilities for social transformation and yet portend a potentially baneful endgame. Nakayama notes that whiteness in the United States finds itself in a shifting situation as white people represent a declining share of the population in a nation increasingly impacted by diverse cultures and practices of globally interconnected societies. Coupled with the upheavals of a global pandemic, these developments broach fundamental questions about belonging and identity in the nation. Drawing from a so-called "great replacement theory," rhetorics of whiteness position white people as the real indigenous inhabitants of the nation. On this basis, white people appear as the victims of a changing society. Speculating about future trajectories, Nakayama wonders if reactionary rhetorics of whiteness will exacerbate the fascistic tendencies of the current era, undermine multiracial visions of democracy, and ultimately seek to destroy the nation from within.

The contributions to this volume invite readers to make connections of scale, intensity, and scope across the chapters. Personal decisions about where to live or send a child to school reflect everyday matters that nonetheless bear the imprint of historical and contemporary rhetorical economies of whiteness, as legally supported segregation may no longer delimit individual decisions, but the legacies of these practices remain in segregated neighborhoods and classrooms. Although they may seem worlds away, media discourses about the public roles of global entertainers and the international recruiting efforts of large PhD-granting universities also invite reflection on the constraints that racial and economic inequalities place on decision-making. Some discourses of whiteness, such as the hatred expressed by advocates for parasitic publics or the graphic, filmic representations of hatred imagined by Black creators, articulate a virulence that commands our attention. And yet, even in generally positive moments, such as the confirmation of the first Black female justice to the US Supreme Court, we should attend to the ways that discourses of whiteness may reframe these moments to justify past wrongs or to excuse ongoing systemic inequities. From institutions to individuals, the scope of these discourses may extend to the work of teaching, research, and public engagement, as university administrators and consultants may seek to reconcile academics' voices with hegemonic discourses of race and economics, as well as their intersections with anti-trans discourses, theories of racial replacement, and other oppressive forces.

CHAPTER 1

"The Cause Is the Consequence"

Biden's Nomination of Justice Ketanji Brown Jackson and the Right to Include

CORINNE MITSUYE SUGINO AND CHARLES ATHANASOPOULOS

During his victory speech after the 2020 US presidential election, Joe Biden expressed his desire to "unify" a politically divided nation and his excitement to serve alongside Vice President Kamala Harris as "the first woman, first Black woman, first woman of South Asian descent, and first daughter of immigrants ever elected to national office in this country."[1] Of course, it is a matter of convention that a president recognizes the vice president in their victory speech. Nevertheless, Biden's comments are significant not only insofar as they marked a historic moment but also because of how he sought to restore faith in American democratic ideals of inclusion in opposition to Donald Trump's explicit racial animosity. Indeed, Biden was celebrated for appointing one of the most diverse cabinets in US presidential history, and he also notably promised to nominate the first Black woman to the Supreme Court of the United States (SCOTUS).[2] These dynamics are indicative of the way public discourse often characterizes his presidency in multicultural

---

1. Joe Biden, "Transcript of President-Elect Joe Biden's Victory Speech," AP News, November 7, 2020, https://apnews.com/article/election-2020-joe-biden-religion-technology-race-and-ethnicity-2b961c70bc72c2516046bffd378e95de.

2. Andrew Chung, Lawrence Hurley, and Steve Holland, "Biden Vows to Nominate Black Woman to U.S. Supreme Court by End of February," Reuters, January 28, 2022, https://www.reuters.com/world/us/retiring-us-justice-breyer-appear-with-biden-white-house-2022-01-27/.

contradistinction from Trump.³ Yet it bears noting that Biden's career has often worked to support related forms of institutionalized racial violence that Trump's platform more explicitly defends. For example, as the author of the infamous 1994 crime bill, Biden played a direct role in expanding a carceral system that criminalizes Black people and targets, deports, and detains immigrant communities.⁴ Consequently, Biden's celebration of Harris as the "first woman, first Black woman, first woman of South Asian descent, and first daughter of immigrants" to be vice president in US history must be placed in context of his own direct contributions to expanding violence against Black, South Asian, and immigrant women. Biden's invocation of Harris as evidence of his administration's antiracism thus highlights how whiteness operates even through its own proclaimed displacement.

In the contemporary era, increasingly visible discourses of overt white nationalism regularly interlace with simultaneous discourses of liberal multicultural harmony.⁵ Biden's attempts to characterize his administration as a championing force for diversity and racial progress thus speak to a larger process by which whiteness reckons with racial difference. Given these dynamics, this chapter asks: how does whiteness (re)secure its dominance within a rhetorical context that often names, invokes, and celebrates racial difference? To consider this question, we examine public discourses surrounding the recent nomination and confirmation of SCOTUS Justice Ketanji Brown Jackson. Once president, Biden nominated Justice Ketanji Brown Jackson to be the next SCOTUS justice, igniting a political firestorm and conservative backlash about "merit," "diversity," "affirmative action," and Black representation. The discourses surrounding the controversy illuminate how whiteness operates to secure its own racial, political, and cultural dominance in relation to racial difference.

In considering how whiteness resecures itself in relation to difference, we place Cheryl Harris's notion of whiteness as property in conversation with Frantz Fanon's theorization of racial fetishism. Harris highlights how whiteness and property both contain the "right to exclude" as an organizing principle, while Fanon considers how whiteness is invested with a transcendent

---

3. Alisha Haridasani Gupta, "Fulfilling a Promise: A Cabinet That 'Looks Like America,'" *New York Times*, January 22, 2021, https://www.nytimes.com/2021/01/21/us/biden-cabinet-diversity-gender-race.html.

4. Sheryl Gay Stolberg and Astead W. Hearndon, "'Lock the S.O.B.s Up': Joe Biden and the Era of Mass Incarceration," *New York Times*, June 25, 2019, https://www.nytimes.com/2019/06/25/us/joe-biden-crime-laws.html.

5. Corinne Mitsuye Sugino, "Multicultural Incorporation in Donald Trump's Political Rhetoric," *Southern Communication Journal* 85, no. 3 (2020): 191–202; and Dylan Rodríguez, *White Reconstruction* (New York: Fordham University Press, 2020).

status that obscures its dependence on anti-Blackness for coherence.⁶ Drawing on this scholarship, we argue that the Jackson nomination highlights how whiteness also relies on the *right to include* to sustain itself in relation to racial difference. That is, whiteness relies on a larger rhetorical economy grounded in anti-Blackness that stabilizes categories of difference in relation to whiteness to shore up its violent boundaries. In this way, white liberal celebrations of diversity frame Blackness within a limited set of predetermined conceptual options that are, from the outset, sterilized of any potential to challenge the foundations of American society. The term *economy* is instructive in context of the ancient Greek term οικονομία (oiko-nomia) insofar as it highlights how rhetorical notions of race circulate in ways that maintain the "family" and "property," or οίκος (oikos), of whiteness through adaptive "management," or νέμειν (nemein), in the face of crises. We are not arguing that Jackson or other marginalized people become white. Rather, we suggest whiteness relies on the rhetorical management of difference in which it seeks to control the *terms* of how racial difference is imagined and staticized in relation to whiteness. Put differently, the right to include describes how whiteness not only works by excluding racial others from its privileges and conceptual nucleus but also by co-opting, defining, and wielding racial difference in its own image.

In theorizing the right to include, our chapter dovetails with ongoing scholarly discussions within rhetoric and critical/cultural studies attending to the way power, race, and communication processes interact.⁷ Moreover, the public commentary surrounding Jackson's nomination not only referenced her positionality as a Black woman but also compared Jackson to other minoritized political figures such as Sri Srinivasan. Consequently, we highlight how the right to include does not impact racial groups in isolation but in relation to one another in distinct ways. In doing so, we build on interdisciplinary scholarship addressing how multiple processes of racialization operate in interrelated yet nonsynonymous ways.⁸ Examining various types of rhetorical

6. Frantz Fanon, *The Wretched of the Earth*, trans. Constance Farrington (New York: Grove Press, 1967); Frantz Fanon, *Black Skin, White Masks*, trans. Richard Philcox (New York: Grove Press, 2008); David S. Marriott, *Whither Fanon: Studies in the Blackness of Being* (Stanford, CA: Stanford University Press, 2018); and Cheryl I. Harris, "Whiteness as Property," *Harvard Law Review* 106, no. 8 (1993): 1707–91.

7. Lisa A. Flores, "Towards an Insistent and Transformative Racial Rhetorical Criticism," *Communication and Critical/Cultural Studies* 15, no. 4 (2018): 349–57; and Armond Towns, "'What Do We Wanna Be?' Black Radical Imagination and the Ends of the World," *Communication and Critical/Cultural Studies* 17, no. 1 (2020): 75–80.

8. Caroline Yang, *The Peculiar Afterlife of Slavery: The Chinese Worker and the Minstrel Form* (Stanford, CA: Stanford University Press, 2020); Lisa Lowe, *The Intimacies of Four Continents* (Durham, NC: Duke University Press, 2015); and Natalia Molina, *How Race Is Made in America: Immigration, Citizenship, and the Historic Power of Racial Scripts* (Berkeley: University of California Press, 2014).

evidence—including political speeches, media coverage, and the confirmation hearing itself—we draw on Louis M. Maraj's discussion of "deep rhetorical ecologies" by identifying a broader interconnected network of racial meaning-making.[9] Because racialization operates not in siloed manners but across communicative mediums, investigating its operations requires an approach that attends to its dynamic, flexible, and interconnected qualities.

Similarly, our discussion of the right to include emphasizes that whiteness wields difference through particularly *gendered* racial processes. Describing neoliberalism as an "epistemological structure of disavowal," Grace Hong articulates familial and gendered respectability as key ideological forces that helped to rearticulate age-old racial and capitalist hierarchies under the guise of inclusion.[10] In the case of Jackson's nomination, we consider how liberal and conservative political discourses figure Justice Jackson's position as a Black woman in distinct yet complementary ways. On one hand, liberal discourses construct Jackson as a symbol of progress via an iconic and respectable image of Black womanhood that ultimately authorizes white neoliberal discourses and policies. On the other, conservatives narrate Jackson's nomination through gendered racial discourses that cast her as a symbol of the threat "identity politics" poses to "objective" standards of merit. In this regard, the right to include points to both the way that liberal and conservative political discourses operate not as opposites but as interlocutors in a broader rhetorical economy of violence as well as how this racialization process remains intimately shaped by gendered normativities.

Merit, Diversity, and Multicultural American Democracy

Early in the 2020 US presidential election primaries, it seemed as if Senator Bernie Sanders was slated to square off in a bombastic clash in the November general election.[11] That shifted on March 3, 2020, when former vice president Joe Biden swept what is known as the "Super Tuesday" of the primary election cycle with ten states pledging their votes to him.[12] Biden used his broader

---

9. Louis M. Maraj, *Black or Right: Anti/Racist Campus Rhetorics* (Logan: Utah State Press, 2020), 7–9.

10. Grace Hong, *Death beyond Disavowal: The Impossible Politics of Difference* (Minneapolis: University of Minnesota Press, 2015).

11. Devan Cole and Jennifer Agiesta, "Sanders Leads Democratic Field in New National Poll," CNN, February 23, 2020, https://www.cnn.com/2020/02/23/politics/bernie-sanders-leads-democrats-national-poll-february-23/index.html.

12. Deirdre Walsh, "Biden Surges on Super Tuesday, Transforming Democratic Primary into 2-Man Race," NPR, March 4, 2020, https://www.npr.org/2020/03/04/811785729/biden-surges-on-super-tuesday-transforming-democratic-primary-into-2-man-race.

support with Black voters to garner much-needed wins in key Southern states. While Biden had no doubt earned at least some of his Black political constituency from his days as vice president under the nation's first Black president, there is a larger political context for the staging of Biden's unlikely comeback: his promise to nominate a Black woman to SCOTUS. As reported by multiple outlets, Biden was coaxed into making this promise by Representative Jim Clyburn, a prominent member of the Congressional Black Caucus who served as the House Majority Whip from 2019 to 2023.[13] During a primary debate in South Carolina on February 2020, Clyburn stood up and walked out when Biden, in Clyburn's view, answered a question about SCOTUS nominations too vaguely. During a pause in the debate, Clyburn critiqued Biden for not living up to what they had discussed in private, prompting Biden to announce his intentions to nominate a Black woman to SCOTUS when the debate resumed. Biden's decision was likely in part informed by Clyburn's influence on the Black voters he needed to defeat Sanders. The following morning Clyburn officially endorsed Biden, setting the stage for Biden's triumphant reversal of fortune on Super Tuesday.

Biden's promise to nominate a Black woman to SCOTUS elicited conservative backlash claiming he was privileging identity politics at the expense of race "neutral" meritocracy.[14] This either/or frame is rooted in the argument that prioritizing diversity means handing people positions simply due to their race or gender, rather than based on "objective" qualifications.[15] For example, Fox News anchor Tucker Carlson argued that Biden's declaration was disrespectful to Judge Jackson because it reoriented what should have been a thorough vetting process into a conversation about her "genetics" and "appearance," asking "what does appearance have to do with ability [to serve on the court]?"[16] Political discourses such as these framing "diversity" versus "meritocracy" mirrored a larger national debate about affirmative action, particularly those leading up to (and following) the recent SCOTUS decision in *Students for Fair Admissions vs. Harvard (2023)*.[17]

Considering the interaction between whiteness and property helps to illuminate the racial dynamics at play in this SCOTUS nomination controversy.

---

13. Greg Stohr, "Clyburn Says He Pushed Biden to Put Black Woman on Top Court," *Bloomberg*, September 16, 2021, https://www.bloomberg.com/news/articles/2021-09-16/clyburn-says-he-pushed-biden-to-put-black-woman-on-supreme-court.

14. Seung Min Kim, "Republicans Telegraph Their Attacks on Ketanji Brown Jackson," *Washington Post*, March 3, 2022, https://www.washingtonpost.com/politics/2022/03/03/conservatives-attacks-ketanji-brown-jackson/.

15. *Tucker: You Are Not Allowed to Ask This*, 2022, https://www.youtube.com/watch?v=zVkS_4bIr98.

16. *Tucker*.

17. *Students for Fair Admissions v. Harvard*, 600 US 181 (2023).

Cheryl Harris theorizes whiteness as a form of property that bestows state-sanctioned privileges on white people. While these privileges are treated as natural, they were formed through the historical processes of Black and Native dispossession.[18] Consequently, whiteness as property does not operate in isolation but in relation to anti-Black and settler colonial violence. Tracing the evolution of whiteness as property through legal history, Harris highlights how *Plessy v. Ferguson* sanctioned white privilege as a form of status property legally protected from violation via segregation. She then turns to the *Brown* decisions in which the court ruled segregation unconstitutional but refused to address the legacy of segregation and slavery. As a result, it outwardly refused racial discrimination but left intact whiteness as a *de facto* form of normative privilege. Harris thus argues that *Brown* "recognized the property interest in whiteness by leaving intact the ability of whites to control, manage, postpone, and if necessary, thwart change."[19] She demonstrates the intertwined nature of property and whiteness as well as how whiteness avoids decline by reinventing itself anew. Importantly, she argues that whiteness and property share a "conceptual nucleus" of the "right to exclude."[20] That is, property involves the *exclusive* rights of possession, use, disposition, and ability to exclude others from those same privileges. Similarly, whiteness involves the right to exclude others from its privileges.[21]

We might consider the conservative backlash to Jackson's nomination as exemplary of a reactionary attempt to enforce the exclusive boundaries of white privilege—in this case, to dominate both legal positions of power and the ability to symbolically occupy meritocracy. The opposition drawn between Biden's decision to nominate a Black woman specifically and a process of "fair" consideration given to all candidates based on "ability" alone further points to how the construction of "qualifications" as neutral indicators of success obscures the state-sanctioned criminalization and exclusion of Black women while upholding whiteness as a normative baseline. Here, Harris's discussion of affirmative action is particularly fitting given the way public discourse and media outlets have characterized Biden's nomination of Jackson as a form of affirmative action.[22] In the landmark 1978 SCOTUS case *Regents of the*

---

18. Harris, "Whiteness as Property."
19. Harris, "Whiteness as Property."
20. Harris, "Whiteness as Property," 1714.
21. Harris, "Whiteness as Property," 1736.
22. Dominique Stewart, "What the Term 'Diversity Hire' Gets Wrong," *Anti-Racism Daily*, March 22, 2022, https://the-ard.com/2022/03/22/what-the-term-diversity-hire-gets-wrong/; and Emil Guillermo, "Judge Ketanji Brown Jackson Is an Example of How Affirmative Action Really Works," *Diverse*, March 1, 2022, https://www.diverseeducation.com/opinion/article/15289128/judge-ketanji-brown-jackson-is-an-example-of-how-affirmative-action-really-works.

University of California v. Bakke, Allan Bakke, a white man, claimed he was denied admission to the University of California's medical school because it favored minority applicants. The court ruled the use of racial quotas unconstitutional but upheld affirmative action broadly by allowing the use of race as one of many factors.[23] As Harris contends, Bakke's case relied on the idea that minority applicants had been privileged over him and, absent the affirmative action program, he would have been accepted based on "merit." Yet this claim ignores how the *standards* for "merit"—such as standardized tests and grades—are themselves subjective measures that implicitly privilege whiteness and the resources white applicants have over Black and minority applicants.[24] The opposition between "merit" and "diversity" relies on a racial construction that privileges whiteness as objective, fair, and *mutually exclusive* with diversity. Similarly, the conservative backlash to Jackson's nomination relied on underlying associations of whiteness with "neutral" meritocracy while casting it as mutually exclusive with racial diversity, thus revealing a larger investment in whiteness as property.

While Jackson's nomination has been touted as a historic moment in the struggle for Black inclusion, it is also clear that Biden's decision was made under pressure to win an election. In response to the pressure placed on him by Rep. Clyburn, and perhaps as a signal to the broader political coalition formed by activists associated with the Black Lives Matter Global Network, Biden wielded Black inclusion as a mechanism for securing political support. This platform has ultimately sought to stabilize citizens' shaken confidence in US political institutions and democracy.[25] Biden's nomination of Jackson thus highlights how whiteness not only involves the right to exclude but the right to include as well. Whiteness is not just about the exclusive right to a particular object but the right to establish the terms upon which difference becomes legible. The right to include describes how whiteness also involves the ability to co-opt, define, and wield racial difference in its own image. This is not to claim that whiteness determines how Black people or racial minorities experience their own identity nor is it to suggest that they become white. Rather,

---

23. Corinne Mitsuye Sugino highlights how this decision set the stage for the recent legal battles over affirmative action that co-opt the language of "antiracism" to reproduce racial violence. Corinne Mitsuye Sugino, "Multicultural Anti-Racism: Anti-Blackness and Asian Americans in *Students for Fair Admissions v. Harvard*," *Western Journal of Communication* 86, no. 4 (2022): 423–42.

24. Harris, "Whiteness as Property."

25. Sou Mi, "Is America Back? Biden and Imperialist Decline," *Left Voice*, January 20, 2022, https://www.leftvoice.org/is-america-back-biden-and-imperialist-decline/; and Andrew Latham, "Forget FDR and LBJ, Joe Biden Is a Modern-Day Justinian," *The Hill*, August 5, 2021, https://thehill.com/opinion/white-house/566433-forget-fdr-and-lbj-joe-biden-is-a-modern-day-justinian/.

we consider how whiteness normalizes a dominant *projection* of Blackness and racial difference for its coherence. Elsewhere, Charles Athanasopoulos describes this as the way contemporary society relies on a "racial iconography" in which both "positive" and "negative" representations of racial difference uphold a similar form and structure of anti-Black violence.[26] Following Hortense Spillers, we consider how anti-Blackness produces a "national treasury of rhetorical wealth" that gives whiteness its coherence.[27] Biden's decision to nominate Jackson at least in part to secure Black voter support highlights how whiteness strategically seeks to incorporate Blackness to buttress its own material and symbolic power.

Biden's attempts to appeal to Black communities highlight how whiteness relies on the right to include. That is, to define not only the boundaries of white identity but the terms of Black inclusion in a larger rhetorical economy. For example, during an interview with Black media personality "Charlamagne tha God," Biden made the peculiar declaration that anyone struggling to decide whether to vote for him or Trump "ain't Black."[28] Statements like these reduce Blackness to a set of political beliefs held by Democrats who patronizingly project their ideology onto Black people because they assume it works in their best interest. Biden's comment garnered immediate backlash. Black conservatives capitalized on the moment to highlight Biden's racism and claim that liberal ideology doesn't serve the interests of Black people. Interestingly, this same discourse is also used to paint Black radicals as aberrations in an imaginary universal Black community.[29] Biden's comments are reminiscent of another interview with Charlamagne: during the 2016 election, Hillary Clinton, when asked what she always carries in her purse wherever she goes, responded "hot sauce" not-so-coincidentally around the time that music artist Beyoncé had popularized the phrase "I got hot sauce in my bag, swag" through her song *Formation*.[30] In both cases, white liberal politicians attempt to conjure cultural imagery (hot sauce) and/or political ideology (you "ain't

---

26. Charles Athanasopoulos, "'A Program of Complete Disorder': The Black Iconoclasm within Fanonian Thought," *Lateral* 10, no. 1 (2021), https://doi.org/10.25158/L10.1.3.

27. Hortense J. Spillers, "'Mama's Baby, Papa's Maybe': An American Grammar Book," in *Black, White, and in Color: Essays on American Literature and Culture* (Chicago: University of Chicago Press, 2003), 203.

28. Quint Forgey and Myah Ward, "Biden Apologizes for Controversial 'You Ain't Black' Comment," *Politico*, May 22, 2020, https://www.politico.com/news/2020/05/22/joe-biden-breakfast-club-interview-274490.

29. Hortense J. Spillers, "The Idea of Black Culture," *CR: The New Centennial Review* 6, no. 3 (2006): 7–28.

30. R. Newkirk II, "Hillary Clinton and Her Hot Sauce," *The Atlantic*, April 19, 2016, https://www.theatlantic.com/politics/archive/2016/04/hillary-clinton-pandering-radio/479004/.

Black" if you're not a Democrat) that they believe to be a natural and objective fact of Blackness. Even in their attempts to include Black people, they define Black difference through the very essentializing web of symbols that uphold anti-Black violence. Blackness is thus made legible via the right to include to help reenforce the dominance of whiteness.

The right to include not only applies to liberal political discourse but conservative ones as well. Amid the nomination, many conservative figures brought up Clarence Thomas as the second Black justice to serve on SCOTUS.[31] In Tucker Carlson's aforementioned news coverage of the Biden nomination, for example, Carlson refers to Jackson as a "garden variety white liberal" in ideology who "will get nowhere near the vetting of a typical Supreme Court Justice" because of her "appearance," with "appearance" referring to Jackson's race and gender.[32] He then goes on to contrast this supposed lack of vetting with Thomas's confirmation as a way of implying that liberals are using Jackson's identity to bypass fair standards. Recall that Thomas's nomination received criticism after Anita Hill, a Black woman, publicly recounted her experiences of Thomas sexually harassing her.[33] Carlson's comments rely on the claim that Jackson and Thomas are in similar situations except for the difference of political ideology, erasing their different positionalities due to gender and—perhaps more importantly—the context of gendered violence.

Carlson invokes Thomas as an example of Black conservativism not only to deny his own racism but also to claim that Black *liberals* specifically receive less vetting due to "identity politics." Paradoxically, Carlson's logic relies on two assumptions. The first is the idea that conservatives unfairly receive more criticism due to their political ideology—a criticism commonly lobbied against liberal "P.C. (politically correct) culture"—*even* if they are Black, which uses racial difference to deny that conservatives are critiqued due to their racism. The second assumption is that had Jackson been a "garden variety white liberal" not only ideologically, but also racially, she would have received a proper amount of vetting. This second assumption thus implies that Jackson received less vetting due to her race and effectively refutes the idea that liberals receive less criticism solely due to their ideology (by implicitly conceding a white liberal would receive the proper vetting). As a result, the first premise cloaks the second premise in the language of inclusion; that is, Carlson rhetorically wields Black difference to effectively make a reverse racism claim that Black

---

31. *Tucker.*
32. *Tucker.*
33. Jane Mayer, "What Joe Biden Hasn't Owned Up to About Anita Hill," *New Yorker,* April 27, 2019, https://www.newyorker.com/news/news-desk/what-joe-biden-hasnt-owned-up-to-about-anita-hill.

people receive privileges from white liberal politics. Doing so reveals how conservatives utilize the right to include by invoking Blackness to *deny* white privilege, thus maintaining whiteness's political, cultural, and material dominance. It also highlights how the right to include and whiteness more broadly operate across political ideologies. Indeed, though they posit one another as opposites, both the Democratic and Republican parties are united in their shared commitment to larger projects of racial hierarchy. They both lay claim to defending American democracy and in doing so, both invoke marginalized people to claim they are the party that properly defends its inclusive values. In this regard, the right to include is an extension of a fundamental tension at the heart of the US nation-state: that is, the promise of equality built on histories of slavery and indigenous dispossession.

The public discourse surrounding Jackson's confirmation not only wielded Black difference in relation to whiteness but Asian American difference as well, revealing how multiple forms of difference circulate and interact within a broader rhetorical economy. For example, in the wake of Biden's pledge to nominate a Black woman to SCOTUS, Georgetown law lecturer and former vice president of the Cato Institute Ilya Shapiro tweeted, "Objectively best pick for Biden is Sri Srinivasan, who is solid prog & v smart. Even has identity politics benefit of being first Asian (Indian) American. But alas doesn't fit into latest intersectionality hierarchy so we'll get lesser black woman. Thank heaven for small favors?"[34] This viral tweet ignited public criticism for his description of Biden's potential nominee as a "lesser black woman." This resulted in Georgetown Law placing him on leave and investigating him for discrimination, though they ultimately reinstated him because he hadn't technically begun his position. Shapiro eventually himself resigned over the fallout from the tweet. It is worth noting that, aside from Shapiro's usage of the explicitly racist phrase "lesser black woman," his comments were broadly in line with socially accepted (though no less violent) conservative criticism that Biden was valuing diversity and over "ability." His decision to name Srinivasan as an example of someone unfairly discounted is significant insofar as it demonstrates a willingness on the part of conservatives to wield racial difference—in this case, Asian American racial difference—for the purposes of justifying their anti-Black rhetoric. It is salient that Shapiro invoked a person

---

34. Bill Bostock, "Georgetown Law Professor Who Said Biden Was Picking a 'Lesser Black Woman' for Supreme Court Resigns after 4 Months," *Business Insider*, June 7, 2022, https://www.businessinsider.com/georgetown-law-ilya-shapiro-resigns-biden-lesser-black-woman-tweet-2022-6; Nadine El-Bawab, "Lecturer Suspended after Comments about Biden's Supreme Court Selection," ABC News, February 1, 2022, https://abcnews.go.com/US/lecturer-suspended-comments-bidens-supreme-court-selection/story?id=82599414.

of color as the "best pick" with an "identity politics benefit" because it enables him to simultaneously accuse Biden of unfairly privileging race while himself invoking race under the auspices of refusing it.

It is also significant that Shapiro invoked an Indian American specifically, as doing so draws on larger tropes about Indian Americans as "model minorities." Indeed, the model minority trope functions in part to uphold Asian Americans as exemplary minorities and has been utilized historically to criminalize Black people by blaming them for their oppression. Shapiro's use of Srinivasan to discredit a Black nominee (Jackson hadn't yet been specifically selected) serves a similar function. Shapiro invokes Asian American racial difference to deflect his own anti-Black claims that Biden's nominee will necessarily be less qualified. Consequently, the right to include does not name a homogenous approach to wielding racial difference; instead, it points to how different yet interrelated anti-Asian and anti-Black racial discourses circulate and interact within a larger rhetorical economy. In the context of Jackson's nomination, Asian Americans are ideal candidates for co-option insofar the figure of the "model minority" fuses notions of colorblind meritocracy with the fact that Asian Americans are nevertheless considered interminably foreign to whiteness.[35] They thus stand in as markers of difference (and cloak conservative anti-Blackness in the language of defending minorities) but also as an ideological argument for supporting racialized notions of "merit" as opposed to "diversity." This rhetorical gesture depends as much on Srinivasan's ability to stand in for "colorblind" meritocracy as does his Asianness as a marker of difference inassimilable to whiteness. Consequently, the right to include is less about assimilating or erasing racial difference than it is controlling and deploying it. It names the ability for whiteness to wield and co-opt racial difference in ways that support its own hierarchical dominance, as well as the way that nonwhite people often internalize the values of whiteness even as they are denied its privileges. Srinivasan as a marker of Asian American racial difference serves a distinct purpose that Jackson does not insofar as his invocation is utilized precisely to discredit and pathologize her as lacking merit. Moreover, it is worth noting that Obama had considered both Srinivasan and Jackson to nominate as a SCOTUS justice. Srinivasan's proximity to Obama as the first Black president and a liberal are important insofar as Shapiro's argument is designed to point out another liberal candidate of color who is supposedly passed over in the promise to nominate a Black woman specifically. Situated between his association with the first Black

---

35. Erika Lee, *The Making of Asian America: A History* (New York: Simon and Schuster, 2016); and David Eng and Shinhee Han, *Racial Melancholia, Racial Dissociation: On the Social and Psychic Lives of Asian Americans* (Durham, NC: Duke University Press, 2019).

president, visible racial distance from whiteness as a South Asian American man, and distance from Jackson as a non-Black Asian American example of "meritocracy," Srinivasan's racialization circulates within and gains coherence in relation to multiple categories of racial and gendered difference.

In addition to Shapiro's viral tweet, Asian American racial difference also played into the dynamics of Jackson's nomination via the then-ongoing legal battles over affirmative action and Asian Americans.[36] In two cases, the anti-affirmative action advocacy group Students for Fair Admissions alleged that the affirmative action programs at the University of North Carolina (UNC) and Harvard discriminated against Asian Americans, who would be admitted at higher rates if admissions were only determined based on supposedly race-neutral, "merit"-based measures such as test scores and grades. Though they focused primarily on making a supposedly "antiracist" claim about defending Asian Americans, the plaintiff's claims rested on the assumption that Black applicants receive an unfair advantage. The conservative leaning Supreme Court would ultimately rule the use of race-based considerations in university admissions unconstitutional in the summer of 2023.[37] One year prior, the US thus witnessed debates about Jackson's nomination and the future of race-conscious admissions intensify simultaneously. As public commentary celebrated Jackson both as an example of why affirmative action is important as well as criticized her nomination as an example of picking someone based on identity rather than "merit," the specter of the Harvard and UNC cases subtended this environment.[38]

During the confirmation hearing, Senator Ted Cruz asked how Ketanji Brown Jackson would evaluate questions of standing in relation to race and gender identity. He asked her to consider if he "could decide I was an Asian man" and make a claim to discrimination as part of the Harvard case.[39] At the core of Cruz's question is how to decide whether someone is part of an oppressed identity. In response, Jackson explained she could not consider a hypothetical scenario but, if presented with the situation, would decide based on the circumstances of the case and relevant legal precedents. Nevertheless,

---

36. Because the cases at UNC and Harvard had been taken up by SCOTUS, Jackson recused herself from the Harvard case due to her connections to the university. Nate Raymond, "U.S. Supreme Court Pick Jackson to Recuse from Harvard Race Case," Reuters, March 23, 2022, https://www.reuters.com/legal/government/us-supreme-court-pick-jackson-recuse-harvard-race-case-2022-03-23/.

37. *Students for Fair Admissions v. Harvard*, 600 US 181 (2023).

38. Guillermo, "Judge Ketanji Brown Jackson."

39. Daniel Anderson, "'Could I Decide I Was an Asian Man?': Sen. Ted Cruz's Question during SCOTUS Nominee Hearing Goes Viral," Yahoo News, March 24, 2022, https://news.yahoo.com/could-decide-asian-man-sen-233409211.html.

that Cruz invokes Asian Americans in relation to the Harvard case is significant insofar as it implicitly conjures the figure of the excluded Asian American being passed over in relation to Jackson. It points to larger white anxieties about Black people receiving special preferences and thus being prioritized not only over Asian Americans but white people as well. Cruz thus wields Asian American difference as an implicit defense mechanism to discredit Blackness and protect whiteness. Moreover, since Cruz is imagining a scenario in which one simply "decides" to be an Asian American to make a discrimination claim, his commentary invokes Asian Americans as rhetorical figures for denying racial categorization as being itself a baseless form of racism. Both Shapiro's invocation of Srinivasan and Cruz's invocation of the affirmative action cases thus operate within and support a larger rhetorical economy that makes whiteness, Blackness, Asianness, and other forms of difference legible in relation to each other, ultimately working to support whiteness's political, cultural, and racial dominance.

Liberals also sought to wield Asian American racial difference in relation to Jackson. After discussing the historic nature of her nomination, Senator Cory Booker stated that "Chinese Americans first forced into near slave labor building our railroads connecting our country saw the ugliest of America, but they were going to build their home here and say, 'America, you may not love me yet, but I'm going to make this nation live up to its promise and hope.'"[40] Knowing that Asian Americans had been repeatedly invoked to discredit Jackson, Booker may have invoked Chinese Americans here as analogy for Jackson's position to bridge perceived tensions between them. Or perhaps he invoked them simply because he wanted to emphasize a common struggle against racism by multiple groups of people of color. Whatever the reason, Booker's comments are interesting for two reasons. First, they strategically fold Asian Americans into a narrative arc of progress that redeems American democracy as a nation built by minorities even as they were consistently excluded. The second reason is his reference to Asian American indentured "coolie" labor as being "near slave labor."[41] Both the reference to slavery and its qualifier "near" are relevant insofar as they highlight how slavery gives legibility to the suffering of other minorities, in this case Asian Americans. Put differently, describing it as "near slave labor" not only obscures the specificity of anti-Blackness as historically distinct but also highlights how it anchors the *imaginative boundaries* of how political discourse makes race-based suffering

---

40. Christina Carrega, "Cory Booker's Full Speech to Ketanji Brown Jackson," *Capital B*, March 25, 2022, https://capitalbnews.org/booker-ketanji-brown-jackson-full-speech/.

41. Edlie L. Wong, *Racial Reconstruction: Black Inclusion, Chinese Exclusion, and the Fictions of Citizenship* (New York: New York University Press, 2015).

understandable. Consequently, Asian American racial difference does not operate in isolation but in relation to Blackness, whiteness, and other signifiers of racial difference within a larger rhetorical economy. The right to include thus names the process by which racial discourses dictate not only exclusionary boundaries of whiteness but the terms of how racial otherness becomes legible.

Given this discussion of the role of anti-Asian racism in relation to the Jackson nomination, it is worth returning to one of the foundational cases Cheryl Harris uses to theorize whiteness as property: *Plessy v. Ferguson*. Harris explains how *Plessy* protected whiteness as a form of status property that required protection and enabled the physical exclusion and separation from Blackness. Curiously, Asian Americans also appear as figures in the case. In his dissent—which argued for "color-blindness" in the area of the law—Justice John Marshall Harlan wrote, "There is a race so different from our own that we do not permit those belonging to it to become citizens of the United States. . . . I allude to the Chinese race. But, by the statute in question, a Chinaman can ride in the same passenger coach with white citizens of the United States, while citizens of the black race" are not allowed to, despite having rights to citizenship.[42] As Edlie L. Wong explains, this rhetorical move to use Chinese exclusion to justify Black inclusion occurred amid entangled histories of Black reconstruction and anti-Asian immigration legislation, including the Chinese Exclusion Act.[43] The point is not to claim that Black people are included at the expense of Chinese people—even when overruled, anti-Black segregation persisted without the authority of *Plessy* in de facto forms. Rather, *Plessy* highlights how Asian American racial categorization is routinely invoked in relation to Blackness, whether to make a case for its exclusion or "inclusion." Here, Harlan deploys the interminable foreignness of Chinese Americans to argue for Black inclusion. Chinese Americans appear as figures that are interminably different from whiteness but also paradoxically serve to justify "color-blind" policies. Moreover, given that *Plessy* occurred during a period in which Asian immigration and the legal abolition of slavery threw prevailing modes of racial categorization into crisis, this example speaks to how anti-Asian and anti-Black tropes circulate in relation to one another to stabilize a larger field of racial meaning. *Plessy* was about more than train cars and segregation; it exemplified a larger crisis and attempt to reckon with whether and how racial differences might be figured and included within a larger (racial) rhetorical framework without unseating whiteness's dominance.

---

42. *Plessy v. Ferguson*, 163 US 537 (1896) (Harlan, J., dissenting).
43. Wong, *Racial Reconstruction*.

Racial discourses about Sonia Sotomayor also surfaced in relation to Ketanji Brown Jackson's confirmation. As the confirmation process for Ketanji Brown Jackson was nearing its start, Justice Sotomayor, the first woman of color to serve on SCOTUS, described how the media coverage surrounding Jackson brought her back to "hurtful" comments made in the past about how she was an "affirmative action" justice.[44] She explained how it felt as though the goalpost of being "enough" was always shifting in order to make women of color like her feel like they aren't "smart" enough to be on SCOTUS. There are striking similarities between the treatment of these two women of color: an argument concerning their qualifications as well as questions about whether they could impartially adjudicate cases according to the facts of the law. Sotomayor was interrogated by Jeff Sessions for her comments about being a "wise Latina" judge who could bring a certain kind of wisdom to the bench that a white male judge could not just as Jackson was criticized for any shallow way she could be linked to critical race theory.[45] Sotomayor was seen as unfit to serve on the court and asked to withdraw her nomination just as conservatives called for Jackson's LSAT scores despite being as credentialed as any candidate to ever appear before the Senate.[46] Yet, also consider how Jackson's nomination is framed as the fulfillment of a Black civil rights struggle rooted in slavery and segregation, whereas Sotomayor functions narratively to represent the symbolic inclusion of Latinx communities.[47] Here, Sotomayor represents Latinx (and perhaps, more broadly, non-Black people of color) who descend from immigrants and rise to success through hard work. In the narratives

---

44. Jordan S. Rubin, "Sotomayor Recalls Confirmation Attacks as Jackson Vote Nears," *Bloomberg Law*, April 5, 2022, https://news.bloomberglaw.com/us-law-week/sotomayor-recalls-confirmation-attacks-as-jackson-vote-nears.

45. Ilya Shapiro, "Sotomayor Pick Not Based on Merit," CNN, May 27, 2009, https://www.cnn.com/2009/POLITICS/05/27/shapiro.scotus.identity/index.html; Andrew Zhang, "Ted Cruz and John Cornyn Question Ketanji Brown Jackson about Anti-Racism Books, Supreme Court's Gay Marriage Ruling," *Texas Tribune*, March 23, 2022, https://www.texastribune.org/2022/03/22/ketanji-brown-jackson-supreme-court-ted-cruz/; and Susan Davis, "Sessions Casts Doubt on Sotomayor's 'Wise Latina' Explanation," *Wall Street Journal*, July 15, 2009, https://www.wsj.com/articles/BL-WB-11322.

46. Arwa Mahdawi, "Tucker Carlson Suddenly Has Questions about Ketanji Brown Jackson's Credentials—I Have Questions about His," *The Guardian*, March 4, 2022, https://www.theguardian.com/media/2022/mar/04/tucker-carlson-ketanji-brown-jackson-lsat-scores-credentials.

47. Mark Walsh, "Justice Sotomayor Urges Immigrant Parents to Aid Their Children's Education," *Education Week*, May 17, 2013, https://www.edweek.org/education/justice-sotomayor-urges-immigrant-parents-to-aid-their-childrens-education/2013/05; and Sahar Aziz, "Judge Brown Jackson and America's Moment of Racial Reckoning," *Al Jazeera*, April 7, 2022, https://www.aljazeera.com/opinions/2022/4/7/judge-jackson-and-americas-current-moment-of-racial-reckoning.

surrounding Sotomayor, she is rhetorically marked as a former resident of a public housing project in the Bronx called Soundview Houses to harken to her proximity to poverty, violence, and indeed, Blackness. Yet, at the same time she, as a hard-working non-Black Puerto Rican who eventually is honored with the renaming of her former projects to "the Sotomayor Houses," becomes a literal model against which the merit of other minorities, and specifically the predominantly Black residents of these houses, are measured.[48] Thus, Sotomayor, as a non-Black Puerto Rican woman, is racialized in interrelated but nonsynonymous ways to how Jackson is, highlighting how whiteness relies on multiple tropes about racial difference within a larger rhetorical economy of racial violence.

You Are Included Because You Are Diverse, You are Diverse Because You Are Excluded

> *The cause is the consequence*; you are rich because you are white, you are white because you are rich. This is why Marxist analysis should always be slightly stretched every time we have to do with the colonial problem.
>
> —Frantz Fanon, *The Wretched of The Earth*[49]

Fanon's analysis of racial fetishism is instructive in considering the relationship between whiteness, property, and the right to include. Fanon discusses fetishism in the context of racial stereotype, which functions symbolically in response to anxiety.[50] Here, anxiety names that which threatens to expose the baselessness of the (white) ego or sense of self and maintains itself by stabilizing Blackness and other forms of racial difference in contradistinction. As a result, David Marriott refers to fetishism as a "defense against an intolerable idea" insofar as it utilizes stereotypes to shore up whiteness against the intolerable idea that it is, essentially, a baseless social construction only possible through violence.[51] When Fanon writes, "You are rich because you are white, you are white because you are rich," he is, for Marriott, inverting the Marxist notion of commodity fetishism. Commodity fetishism refers to the

---

48. "Bronxdale Houses Renamed for Supreme Court Justice Sonia Sotomayor," abc7NY, June 4, 2010, https://abc7ny.com/archive/7478225/.
49. Fanon, *Wretched of the Earth*, 31.
50. Fanon, *Black Skin, White Masks*.
51. Marriott, *Whither Fanon*, 125.

notion that inherent value emanates from a commodity itself as a discrete and self-contained object, rather than being the product of social relations and capitalist exploitation.[52] In inverting this formulation, Fanon names how whiteness is constructed as inherently valuable, transcendent, and nontransferable, obscuring its origins in racial violence. Whiteness's status as property is thus made possible in part through its fetishism; that is, its associated qualities of merit, value, objectivity, purity, and so forth are assumed to be inherent, neutral qualities of whiteness, obscuring the reliance of these associations on anti-Blackness. Fanon's commentary on the need to stretch Marxist theory to account for the colonial situation dovetails with Cedric Robinson's theory of racial capitalism, which importantly displaces a focus on the European proletarian subject. At the same time, Robinson's theory remains wedded to a more materialist reading of Fanon that risks leaving underexamined the role of cultural and rhetorical processes.[53] Thinking through the materiality of rhetoric, we proceed from a Fanonian perspective that emphasizes the co-constitutive nature of cultural symbols and materiality.[54] Thus, if whiteness operates as a form of property, that property circulates within, and is only legible in relation to, a larger rhetorical economy of racial difference grounded in anti-Blackness. The right to include thus names how whiteness operates not only by denying that differences matter but by dictating whether and how categories of difference become legible and incorporable into an existing value system.

The right to include works to manage racial anxiety by wielding difference in its own image. When campaigning for the Obama-Biden 2012 reelection bid, Biden promised to put Wall Street companies in check.[55] Addressing the majority-Black city of Danville, Virginia, he stated, "Romney wants to let the—he said in the first hundred days he's going to let the big banks once again write their own rules, '*unchain* Wall Street.' They're going to put *y'all back in chains*." Biden's references to Wall Street and chains also call to mind Marx and Engel's claim that "the proletarians have nothing to lose but their chains."[56] Fanon argues that Marxism needs to be "slightly stretched," because "instead of objects veiled by the social conditions of production, in brief, Fanon suggests that race is the fetish by which money as a value-form appears

---

52. Karl Marx, *Capital: A Critique of Political Economy*, Vol. 1, trans. Ben Fowkes (London: Penguin Books, 1976).
53. Cedric J. Robinson, *Black Marxism: The Making of the Black Radical Tradition* (Chapel Hill: University of North Carolina Press, 2000).
54. Athanasopoulos, "'A Program of Complete Disorder.'"
55. Mark Mardell, "On Biden's 'Wall Street Chains' Remark," BBC News, August 15, 2012, https://www.bbc.com/news/world-us-canada-19275484.
56. Karl Marx and Frederick Engels, *Manifesto of The Communist Party* (Moscow: Progress Publishers, 1969), 34, 67n5.

as the equivalence between whiteness and wealth."[57] Biden's claim that conservatives will "unchain Wall Street" to put Black people "back in chains" thus not only obscures anti-Blackness by rendering it synonymous with class oppression but also relies on a conceptual slippage between slave and worker. Here, the figure of the slave-bound-in-chains grounds the imagined fears of class inequality while symbolically linking whiteness and wealth.[58] Indeed, Biden is responding to conservative calls to "unchain Wall Street" and "unshackle the private sector."[59] Slavery thus operates as an organizing rhetorical template through which both Biden and conservatives make sense of oppression. The claim that proletarians have "nothing to lose but their chains" relies on a similar slippage, highlighting how fears of class exploitation are tied up in anti-Blackness. The notion that "you are rich because you are white, you are white because you are rich" is thus part and parcel to a larger rhetorical economy that relies on racial fetishism as a "defense" against the "intolerable idea" of Black difference by working to recast that difference in its own image. It is through this type of inclusive reimagining that we can see Fanon's warning that "there is but one destiny for the Black man. And it is white" coming to fruition.[60] Similarly, Biden and Harris reimagine white hegemony through a "diverse cabinet" that "looks like [the promise of a multicultural] America" that they imagine we should all be striving toward as our shared destiny.[61] Of course, this imagined community and shared destiny is nothing other than the ideals of Western Man transposed onto Blackness. This rhetorical wielding of the right to include reduces the Black freedom struggle to the political platform of centrist-liberals, highlighting how whiteness works to recast Black agency within its own image.

Considering this analysis, and in the context of Jackson's nomination, we might say that *the cause is the consequence*: you are included because you are diverse, you are diverse because you are excluded. As Fanon explains, the colonized intellectual is offered as a symbol to mediate across the chasm. Quite literally, figures like Ketanji Brown Jackson and Sonia Sotomayor are included in SCOTUS because they represent a broader narrative about racial

---

57. Marriott, *Whither Fanon*, 143.

58. Another example of this might be gleaned in Biden's statement that "poor kids are just as bright and as talented as white kids." Matt Stevens, "Joe Biden Says 'Poor Kids' Are Just as Bright as 'White Kids,'" *New York Times*, August 9, 2019, https://www.nytimes.com/2019/08/09/us/politics/joe-biden-poor-kids.html.

59. Elspeth Reeve, "Joe Biden Threatens Republicans Will Put You in Chains," *The Atlantic*, August 14, 2012, https://www.theatlantic.com/politics/archive/2012/08/joe-biden-threatens-republicans-will-put-you-chains/324728/.

60. Fanon, *Black Skin, White Masks*, xiv.

61. Gupta, "Fulfilling a Promise."

progression, and their inclusion offers an opportunity to communicate to *les damnes de la terre* [the wretched of the Earth] toward the goal of having them internalize the values of, and participate in, this larger rhetorical economy. Harris makes this clear in her celebration of Justice Jackson's confirmation to SCOTUS, saying, "Judge Jackson, you will inspire generations of leaders. They will watch your confirmation hearings and read your decisions," before explaining how she wrote her goddaughter a letter about how this moment demonstrates that her potential for success in this country as a Black woman is truly unlimited.[62] She continues:

> So, indeed, the road toward our more perfect union is not always straight, and it is not always smooth. But sometimes it leads to a day like today—(applause)—a day that reminds us what is possible—what is possible when progress is made and that the journey—well, it will always be worth it.[63]

The cause is the consequence: missing the forest for the trees, *les damnes de la terre* strive to become the next public symbol wielded through the right to include—the next Jackson or Sotomayor—rather than try to disassemble the underlying racial iconography. Again, the imagined universal Black community functions as an absent referent point that, due to Justice Jackson's nomination, should have faith in the "grand experiment"[64] of multicultural American democracy. Considering this, it is worth asking if fetishism—and by extension, whiteness's operation as property—involves a "defense against an intolerable idea." What is the "intolerable idea" that Jackson's nomination defends against? Given her centrality to a narrative arc that casts America as progressively moving toward justice, we might say that her inclusion defends against the idea that American democracy does not live up to its ideals of freedom and equality. Slavery, indigenous genocide, and centuries of violence against people of color expose fractures in the democratic promise of freedom and equality, and narratives of progress function to smooth over these

---

62. "Remarks by President Biden, Vice President Harris, and Judge Ketanji Brown Jackson on the Senate's Historic, Bipartisan Confirmation of Judge Jackson to Be an Associate Justice of the Supreme Court," White House, April 8, 2022, https://www.whitehouse.gov/briefing-room/speeches-remarks/2022/04/08/remarks-by-president-biden-vice-president-harris-and-judge-ketanji-brown-jackson-on-the-senates-historic-bipartisan-confirmation-of-judge-jackson-to-be-an-associate-justice-of-the-supreme-court/.

63. "Bipartisan Confirmation of Judge Jackson."

64. Moira Warburton, Lawrence Hurley, and Andrew Chung, "U.S. Supreme Court Pick Jackson Stresses God and Country amid Republican Attacks," Reuters, March 21, 2022, https://www.reuters.com/world/us/historic-us-supreme-court-nominee-ketanji-brown-jackson-faces-senate-showdown-2022-03-21/.

fractures and shore up the value system of American democracy. Jackson is thus central to this narrative insofar as she redeems "the grand experiment."

On the other hand, however, it is significant that Jackson's nomination occurs amid rising racial tensions in the US, including nationwide protests against state-sanctioned anti-Black police violence and calls to defund and/or abolish the police and other forms of white institutional dominance. Despite conservative fears that Jackson would disproportionately side with Black plaintiffs and otherwise exemplify "radical" leftist political ideology, her record tells a different story. For example, from 2013 to 2021, in twenty-two cases involving Black plaintiffs seeking retribution for discrimination, primarily in the workplace, Jackson ruled against nineteen of them.[65] Media outlets *championed* this statistic as evidence that she would not be biased in favor of Black plaintiffs and is willing to rule against them.[66] Following her nomination, Jackson was endorsed by the Fraternal Order of Police, which released a statement expressing support for her confirmation, stating they had reviewed her record and approved of her approach, noting that she had two uncles and a brother who worked in US law enforcement.[67] These examples highlight that Jackson's nomination is not only significant because she is a Black woman. It is significant because she is a Black woman that is figured within the dominant ideological framework of white institutional democracy. Her inclusion is possible, in fact it is *necessary*, to both make the US political system appear just without substantially altering its commitments to hierarchy. That she is celebrated for her record of ruling *against* Black plaintiffs is indicative of how the terms of inclusion only allow for a Black woman justice insofar as she maintains the dominant power structure while making it *seem* both fair and diverse. It also highlights how her nomination functions as a neutralizing response to growing demands for dismantling anti-Black policing apparatuses. In this sense, then, a second "intolerable idea" comes into view: the intolerable idea of Black equality and antiracism.

Jackson's confirmation hearing highlights how she distanced herself from radical antiracism. When questioned by Senator Ted Cruz on whether she would utilize critical race theory in her work as a justice, Jackson emphasized that she had never used and did not plan to utilize the theory in her

---

65. Andrew Chung and Lawrence Hurley, "U.S. Supreme Court Nominee Jackson a Tough Sell on Racial-Bias Claims," Reuters, March 17, 2022, https://www.reuters.com/world/us/us-supreme-court-nominee-jackson-tough-sell-racial-bias-claims-2022-03-17/.

66. Chung and Hurley, "U.S. Supreme Court Nominee."

67. "FOP National President Patrick Yoes Statement on Nomination of Ketanji Brown Jackson to SCOTUS," Fraternal Order of Police, February 25, 2022, https://fop.net/2022/02/fop-national-president-patrick-yoes-statement-on-nomination-of-ketanji-brown-jackson-to-scotus/.

work.⁶⁸ When questioned by Senator Cornyn about whether and how race would impact her decisions, she stated it would not.⁶⁹ In these moments, she attempted to distance herself from conservative fears about leftist critical race theory in American schooling and identify with colorblindness. When asked whether she agreed with the SCOTUS decisions to overrule the infamously racist Dred Scott and *Plessy v. Ferguson* decisions, Jackson agreed but qualified her answer.⁷⁰ Jackson was no doubt under immense political pressure to appear politically "neutral" and "reasonable," but it is not a stretch to say that her answers were hardly the radical antiracism that conservatives feared. Of course, that Jackson is repeatedly associated with these ideologies is a testament to how anti-Blackness overdetermines her as a threat to whiteness regardless of her actions, qualifications, or political beliefs. Moreover, it is reasonable to assume that Jackson was giving the answers that she had to in order to navigate a hostile white political environment and confirmation process. Indeed, not unlike Booker and Sotomayor, who similarly align themselves with a narrative of progress, Jackson is in many ways constrained by her role as a visible figure representing US institutions. The point here, then, is not about disparaging Jackson personally. Rather, our analysis illustrates how the right to include dictates the terms of how racial difference can be incorporated into an existing system while defanging its antiracist potential.

Coda

Despite her confirmation being a virtual certainty due to Democrats having the requisite number of votes, Ketanji Brown Jackson no doubt endured racially motivated questions that probed whether she could adequately maintain the neutrality, and thus integrity, of America's judicial institutions by setting aside her personal identity to pursue a consideration of the law *free from passion*. She had to comport herself in particular ways and restrict herself to a carefully curated moderate rhetorical platform in order to pass the trial of public opinion. Stuck between the "anti" of American law and the Black of her nonbeing, Associate Justice Ketanji Brown Jackson slashes through the political tension in her confirmation speech by referencing Maya Angelou's

---

68. Jonathan Weisman and Jazmine Ulloa, "Judging a Judge on Race and Crime, G.O.P. Plays to Base and Fringe," *New York Times*, March 22, 2022, https://www.nytimes.com/2022/03/22/us/politics/ketanji-brown-jackson-race.html.

69. Weisman and Ulloa, "Judging a Judge on Race and Crime."

70. Madison Carlisle, "What We Learned During Ketanji Brown Jackson's Hearings," *Time*, March 23, 2022, https://time.com/6160149/what-we-learned-ketanji-brown-jackson/.

iconic "Still I Rise" poem[71] to declare, "I am the dream and the hope of the slave.... We have come a long way toward perfecting our union. In my family, it took just one generation to go from segregation to the Supreme Court of the United States."[72] Displacing the original context of Angelou's poetic statement—a commentary on the daily degradations faced by Black women in an anti-Black world—Justice Jackson flattens Angelou's declaration that Black women can rise *against* this power structure by harkening instead to how they can rise *within* it.

This chapter's consideration of Jackson's nomination and the surrounding political discourse highlights the operations of whiteness as property within a larger rhetorical economy grounded in anti-Blackness. Drawing on Harris's notion of whiteness as property and Fanon's work on racial fetishism, we highlight how whiteness relies on the right to include for its symbolic and material dominance. Jackson's nomination reveals how whiteness is grounded not only in the ability to exclude marginalized identities but also to dictate the terms of their inclusion. Because it is socially constructed, whiteness is only legible insofar as it can define itself against Blackness and other forms of racial difference, which is to say it is only possible through violence. As a result, its coherence depends not only on maintaining the boundaries of whiteness but also on maintaining the boundaries of racial difference. The Jackson nomination thus highlights how whiteness relies on the right to include as the process by which it defines, co-opts, and wields racial difference in its own image. In doing so, the right to include describes how whiteness functions as part of a broader rhetorical economy that dictates how racial otherness can be rendered legible and incorporable so that it won't substantively alter the existing value system. Though these forms of difference are not all the same—the racial discourses about Asian Americans like Srinivasan and Black women like Jackson, for example, circulate and follow different tropes about what Asian American and Black "difference" represent, respectively—they work to stabilize a larger value system that ultimately redeems whiteness's dominance.

Despite whiteness's continued political, economic, and racial dominance, claims to multicultural harmony circulate in US political discourse. We are inundated daily with a variety of corporate ad campaigns, political promises, diversity initiatives, and claims to media representation that promise to undo whiteness's societal ubiquity. Even former president Donald Trump

---

71. Maya Angelou, "Still I Rise," Poetry Foundation, August 14, 2022, https://www.poetryfoundation.org/poems/46446/still-i-rise.

72. Dylan Stableford, "Ketanji Brown Jackson on Her Historic Confirmation to Supreme Court: 'I Am the Dream and the Hope of the Slave,'" Yahoo News, April 8, 2022, https://news.yahoo.com/ketanji-brown-jackson-i-am-the-dream-and-the-hope-of-a-slave-174858624.html.

consistently claimed to represent the interests of Black, immigrant, and other marginalized people.[73] As a result, whiteness seeks not only to deny racial difference but also to define its terms. The right to include speaks to the way that whiteness maintains its dominance despite—or perhaps *because* of these promises of multicultural inclusion—precisely by dictating the terms upon which racial difference is rendered legible and incorporable. In doing so, it gets at how whiteness operates and circulates within a larger rhetorical economy that works to stabilize hierarchies of racial difference while simultaneously claiming to dismantle them. Because whiteness is coherent only in relation to these categories of difference, it requires consistent, ritualistic, and repeated stabilization in the face of resistance to it. It thus speaks to the imperative that scholars attend to the ongoing evolution of this racial rhetorical economy as it attempts to incorporate difference in new ways over time.

At the same time, given that whiteness operates in part through fetishism—in which whiteness is (mis)perceived to be normative, transcendent, and having inherent qualities rather than being defined through anti-Black and colonial violence—this chapter speaks to the importance of attending to whiteness not as an isolated or generalized phenomenon but *in relation to* categories of racial difference fashioned from an anti-Black treasury of rhetorical wealth. Rather than claiming to be comprehensive, this chapter attempts to open avenues for scholars to ask questions such as: How does whiteness produce itself through/against difference? How does it do so differently (or similarly) in relation to multiple marginalized groups and how do those processes work together? How does whiteness rhetorically and imaginatively limit the existing conceptual frames for imagining difference? Considering these questions opens avenues for interrogating not only how whiteness maintains itself by controlling the terms of racial difference but also how scholars might think beyond the existing conceptual frameworks that dictate them.

---

73. Sugino, "Multicultural Incorporation," 191–202.

CHAPTER 2

Racially Restrictive Covenants and the Spatialization of Race

Whiteness as Property and the Rhetorics of Whiteness

DEREK G. HANDLEY AND ANNE BONDS

> But what is whiteness that one should desire it? ... But then always, somehow, some way, silently but clearly, I am given to understand that whiteness is the ownership of the earth forever and ever, amen!
>
> —W. E. B. Du Bois, *Darkwater*, 1920[1]

> There can be no life, liberty, and the pursuit of happiness if a man cannot work where he wants, and live in a clean respectable home wherever he can afford to buy or build it.
>
> —George Hamilton, Milwaukee resident, 1944[2]

Introduction

In 1871 iconic Milwaukee brewer Captain Frederick Pabst purchased 178 acres of land just west of Milwaukee, Wisconsin, in the town of Wauwatosa, which would later become a Milwaukee suburb. This was land originally inhabited by the Menominee and Potawatomi prior to the US federal government's seizure of Potawatomi territory in 1833 and the displacement of the area's original peoples from their homelands. The land was then surveyed and platted, opening the area for white settlement. We begin here because the historical geography of whiteness and racial covenants in Milwaukee, like all stories of property in

---

1. W. E. B. DuBois, *Darkwater: Voices from within the Veil* (1920; New York: Schocken, 1999), 18.

2. "Rally Attacks 'Racial Action' City Hall is Target," *Milwaukee Journal*, September 11, 1944, 22.

the United States, begins with the settler colonial displacement of Indigenous peoples and the appropriation of Indigenous territories.

Pabst purchased the land in Wauwatosa to grow hops and to raise Percheron horses, and by 1888 the farm included a residence, three dwellings, an office, six barns, and some additional buildings.[3] By 1891, Pabst had built a road through the property—known today as Lloyd Street—and begun subdividing and developing the land north of the road. Following his death in 1904, Pabst's inheritors proceeded to subdivide and fully develop the farm. The area would be connected to Milwaukee's prestigious Washington Boulevard, which was platted in 1914 as part of the development of the city's expansive parks and boulevard system.[4] The Pabst family hired internationally renowned architects to design a land plan for the residential development that would be called Washington Highlands. The plan was heavily influenced by the ideals of the Garden City movement, a progressive urban reform movement that gained momentum when segregationist thinking was at full tide, premised on the development of a "healthful and peaceful environment, shielded from the intrusions of industrialization."[5] The ideals of the Garden City movement can be seen in Washington Highland's private parks and in the curved streets following the topography of the area, designed to minimize traffic through the neighborhood.[6] Building permits for the development were issued in 1918, and by the 1940s the Washington Highlands subdivision was nearly complete. It was listed on the National Register of Historic Places in 1989 and received Landmark Status in 1991.

Indeed, every detail of the community was meticulously planned and restricted, from the scale and style of housing to home and garage setbacks, the height of fences, and allowed building uses, as specified in the twenty-seven-page Washington Highlands Covenants document, maintained and

---

3. Bruce Lynch and Cynthia Lynch, "A Walking Tour of Washington Highlands," Wauwatosa Landmarks Commission, 1991, http://historicalhighlands.net/media/walking-tour-print.pdf.

4. Milwaukee's park landscape includes three parks designed by Frederick Law Olmstead and reflects the ideals and planning imperatives of Charles Whitnall, one of Milwaukee's notable Socialist municipal leaders during the first part of the twentieth century. Whitnall planned and developed Milwaukee County's system of parks and parkways. While Whitnall endeavored to support the urban poor, he also embraced the notion that the problems of urban poverty could be solved by decongestion and urban decentralization. Consequently, most of Milwaukee's parks are located in its suburban periphery, connected through a system of parkways. Lorne Platt, "Planning Ideology and Geographic Thought in the Early 20th Century: Charles Whitnall's Progressive Era Park Designs for Socialist Milwaukee," *Journal of Urban History* 36, no. 6 (2010): 771–91.

5. Lynch and Lynch, "Walking Tour," 3.

6. Lynch and Lynch, "Walking Tour," 3.

enforced by the Washington Homes Association. The original document included a restriction titled "Article IV: Limitations of Ownership," which was removed from the most recent version of the covenants, updated in 1994. Though now missing in the document, we know what was stated in Article IV:

> Article IV: Limitation of Ownership: At no time shall the land included in Washington Highlands or any part thereof, or buildings thereon be purchased, owned, leased, or occupied by any person other than of white race. This prohibition is not intended to include domestic servants while employed by the owner or occupant of any land included in this tract.

This racially restrictive deed covenant, filed with the Register of Deeds on May 6, 1919, is one of the earlier racial covenants introduced in Milwaukee County.[7] This covenant draws attention to an element particularly common in US economic, political, and legal discourse. It implicates the rhetorical economies of whiteness by producing and circulating racial restrictions on the owning, selling, or transferring of land. Whiteness is required by all those involved in order to have a successful financial transaction. Indeed, the imperative of whiteness in this contract both reified whiteness and naturalized it within the geographic and economic order of the neighborhood. The restrictions stipulated in the Washington Highlands covenants were set to remain with the land until 1950, with an automatic renewal for twenty-year terms unless, five years prior to the end of the term, at least 60 percent of the owners in the subdivision agreed to make changes.[8] Such appeals to the supremacy of whiteness in real estate would spread throughout the early twentieth century as white populations moved from urban centers. Opposition to integrated neighborhoods on the part of white homeowners, the real estate industry, and federal and local policies strengthened urban racial boundaries and intensified postwar housing crises in cities across the United States. These practices rely on the "insidious belief that white people matter more than others." Drawing from the work of James Baldwin, Eddie Glaude Jr. refers to this belief as a lie. This lie creates a "value gap." Glaude writes, "If what I have called the 'value gap' is the idea that in America white lives have always mattered more than the lives of others, then the lie is a broad and powerful architecture of false

---

7. However, our current research finds racially restrictive covenants in Milwaukee County prior to 1919, indicating that these race restrictions have a longer history.

8. Lois M. Quinn, "Racially Restrictive Covenants: The Making of All-White Suburbs in Milwaukee County," *ETI Publications*, 178, https://dc.uwm.edu/eti_pubs/178 (accessed September 1, 2022).

assumptions by which the value gap is maintained."[9] Racial covenants are a material embodiment of this value gap.

Though the Washington Highlands was an early adopter of racial covenants, it was certainly not alone. In fact, during the 1920s, our research indicates that at least twenty-nine other subdivisions in Wauwatosa included racial covenants in property deeds. And while Wauwatosa stands out as a flashpoint for racial covenants and an important case study for suburban development premised on whiteness and racial exclusion[10]—the town even advertised their restrictions on city signs[11]—racial deed restrictions were implemented throughout Milwaukee County. With the building of new subdivisions and housing developments in the 1920s and 1930s, racial covenants became commonplace within the city of Milwaukee and in neighboring Milwaukee County suburbs, including Cudahy, Whitefish Bay, West Allis, West Milwaukee, St. Francis, Bay Side, Greendale, Greenfield, Glendale, and Fox Point.

To demonstrate the rhetorical force and the symbolic power of racial covenants, this chapter examines the language, register, and terms used in the covenants. We situate our analysis within the geographies of whiteness and white supremacy, within which the value of whiteness is preserved, vigorously protected, and reproduced through rhetorical and material processes that are grounded *in place*.[12] Building on scholarship examining the mutual articulation of property and race, we situate racially restrictive covenants within racial regimes of property and the persistence of whiteness *as* property.[13] Modern property is not just a central component of capitalist political economy, an apparently "self-evident category,"[14] but also a shifting social formation, animated by intersecting configurations of race, gender, ethnicity, class, and

---

9. Eddie S. Glaude Jr. and Cornel West, "Begin Again: James Baldwin's America and Its Urgent Lessons for Our Own," YouTube, July 1, 2020, https://www.youtube.com/watch?v=RdHlORnIqTo&t=4661s

10. Quinn, "Racially Restrictive Covenants."

11. John Schmid, "Milwaukee's Trauma Care Initiatives Are Meant to Heal. Now They Are at the Heart of the City's Racial Divide," *Milwaukee Journal Sentinel*, June 18, 2019, https://www.jsonline.com/story/news/solutions/2019/06/18/centuries-old-racism-haunts-efforts-treat-milwaukee-trauma-epidemic/2580146002/.

12. Anne Bonds and Josh Inwood, "Beyond White Privilege: Geographies of White Supremacy and Settler Colonialism," *Progress in Human Geography* 40, no. 6 (2016) 715–33.

13. Malini Ranganathan and Anne Bonds, "Introduction: Racial Regimes of Property," *Environment and Planning D: Society and Space* 40, no. 2 (2022): 197–207; Cheryl I. Harris, "Whiteness as Property," *Harvard Law Review* 106, no. 8 (1993): 1707–91.

14. Nicholas K. Blomley, *Unsettling the City: Urban Land and the Politics of Property* (New York: Routledge, 2004), 2.

citizenship.[15] Relations of property both construct and exploit social difference. In her iconic essay "Whiteness as Property," Harris illustrates how property rights in the US are rooted in racial violence, domination, and exclusion. Whiteness, first constructed as a racial identity, became a legally recognized and protected form of property, conferring measurable benefits and advantages in a system of white supremacy.[16] Her theorization of the contingency of whiteness and property emphasizes whiteness as both a social identity and material structure that secures power and dominance and can be possessed, protected, and invested in, reproducing and maintaining the "value gap" mentioned above. We take up this critique to examine racially restrictive covenants as embedded within the ongoing production of whiteness *as* property, rhetorically and materially constituted *through* property.

The first part of the chapter provides a brief background on the history of covenants and some of the ways that Black Milwaukeeans challenged them. The chapter then moves beyond the histories of covenants to examine the rhetorical efforts and effects of the restrictive covenants and setting them in the broader context of twentieth-century rhetorical economies of whiteness. Examining closely the racist language used in the housing covenants, this chapter argues that restrictive housing covenants were critical in reproducing whiteness as "treasured property" in a system of white racial domination and economic exploitation.[17] Racial covenants both reflected, remade, and renewed racial hierarchies and the racial segregation of space, anchoring whiteness to homeownership and white propertied power including the ability to prohibit nonwhites from certain neighborhoods and communities and to accumulate public and private resources based on these exclusions.[18] We argue that the accumulation and circulation of language restricting owners from conveying, leasing, or selling property to anyone "not of the Caucasian race" and permitting the presence of nonwhite people on properties only in roles of "domestic servitude" underscore how whiteness and white supremacy are discursively and materially enacted through "a sense of ownership and the right to exclude" that "systematically undermine the well-being of people of color."[19]

---

15. Ranganathan and Bonds, "Introduction"; Aileen Moreton-Robinson, *The White Possessive: Property, Power, and Indigenous Sovereignty* (Minneapolis: University of Minnesota Press, 2015); Harris, "Whiteness as Property."

16. Harris, "Whiteness as Property."

17. Harris, "Whiteness as Property."

18. Anne Bonds, "Race and Ethnicity I: Property, Race, and the Carceral State," *Progress in Human Geography* 43, no. 3 (2019): 574–83.

19. Laura Pulido, "Geographies of Race and Ethnicity 1: White Supremacy v. White Privilege," *Progress in Human Geography* 39, no. 6 (2015): 809–17.

Within this framework, we argue that the language of the covenants materializes whiteness as property in several ways, including within (1) the legal register of the documents, (2) the choices of racial restriction, (3) the description of how nonwhites are permitted on the property, and (4) where in the property deed the racial language is placed within the document. The cumulative force of this rhetorical economy of whiteness within restrictive covenants both spatialized and racialized economic and social inequalities in the sub/urban landscape in the early twentieth century, and their legacy is still present.[20]

Defining and Resisting Racial Covenants

This chapter emerges from an ongoing public humanities project called "Mapping Racism and Resistance in Milwaukee County" (MRR-MKE) developed by the authors, working in collaboration with the Mapping Prejudice project.[21] Our collaborative mapping project documents, maps, and analyzes racial language in racial covenants identified in Milwaukee County property records between the years of 1910 and 1960. Using digitized property records, we use optical character recognition to flag and identify covenants that include racial language. Each flagged deed needs to have the covenant verified and transcribed by five community members. At this stage of writing, we are currently in the transcription phase of our research. Our proof of concept indicates that, once completed, we are likely to identify over 20,000 racially restrictive covenants in Milwaukee County. Covenants are clauses added to property deeds that attach conditions or restrictions to real estate. The violation of covenant conditions comes with the risk of foregoing a property. In fact, many deeds list in detail how transgressing covenants and restrictions would result in property loss.[22] Racial covenants, then, were legally enforceable contracts that prevented people who were not white from buying or occupying land. Often framed in terms of preserving neighborhood character and property values, racially restrictive covenants began appearing in deeds with greater frequency at the turn of the century, becoming commonplace and withstanding court challenges brought by activists and the National Association for the

---

20. We understand race as produced across intersectional forms of difference, including gender.

21. We work in collaboration with the *Mapping Prejudice* project. See https://mappingprejudice.umn.edu.

22. This observation comes after reading and transcribing many racial covenants in Milwaukee.

Advancement of Colored People (NAACP) throughout the 1910s, '20s, and '30s.[23] The legitimacy of racially restrictive covenants withstood these challenges through the juridical underpinnings of private property: covenants were private contracts enabling racist exclusion rather than formal legislation or mechanizations of the state.[24] Though racial covenants often included language identifying a range of racial, ethnic, and religious groups prohibited from occupying properties, in practice they primarily targeted Black Americans.[25]

The use of race restrictive deed covenants became increasingly common following the 1917 Supreme Court decision in *Buchanan v. Warley*, which found that municipal ordinances segregating Black populations—also known as racial zoning ordinances—were unconstitutional.[26] Following this, realtors, developers, homeowners turned to race-restrictive deed covenants, sometimes referred to as "private zoning," to prevent nonwhite people from living in white areas. Historian Jeffrey Gonda points out that racial covenants predated municipal zoning[27] and thus were a readily available and established practice that could quickly be mobilized to "seal burgeoning Black populations into relatively small and deteriorating sections of cities."[28] Concerted opposition to integration on the part of white homeowners, together with federal and local policies, strengthened urban racial boundaries and intensified wartime and postwar housing crises in cities across the United States. By 1928 half of all homes owned by white people in the US had race-restrictive deed covenants.[29]

But for as long as restrictive covenants have existed, Black Americans have organized and struggled against them. Battling racism and exclusion in housing was a central focus of the organizing efforts of the NAACP throughout the early part of the twentieth century. For decades, the NAACP led a coordinated effort to outlaw racial covenants and racial discrimination in housing deeds. As Gonda notes, the NAACP's victory in the case of *Shelley v. Kramer* in 1948 followed three decades of legal challenges to exclusionary housing practices,

---

23. David M. P. Freund, *Colored Property: State Policy and White Racial Politics in Suburban America* (Chicago: University of Chicago Press, 2007).

24. Jeffrey D. Gonda, *Unjust Deeds: The Restrictive Covenant Cases and the Making of the Civil Rights Movement* (Chapel Hill: University of North Carolina Press, 2015).

25. Kevin Fox Gotham, "Urban Space, Restrictive Covenants and the Origins of Residential Racial Segregation in a U.S. City, 1900–1950," *International Journal of Urban and Regional Research* 24, no. 3 (2000): 616–33.

26. Gonda, *Unjust Deeds*; Colin Gordon, "Dividing the City: Race-Restrictive Covenants and the Architecture of Segregation in St. Louis," *Journal of Urban History* 49, no. 1 (2021): 160–82.

27. Here we refer to the regulation and designation of land use by municipal authorities.

28. Gonda, *Unjust Deeds*, 5.

29. Freund, *Colored Property*.

including against municipal racial zoning ordinances and other forms of private and municipal discrimination.[30]

The local fight against rampant racism in housing was also a central focus of the Milwaukee chapter of the NAACP. For example, when the Milwaukee Board of Realtors discussed the possibility of establishing a municipally zoned area for Black residents to live in 1924, which they termed a "Black Belt," the local NAACP chapter immediately protested with marches and written condemnation of the idea in the local newspaper.[31] Upon hearing news about the proposed "Black Belt," Wilbur and Ardie Halyard, Black American activists who had been working in Beloit, Wisconsin, were compelled to move to Milwaukee and work to improve the housing situation for Black Milwaukeeans. They cofounded Columbia Savings and Loan to provide loans to Black homebuyers in 1924.[32] In a 1978 interview, Ardie Halyard explained, "We found it difficult to get a charter. . . . People were not loaning to [B]lack people because they did trust them to repay loans. There was a limit to how far north they [Black people] could go. A very narrow space in which they could buy a home, and in that area, no loans were made."[33] Describing the deep racism characterizing the Milwaukee area, she further recalls that when Columbia Savings and Loan reached its first one million dollars, sometime around 1950, they found it very difficult to secure a venue willing to host their celebration. Mrs. Halyard was instrumental in establishing the NAACP chapter in Kenosha and in reviving the Milwaukee and Racine chapters. She organized the first state conference of the branches, was elected president, and established the NAACP Youth Council, which played a critical role in Milwaukee's historic marches for open housing in 1967 and 1968.[34]

Housing shortages for growing Black populations in cities in the urban north were particularly acute due to the "double barrier"[35] that they faced: deteriorating and limited housing stock combined with entrenched racism that prevented access to affordable, decent housing and that intensified overcrowding. In Milwaukee, landlords exploited these conditions through

---

30. Gonda, *Unjust Deeds*.

31. Box 1, folders 19, 17, Milwaukee Board of Realtors, Milwaukee County Historical Society Archives, Milwaukee, Wisconsin, August 10, 2021.

32. "Nation Observes Negro History Week: Columbia Savings and Loan Hailed on Local Scene," *Milwaukee Defender*, August 19, 1957.

33. Black Women Oral History Project, Interviews, 1976–1981, Ardie Clark Halyard, OH-31. Schlesinger Library, Radcliffe Institute, Harvard University, Cambridge, MA, https://nrs.lib.harvard.edu/urn-3:rad.schl:10043345.

34. Patrick D. Jones, *The Selma of the North: Civil Rights Insurgency in Milwaukee* (Cambridge, MA: Harvard University Press, 2010).

35. Gonda, *Unjust Deeds*, 21.

rent increases targeting Black families with few other options for housing.[36] According to historian Joe Trotter, in the early 1940s, Milwaukee NAACP Attorney George Brawley made a survey of the plats filed with the Register of Deeds Office of Milwaukee County, finding that approximately "90 percent of the subdivisions which had been platted in the city of Milwaukee since 1910 contained some type of restrictive covenant that pledged the owner not to sell or rent to anyone other than caucasian [sic]."[37] Also, NAACP activist and lawyer Lloyd Barbee, who led protests to integrate Milwaukee Public Schools, had copies of Milwaukee racial covenants in his official papers.[38]

The battle against racial covenants also involved efforts to purchase or build homes in areas with racial restrictions. For example, Zeddie Quitman Hyler was one person who directly confronted the covenants. In 1944 Hyler left New Albany, Mississippi, as part of the Great Migration of Black Americans traveling for better opportunities in the urban north. Once in Milwaukee, Hyler worked at a grocery store, Allis-Chalmers, and other industrial jobs and then got a job as a United States postal clerk. He occasionally held two jobs at a time in order "to help us get ahead."[39] He eventually bought and lived in a three-unit building in the heart of the Black neighborhood of Bronzeville. But for so many Americans, the dream of a bigger, newer home and more space made living in the suburbs appealing. For Hyler and other middle-class Black Americans, this dream of a house outside the city core was hindered by restrictive covenants.

To subvert the restrictive housing covenants, Hyler was forced to engage in the rhetorical economy of whiteness by asking his white friend to buy the property and then sell it to Hyler who would build a house for his family. As a result of this transaction, Hyler became the first Black person to buy property in Wauwatosa. Though his home was repeatedly vandalized during construction, Hyler resided in the highly restricted community until his death in 2004. Hyler was just one example that demonstrates how Black residents' efforts to overcome racial covenants in Milwaukee were multilayered and strategic, taking many forms, including protest, establishment of Black lending institutions and organizations, pursuit of open housing legislation, and individual attempts to buy or build homes.

---

36. Joe William Trotter Jr., *Black Milwaukee: The Making of an Industrial Proletariat, 1915–45* (Urbana: University of Illinois Press, 1985).

37. Trotter, *Black Milwaukee*, 71.

38. Barbee Papers, box 203, folder 11, Restrictive Real Estate Covenants, 1929–1946, *March On Milwaukee Civil Rights History Project*.

39. Larry Sandler, "Hyler Overcame Racism to Build his House in Tosa," *Milwaukee Journal Sentinel*, January 1, 2005.

Property as Whiteness

Racial covenants were often written into deeds by private developers and homebuilders, drawing on language and examples developed by the real estate industry. Yet they were enforced by the courts, endorsed and encouraged by the Federal Housing Administration (FHA), and their implementation required the mutual cooperation of a number of parties situated across local, state, and federal contexts.[40] This included white property owners agreeing not to sell or rent to nonwhite people; federal, county, and municipal authorities enforcing and supporting the covenants; and the real estate boards, neighborhood associations, property developers, and individuals enacting and applying the deed restrictions.

The initial set of covenants that we have examined to date illustrate how racial covenants work to create property as whiteness as a rhetorical force to buttress the notion of white supremacy. As we have discussed, property regimes, including the laws, technologies, and logics of ownership that underpin their capacity, emerged and unfolded together with schemas of race, producing the (settler) colonial subject and the capacity to define humans as property.[41] Iyko Day suggests a reversing of Cheryl Harris's concept of "whiteness as property" to suggest "how property, too, was constituted by the white male colonizers['] capacity to appropriate."[42] Day's work examines how in "settler colonies like the United States and Canada, this racial regime of property-as-whiteness rendered Native peoples occupants rather than possessors, and enslaved Black people as objects of possession."[43] Also emphasizing the logics of possession, Aileen Moreton-Robertson's book, *The White Possessive*, examines how "racialization is the process by which whiteness operates possessively to define and construct itself as the pinnacle of its own racial hierarchy."[44] Her notion of "possessive logics" refers to "a mode of rationalization . . . reaffirming . . . ownership, control, and domination."[45] White possessive logics, she contends, are operationalized within discourses circulating sets of meanings, commonsense understandings, conventions, and decision-making. Racial covenants circulated among homeowners, real estate developers, insurers, and municipal leaders as normalized and unquestioned rationalities of white

---

40. Gonda, *Unjust Deeds*.
41. Ranganathan and Bonds, "Introduction"; and Brenna Bhandar, *Colonial Lives of Property: Land, Law, and Racial Regimes of Ownership* (Durham, NC: Duke University Press, 2018).
42. Iyko Day, "Property," *Amerasia Journal* 46, no. 2 (2020): 147–48.
43. Day, "Property"; see also Bhandar, *Colonial Lives*; and Moreton-Robinson, *White Possessive*.
44. Moreton-Robinson, *White Possessive*, xx.
45. Moreton-Robinson, *White Possessive*, xii.

possession that tied homeownership, property rights, and property values inherently to whiteness.

Byrd, Goldstein, Melamed, and Reddy theorize economies of dispossession emerging from the "multiple and intertwined genealogies of racialized property, subjection, and expropriation through which capitalism and colonialism take shape historically and change over time."[46] The political, economic, and social processes necessary to contain, dispossess, and permanently occupy territory are premised on a continuously reworked racial differentiation that underwrites racial capitalism. Therefore, as Harris so lucidly clarifies, within a system of white supremacy premised on the economic exploitation and dispossession of those classified as "other," whiteness operates both as a racial category and as a structure guaranteeing power, dominance, and material benefits.[47] As Du Bois reminds us, "Whiteness is the ownership of the earth forever and ever, amen!"[48] The rhetoric of whiteness in covenants, posited in claims to title and ownership against those deemed not white, spatializes whiteness even as "white's only" neighborhoods and communities depended upon the elaboration and reproduction of racial difference to retain and preserve the "value gap."[49] The spatialization of whiteness thus depends upon the relational spatialization of Blackness through collective and cumulative forms of racist exclusion and extraction that concentrated Black Milwaukeeans in impoverished, underresourced neighborhoods.

We situate our analysis of racial covenants in Milwaukee within mutually produced and reinforced regimes of race and property structured around white ownership and the material and social benefits associated with whiteness. The dividends of whiteness, secured within a system of racial exploitation and dispossession, accumulate in place at the expense of nonwhite people and places. Just as the Great Migration was underway, developers and the burgeoning real estate industry advanced the idea that residential property values were tied to the racial homogeneity of neighborhoods, associating highly segregated white neighborhoods with high property values while equating the presence of nonwhite people with property value decline.[50] In the context of

---

46. Jodi A. Byrd, Alyosha Goldstein, Jodi Melamed, and Chandan Reddy, "Predatory Value: Economies of Dispossession and Disturbed Rationalities," *Social Text* 36, no. 2 (2018): 1–18.

47. Harris, "Whiteness as Property."

48. Du Bois, *Darkwater*, 18.

49. Eddie S. Glaude Jr., *Democracy in Black: How Race Still Enslaves the American Soul* (New York: Crown, 2017).

50. Scott N. Markley, Taylor J. Hafley, Coleman A. Allums, Steven R. Holloway, and Hee Cheol Chung, "The Limits of Homeownership: Racial Capitalism, Black Wealth, and the Appreciation Gap in Atlanta," *International Journal of Urban and Regional Research* 44, no. 2 (2020): 310–28.

an urban housing crisis, a growing Black population, and virulent anti-Blackness, white Milwaukeeans mobilized racial covenants and other technologies of property to confine Black residents to the city's so-called "inner core" to enshrine and protect geographies of whiteness and the benefits and possessions associated with such geographies.

The language of the restrictive covenants and their long-lasting effects on housing speaks to how rhetoric can serve as a social process or "rhetorical materialism."[51] McGee and other material scholars have examined the ways in which rhetoric is substantial and physically concrete.[52] The language used in documents derives its power from the context in which it is used and the cultural and power dynamics involved in its production. In other words, the language of the documents is a "dense reconstruction" of all the bits (or "fragments") of other discourses from which it is made.[53] Racist language in particular was constructed and reconstructed in various forms, documents, and mediums through the early twentieth century, and racial covenants codified and made that racism material within property deeds. The covenants reconstructed fragments of discourse from Jim Crow laws of segregation prevalent in the American South and the colonial/antebellum slave codes where enslaved persons were not permitted to own property.[54] These laws, like the covenants themselves, restricted the movements of Black people and determined where they were permitted to live or the spaces they could occupy. Whether intended or not, Black mobility was restricted by racial covenants. The rhetorical force of the covenants and their repeated usage helped to create a material reality of segregation in the housing industry. In other words, the race restrictive housing covenants created material spaces as white, both ensuring that nonwhite people were confined to highly segregated neighborhoods and also denying them access to the housing equity and wealth associated

---

51. Michael Calvin McGee, "A Materialist's Conception of Rhetoric," in *Explorations in Rhetoric: Essays in Honor of Douglas Ehninger*, ed. Ray E. McKerrow (Glenview, IL: Scott, Foresman, 1982), 23–48.

52. Ronald Walter Greene, "Another Materialist Rhetoric," *Critical Studies in Media Communication* 15, no. 1 (1998): 21–40; Laurie Gries, Jennifer Clary-Lemon, Carolyn Gottschalk Druschke, Nathaniel Rivers, Jodie Nicotra, John M. Ackerman, David M. Grant, Gabriel R. Ríos, Byron Hawk, Joshua S. Hanan, Kristin L. Arola, Thomas J. Rickert, Qwo-Li Driskill, and Donnie Johnson Sackey, "Rhetorical New Materialisms (RNM)," *Rhetoric Society Quarterly* 52, no. 2 (2022): 137–202.

53. Michael Calvin McGee, "Text, Context, and the Fragmentation of Contemporary Culture," *Western Journal of Speech Communication* 54, no. 3 (1990): 279.

54. Thomas N. Ingersoll, "Slave Codes and Judicial Practice in New Orleans, 1718–1807," *Law and History Review* 13, no. 1 (1995): 23–62; Frances L. Edwards and Grayson Bennett Thomson, "The Legal Creation of Raced Space: The Subtle and Ongoing Discrimination Created through Jim Crow Laws," *Berkeley Journal of African-American Law and Policy* 12, no. 1 (2010): 145.

with suburban homeownership. The borders and boundaries of whiteness and white spaces are vigorously defended through the logics of property and the legal and state apparatus underpinning them.[55] Because only white people could live and own racially restricted properties, covenanted neighborhoods and homes, and the manicured and regulated spaces surrounding them, were imbued with a white racial identity. In this sense, whiteness is embedded in both social and physical environments. Racial covenants are material manifestations of the white supremacist ordering of space and bodies.

Legal Language

Because racial covenants were legally binding and enforceable contracts, the racist language used in them appears in the legal syntax or register. The linguistic feature of legal language is often long, complex sentences deployed "to remove all ambiguity from a document, or to make it ambiguous in only the ways the writer wants it to be ambiguous."[56] The effect of this register is twofold. First, it disrupts the familiar narrative of where racism takes place and how it operates. It displaces dominant understandings of racism and caricatures of white supremacy that locate anti-Blackness and racist violence within the purview of extremists like the Ku Klux Klan, as seen in the oft-used image of a sweaty Southern sheriff yelling through a bullhorn at civil rights protestors being blasted with a fire hose. Here racism is presented in legalese; routinized within the language of private property; and administered, acknowledged, and enforced by the state. Consequently, this language makes the covenants seem less discriminatory because it is more official.

Racism in this legal register transfers focus away from acts of racial aggression or violence and the wide-eyed hatred of "colored people," instead locating it within the everyday and mundane actions of "regular" white people. This unsettles easy associations—and dismissals—of racism as emanating from a few "bad apples," revealing instead how racism is systematized in ways that facilitate and reinforce the structural benefits of whiteness. For example, an excerpt from a racial covenant from South Milwaukee identified in our research reads as follows:

> At no time shall the Lot of any building thereon be purchased, owned, leased, occupied or used by any person other than citizen of the United States of

---

55. Bonds, "Race and Ethnicity."
56. Barbara Johnstone, *Discourse Analysis* (Hoboken, NJ: John Wiley and Sons, 2007), 175.

America, of the White Race. This provision shall not apply to domestic servants which may be employed by the owner or occupant of any such Lot or building thereon.
Date Recorded: Dec. 13, 1937
Length of Term: Jan. 1, 2024

The racial language is presented in legal registers that confirm the officialism of race restrictions. Terms like "heretofore," "thereon," and "whereby" convey a formalism, sanitizing and obscuring the violence of racism and racial exclusion. Another racial covenant from 1926 uncovered in our research is particularly illustrative of how the legal language detailing racial restrictions obscures both the restriction's meaning and its violent intent. The covenant reads:

> That the premises herein described shall not be conveyed or leased to the grantor hereof or any of the successors in title of the grantee to any person who is not Caucasian, and that neither the said premises herein described nor any of the improvements thereon shall be occupied by anyone who is not a Caucasian; that in the event that the premises herein described shall be conveyed or leased by the grantee or any successors in the title of the grantee to any person who is not Caucasian, the property herein described shall revert to the grantor free and clear from any claim of the grantee or the successors in the title of the grantee, such reversion, however, to be subject to any then-existing encumbrance.

Here the repetition of the word "Caucasian" occurs within a confoundingly long sentence written in the language of real estate, with terms like "grantee," "grantor," and "successor" appearing with similar frequency. This racial covenant is also notable in that it also clarifies the consequences of violating the racial restriction. In most cases, details about the violation of restrictions appear elsewhere in the document.

Indeed, in our research we find instances where racial covenants are barely noticeable within property deeds. Embedded within dry legalese describing lot size, restrictions on building height and setbacks, we find restrictions on human beings—restrictions that, while formalized and presented in official language, facilitated the racist denial of opportunity and access for Black American home seekers. As deed after deed containing racial covenants was signed and sealed, new geographies of whiteness were made premised on the exclusion of nonwhite "others." The rhetoric of the racial covenant is made material by the signers of the deed. The legal weight and authority of racial covenants and the sheer number of them across the suburban landscape created a naturalized reality of race and real estate premised on the premium of whiteness and white spaces. White people were not only authorized to engage in legal racist practices regarding real estate, they were also required to by the covenants or risk forfeiture.

These dynamics reveal the fact that whiteness is not a reality, but rather a creation made concrete through language, actions, and beliefs and their repetition and recirculation. As mentioned earlier, whiteness is a product of the value gap between white people and nonwhite people.[57] Racial covenants embedded the hierarchal ordering of bodies and places within the built environment. Though no longer enforceable, these covenants remain in property deeds as evidence of the racialization of space. In Milwaukee County, one of the last racial covenants registered in the Village of Wauwatosa was filed in 1955, seven years after the 1948 *Shelley v. Kraemer* Supreme Court decision that racial covenants could not be enforced. A racial covenant was registered three years later in the Milwaukee suburb of Greendale. Clearly, even after they were no longer legally enforceable, the symbolic power of racial covenants remained: whites only. Legal enforcement evolved to a "gentleman's agreement" between interested parties, and thus the legal language of whiteness remained. This occurred and recurred in city after city, community after community, and deed after deed.[58]

Racial Restrictions and Anti-Blackness

As mentioned earlier, racial restrictions were implemented throughout Milwaukee County in the 1920s and 1930s. Though racial covenants were utilized throughout cities, they were particularly concentrated in suburban areas where it was easier for developers and real estate agencies to apply covenants to large plots of land before parcels were sold and developed. Even so, the racial language in the covenants took various forms. For the builders and real estate officials, the primary imperative that no one other than "the white race" or "Caucasians" lived or occupied the properties underscored assumptions about the premium of whiteness and its connections to property value. For instance, the Weber-Fleming Realty company entered into a covenant agreement with William and Linda Schaus on January 18, 1940, in Whitefish Bay, a prominent north shore suburb of Milwaukee. The racial language in the covenant stated:

---

57. Glaude, *Democracy in Black*, 29–50.
58. Freund, *Colored Property*.

That it is mutually understood and agreed by and between the parties hereto that this deed is executed and delivered upon the following express conditions and restrictions. . . . That no part of within described premises or any building erected thereon shall at any time be owned or occupied by colored people.

The language is jarring because of its matter-of-fact statement of racist exclusion, written in the same legal language as the rest of the document, reflecting and reinforcing the anti-Black racism that devalued Black Americans and associated them with neighborhood decline. This particular covenant and its restrictions were to "remain in full force and effect until the first day of January, 1950." Another Whitefish Bay subdivision called Zingen and Braun's Strathmoor was covenanted in 1927, with the racial covenants set to expire in 1975.[59] This subdivision was enthusiastically advertised to potential white buyers as "a highly distinctive and restricted district."[60] These covenants were set to last over a period of years to ensure that the community would remain white. Whether the covenant language specified "Caucasians only" or that the land shall not be conveyed to "colored people," the logics and intent were equivalent: Blackness and the presence of Black people devalued property and neighborhoods. In other words, the rhetorical economies of whiteness within the covenants hinged on anti-Blackness.

The intentionality in the language choice highlights and reinforces—in a legal document—the racial hierarchies of white supremacy. As a result, every other restriction and property requirement listed in the document can now only be viewed through the lens of whiteness and efforts to create "highly restricted and distinctive" spaces for "whites only." The language in the document infuses whiteness into the parcel, buildings, and dwellings on the property. Whiteness clouds the requirements for the placement of the garage, the size of the fence, or building purposes that are also listed in housing covenants. Whiteness becomes synonymous with neighborhoods that are perceived as "first-class residence[s]." Whiteness, like the beautiful suburban homes, is something to aspire to and possess, and yet its value is preserved through what is excluded. The language of the covenants authorizes this aspiration and protects it with its clear and direct restrictive language. The covenants clearly let the buyer and seller know that whiteness is supreme, and there is no question of its place in the racial hierarchy.

---

59. Zingen and Brauns continues to operate today, offering real estate insurance.
60. Many new subdivisions were advertised to potential homebuyers in local newspapers. Analysis of these advertisements provides an opportunity to see how restrictions—both racial and otherwise—were promoted to convey the distinctiveness and "quality" of the neighborhood.

Inversely, this language or restriction implicates directly how the presence of "colored people" in an ownership role is a direct threat to the value of the property and the surrounding properties. The structures too would become "colored" and thus be incompatible with the whites-only structures in the surrounding neighborhood. This new logic of restriction, as coined by David M. P. Freund, legally grounded racially restrictive covenants "upon the assumption that certain land uses and certain populations categorically threatened the value of private property and the 'health and welfare' of white property owners."[61] Ironically, in the case of this particular covenant, white is even in the name of the community—Whitefish Bay. It is perhaps not surprising that Black Milwaukeeans colloquially refer to the village as "white folks bay," and that in the past it was referred to as "white face bay." Regardless of economic status, education level, or occupation, Black homeowners could never make the transition from urban dwellings to suburban living because their presence would disrupt racial hierarchies and devalue properties. The suburbs were representative of this hierarchy, which meant that Black people remained "hemmed in" urban neighborhoods.[62]

It is critically important to emphasize that the racial restriction is the only place in a deed document, outside of the names of the people involved in the transaction, where human beings appear or are mentioned. Rather, the bulk of language contained within property deed documents describes how the property can be used, what kinds of buildings or structures can be erected on the property, the value of the homes to be built on the land, uses of the garages, types of signs permitted on the premises, and restrictions against creating or selling "intoxicating liquors." Often, the only human beings that are explicitly mentioned in the document are "colored people." Conversely, in covenants stipulating that "said premises shall never be occupied by or conveyed to anyone other than the white race," people of color appear in the deed only insofar as what they are not (white), underscoring Moreton-Robinson's assertion that "whiteness operates possessively to define and construct itself as the pinnacle of its own racial hierarchy."[63] It is here where we see the weight and the power of white supremacy creating and enforcing racially segregated spaces.

Examining racial covenants lays bare the myths of American bootstrap individualism and homeownership as the key to prosperity: the ethos of hard work and merit do not apply in the Jim Crow urban/suburban north, where racial restrictions combined with other racist policies and practices that

---

61. Freund, *Colored Property*, 92.
62. Langston Hughes, *The Collected Poems of Langston Hughes* (New York: Knopf, 1994), 362.
63. Moreton-Robinson, *White Possessive*, xx.

denied access and opportunity and confined growing Black populations in disinvested urban areas. Growing Black populations in cities in the Midwest and Northeast created a heightened sense of fear among developers and the real estate industry. In fact, in 1924 the National Association of Real Estate Boards (NAREB) introduced Article 34 into its Code of Ethics, which stipulated that "a Realtor should never be instrumental [in] introducing into a neighborhood a character of property or occupancy, members of any race or nationality, or any individuals whose presence will clearly be detrimental to property values in a neighborhood." Indeed, the penalty of violating the restrictive agreement was explicit and harsh, reverting the property back to the realty company without any compensation to the owners. And indeed, many Black property owners who purchased racially covenanted properties, knowingly or otherwise, did lose their homes.[64]

The real estate industry, homebuilders, and private homeowners, capitalized on and reinforced the rhetorical economy of whiteness, further enshrining racism in new suburban developments. As a result, Black Americans and other ethnic minorities were confined to highly segregated neighborhoods whereas white exclusive enclaves were being created. These areas of whiteness were made so through conscious design and provided only whites access to the housing equity and wealth associated with suburban homeownership.

Delineating "Domestic Servants" and the Rhetorics of Whiteness

Analysis of racial covenants also reveals the hierarchies of labor underpinning white supremacy within a system of racial capitalism.[65] Although Black Americans were not permitted to own or rent the properties as described by racial restrictions, they could occupy the properties as domestic servants or as employees of white homeowners. This is an extremely common caveat that appeared in racial covenants within and beyond Milwaukee County. Here we can see such an example in the Beverly Hills neighborhood in the town of Wauwatosa:

> At no time shall the land included in Beverly Hills or any part thereof or any building thereon, be purchased, owned, leased or occupied by any other person other than of the White Race. This prohibition is not intended to

---

64. Gonda, *Unjust Deeds*; and Freund, *Colored Property*.
65. Cedric J. Robinson, *Black Marxism: The Making of the Black Radical Tradition* (1983; Chapel Hill: University of North Carolina Press, 2000).

include *domestic servants* [emphasis added] while employed by the owner or occupant of any land included in the tract.

This language similarly appears in the Washington Highlands covenants that we discussed earlier in the chapter:

At no time shall the land included in Washington Highlands or any part thereof, or any building thereon be purchased, owned, leased or occupied by any person other than of white race. This prohibition is not intended to include *domestic servants* [emphasis added] while employed by the owner or occupant of any land included in the tract.

The language is clear and explicit, stipulating all possibilities in which nonwhites could occupy properties, but ensuring that white supremacist hierarchies of labor and exploitation remained intact. The racial covenants ensured that nonwhites could continue to deliver the socially reproductive labor—the childcare, housekeeping, landscaping, and building maintenance—necessary for sustaining white supremacy and white spaces. Nonwhite bodies, therefore, must be permitted to occupy white spaces under specific, legally defined circumstances specifying the proper place in which they can exist in such close proximity to whiteness.

This language, appearing repeatedly in racial covenants throughout Milwaukee County, asserts and reaffirms the social status of Black Americans within the ideology of white supremacy. As noted by Michael Jones-Correa, "The diffusion of racial restrictive covenants was ensured by the National Association of Real Estate Boards (NAREB), which was eager to foster segregated neighborhoods and actively propagated the use of covenants toward that end."[66] The covenants were used by NAREB in community after community in neighborhoods all over the country, creating a geography of whiteness that was vigorously maintained by legal means and violence when necessary. Within racial covenants, whiteness and white supremacy were fundamentally secured to the land and property with racial language and restrictions stipulating how and in which ways race could *take place*. Property as whiteness and whiteness as property was clearly defined and systematized in real estate and housing markets. Indeed, white propertied power—the political, economic, and social power afforded to white homeowners via property relations[67]—is further asserted in conditions allowing for nonwhites laboring in devalued

---

66. Michael Jones-Correa, "The Origins and Diffusion of Racial Restrictive Covenants," *Political Science Quarterly* 115, no. 4 (2000): 541–68.

67. Bonds, "Race and Ethnicity."

domestic labor. The logic of this spatial dynamic idea is both ironic and perplexing: the racial covenants create a narrative within which the presence of Black Americans and other nonwhite bodies is allowed in service to whiteness and white supremacy. Thus, it is not only the absence of Blackness that enhances the properties as white but rather a presence of Blackness under certain requirements that ensures relations of white supremacy. The geographies of whiteness and white supremacy must be defined against the Black American bodies and spaces that they are not, harkening to the main character in Ralph Ellison's *Invisible Man,* who must add drops of a dark black mixture to an original dull gray substance in order to make Liberty Paints' Optic White color.[68]

Location of Racial Language

The rhetorical force of the racist language in covenants can also be viewed in *where* the language is located in the document and the context in which the racial covenants are embedded within the deed. Our research on racial covenants finds that there doesn't seem to be a clear or consistent pattern to where such language might appear within the property deed, which is one of the reasons that they can be difficult to identify. Some racial covenants might appear early in the deed, while others appear pages later. For instance, a deed may have language detailing restrictions against "manufacture, sale or disposal of intoxicating liquors" or the prohibition of "building detrimental to a rural residential subdivision" in sentences just before statements that "no person other than of the white race" is permitted on the property. In other instances, we find the racial restriction is couched between the yard features of shrubbery and where fences and boundary walls can be placed. The effect of which is that nonwhite people are compared with and reduced to the nonhuman and inanimate objects that could also not be on the land/property. The racial covenants in some deeds appear alongside descriptions of livestock, poultry, and other animals prohibited on properties. For instance, a racial covenant in Greenfield, a suburb of Milwaukee, states that "the premises shall never be occupied by or conveyed to a colored person," followed by language in the same paragraph specifying "that no cows, horses, or livestock of any kind (poultry excepted) shall be kept on the premises." Even more striking, the following 1927 covenant referring to a property in Milwaukee states:

---

68. Ralph Ellison, *Invisible Man* (1952; New York: Vintage, 1995), 217.

> Provided, further, that no part of the lands herein conveyed shall be sold, leased to, or occupied by any person except one of the Caucasian race, and that no animals, fowl or birds, except domestic fowl, not to exceed 50 in number kept within an enclosure, and except song birds, and no more than two canine animals, shall be kept on said lands.

In this covenant, restrictions applying to nonwhites are included within the same sentence clarifying limitations on domestic fowl—excluding song birds—and canines. The sinister animalization and violent equation of grouping people of color with unwanted animals hearkens back to the language of chattel slavery that defined Black people as property.

This dehumanization appears in many forms. For example, another racial covenant registered in 1927 in the Lincoln Park neighborhood states that "the premises herein described shall not be conveyed or leased to or be occupied by any person other than of the white race. Servants, other than of the white race, of an owner or tenant of said premises, while engaged in the capacity of servants, shall be permitted to occupy said premises." The intended effect of this dehumanizing language is that Black people who worked in these homes as domestic servants were constantly reminded that these spaces, according to the covenants, would never belong to them or their children. It also reinforces their belief that they are not full citizens where "the emblem of American citizenship" is homeownership.[69] For Black people, hard work and saving money would never overcome the economic threshold of whiteness in the covenants.

Another example of dehumanization is evident in the statement that follows directly from the sentence above. It states, "No unused building material, junk or rubbish shall be left exposed on said land except during operations." Here the restrictions of those "other than the white race" are situated alongside restrictions on refuse and waste, the presence of which disrupts the orderly landscape and therefore should remain invisible. The surrounding text reinforces the traditional rhetorical economies of whiteness justifying exploitation, inequality, and resource disparities. For those Black Americans who worked in these spaces, their humanity, agency, and relationship to their surroundings was reduced to convoluted calculations of white supremacy that were written in these covenants. The historical distortion of Black Americans in the United States is rooted in white supremacy as a system of exploitation and domination of Black and Indigenous peoples, from which racially

---

69. Ta-Nehisi Coates, "The Case for Reparations," *The Atlantic,* June 2014, https://www.theatlantic.com/magazine/archive/2014/06/the-case-for-reparations/361631/.

contingent forms of property emerge.[70] No longer defined as property, in the Jim Crow Midwest, Black Milwaukeeans were equated to property restrictions, not permitted alongside certain land uses, buildings, animals, and plant life. This violence of language and the conscious choice of it, shaped the context in which housing would be discussed, negotiated, and purchased, resulting in racially segregated white neighborhoods premised on the exclusion and exploitation of Black Americans and other unwanted ethnic groups. Racial covenants reaffirmed the persistence of whiteness as property and ensured the legacy of material disinvestment in Blackness and its catastrophic impacts.

Conclusion

While racial covenants and other discriminatory housing policies have been eliminated and even outlawed, their consequences live on.[71] They remain embedded in property deeds throughout the United States as evidence of the ways in which white supremacy and segregationist systems mapped race and urban development. Working together, they channeled investment into the growing white suburbs and facilitated disinvestment in urban areas occupied by nonwhite, working-class communities.

Of course, racial covenants were just one mechanism explicitly designed to separate urban populations by race and class. The rhetorical force of their language worked in conjunction with an array of other federal policies, patterns of lending, municipal ordinances, and private practices that ensured the racial segregation of American cities. At the local scale, municipalities and private actors backed real estate practices and patterns of lending that further guaranteed the racial homogeneity of neighborhoods. The real estate industry and homebuilders capitalized on and reinforced the rhetorical practices of racial segregation, further enshrining racism in urban and suburban housing markets. People of color and ethnic minorities were not only confined to highly segregated neighborhoods that were made so through conscious design; they were denied access to the housing equity, wealth, and security associated with suburban homeownership, inscribed and produced as white.

In this chapter, we emphasize residential property and racial covenants in Milwaukee County to illustrate whiteness as property and the legal

---

70. Harris, "Whiteness as Property"; and Bonds and Inwood, "Beyond White Privilege."
71. Though restrictive covenants are no longer legal, other mechanisms of African American confinement have emerged in their wake, including carceral strategies of containment in the era of mass criminalization. See Rashad Shabazz, *Spatializing Blackness: Architectures of Confinement and Black Masculinity in Chicago* (Champaign: University of Illinois Press, 2015).

mechanisms preventing people of color from owning, or even occupying, property. Racist housing policy has often been viewed, as we have at various points in this chapter, as an extension of Jim Crow-era segregation policies. But what sorts of new questions might emerge when we think through racist housing policy in the urban industrial North and Midwest as part of an ongoing colonial project predicated on the logics of white possession and displacement? Such a reframing contests white epistemologies that exclude Indigenous histories and challenges us to consider residential property within a much longer history of white settlement and territorial appropriation. This focus resists static understandings of race that are unmoored from places by revealing the fluidity of racial categories and the ways in which practices of racialization are possessively defined and constructed in specific geographic contexts. White supremacy—produced through structures of domination—is not inexorable, nor is it unchanging. But it has always been intimately bound up with hegemonic notions of dis/possession: from the propertizing of human life via slavery, to the creation of liberal norms of property aimed at abolishing communal property holdings, to structures and policies excluding people of color and women from the material advantages and benefits of property. Examining systems of property and race as they are continuously remade in place through hierarchies of value and power, we argue, allows us to think about the ongoing production of white supremacist logics and their geographies.

CHAPTER 3

Gradations of Self-Reflexivity

Reckoning with Racial Privilege in Progressive White Parents' School Choice Discourse

KELLY JENSEN

White racial identity formation in the US is riddled with tensions and contradictions. One such context that magnifies this complexity is the way in which white parents discuss how they choose "good" schools for their children. Rife with subjective measures of quality, justifications of unique circumstances, and often coded racism, the language of school choice carries historical baggage that dates to the mid-twentieth-century era of white opposition to school desegregation in the US. In its contemporary manifestations, school choice signals a broader reform movement that advocates for a parent's right to use public tax dollars to choose the best fit school for a child. School choice references a spectrum of policy reforms, including open enrollment, magnet or specialty schools, charter schools, scholarship tax credit programs, and private school vouchers. These education policy reforms range in their degree of controversiality, from less controversial open enrollment programs to more controversial private school voucher programs. Although parents of all races advocate for various forms of school choice, the historical legacy of the US education system unfairly benefiting white families bears significance on its meaning. A glimpse into the historical uses of school choice demonstrates how this language has long been used to perpetuate unequal access to a quality education based on privilege and race.¹ This history of institutionalized racism in K–12 education warrants scrutinization of how white parents employ school choice in the present-day in ways that reaffirm white privilege. Indeed, contemporary school enrollment patterns reflect the ways that socioeconomically advantaged white parents reproduce racial segregation in schools. White, advantaged parents leverage their social networks to influence the educational decisions of other white parents in ways that concentrate white families in specific schools and districts, hoard educational opportunities, influence school reputations, and redirect funding streams.²

Given the connections between access to education and upward economic mobility, school choice exacerbates uneven race and class relations. A particular quandary presents itself for white parents who identify as politically progressive, given the assumptions that accompany their left-leaning values. I define white progressives as white people that politically identify as left of center with nominal commitments to social justice values like educational equity, antiracism, and multiculturalism. Progressive white parents must navigate the tension between their nominal commitments and their privileged positioning in the education system. White progressives, like their conservative counterparts, benefit from complex systems of neoliberalism and racial capitalism. Neoliberalism exerts a hegemonic influence as an orientation that applies a market-based lens to previously noneconomic public realms, like education, to promote values such as the freedom of competition and individual choice that position parents as consumers.³ Through emphasis on individual responsibility, the racist logics of neoliberal ideology depoliticize

---

1. Candace Epps-Robertson, *Resisting Brown: Race, Literacy, & Citizenship in the Heart of Virginia* (Pittsburgh, PA: University of Pittsburgh Press, 2018); and Kelly Jensen, "Localized Ideographs in Education Rhetoric: Polly Williams and a Justice-Driven Ideology of Choice," *Quarterly Journal of Speech* 107, no. 3 (2021): 305–27.

2. Jennifer J. Holme, "Buying Homes, Buying Schools: School Choice and the Social Construction of School Quality," *Harvard Educational Review* 72, no. 2 (2002): 177–206; Heather Beth Johnson, *The American Dream and the Power of Wealth: Choosing Schools and Inheriting Inequality in the Land of Opportunity* (New York: Routledge, 2015); Linn Posey-Maddox, *When Middle-Class Parents Choose Urban Schools* (Chicago: University of Chicago Press, 2014); and Jeremy Singer and Sarah Winchell Lenhoff, "Race, Geography, and School Choice Policy: A Critical Analysis of Detroit Students' Suburban School Choices," *AERA Open*, 8 (2022), https://doi.org/10.1177/23328584211067202.

3. Wendy Brown, *Undoing the Demos: Neoliberalism's Stealth Revolution* (New York: Zone Books, 2015); Michael J. Dumas, "My Brother as 'Problem': Neoliberal Governmentality and Interventions for Black Young Men and Boys," *Educational Policy* 30, no. 1 (2016): 94–113; and David Harvey, *A Brief History of Neoliberalism* (Oxford, UK: Oxford University Press), 2005.

structural difference and discount race and racism as individual concerns.[4] In purporting a supposedly universal, race-absent individual, neoliberalism produces a mold that adheres to cultural standards of whiteness, thus reproducing racial hierarchies that reinforce white hegemony.[5] This raises questions as to how white progressive parents may intend to contribute to equity efforts while bound up in violent systems of racial oppression. Moreover, a racial capitalist framework highlights the interdependent relationship between racism and capitalism and how progressive white parents with socioeconomic privilege benefit from greater access to mechanisms of choice due to the material advantages they enjoy as a result of their class position.

This chapter spotlights K–12 education as a key site for the production of racial subjectivity and racial socialization. Joining fellow contributors to this volume interrogating whiteness as a rhetorical identity, I explore the extent to which progressive white parents are critically aware of their white racial identity when talking about their school choice decisions. To assemble a text of this discursive phenomenon, I engaged rhetorical field methods, drawing from interview and focus group data with white, politically progressive, socioeconomically advantaged parents of K–12 school-aged children living in the Madison, Wisconsin, area. Through the frame of critical self-reflexivity, I demonstrate the varying degrees to which participants name and recognize their whiteness as a racial identity associated with privilege. I critically examine white identity formation in parents' discourse through three analytical themes: ambiguity in articulating white identity, ease and comfort in school spaces, and relationality to other white people. In doing so, I argue that the gradations of self-reflexivity within each theme reveal varied understandings of whiteness as part of a hegemonic structure for which parents might assume a broader sense of responsibility.

In the absence of a nominalist rhetoric that recognizes white parents' privileged positioning in the K–12 education system, existing white privilege continues to entrench established relations of power within this area of

---

4. Kevin L. Clay, "Despite the Odds: Unpacking the Politics of Black Resilience Neoliberalism," *American Education Research Journal* 20, no. 10 (2018): 1–36; Pauline Lipman, *The New Political Economy of Urban Education: Neoliberalism, Race, and the Right to the City* (Chicago: University of Chicago Press, 2011); Bradley Jones and Roopali Mukherjee, "From California to Michigan: Race, Rationality, and Neoliberal Governmentality," *Communication and Critical/Cultural Studies* 7, no. 4 (2010): 401–22; and Darrel Wanzer-Serrano, "Barack Obama, the Tea Party, and the Threat of Race: On Racial Neoliberalism and Born Again Racism," *Communication, Culture & Critique* 4, no. 1 (2011): 23–30.

5. Jeong-eun Rhee, "The Neoliberal Racial Project, Governmentality, and the Tiger Mother," *Educational Theory* 63, no. 6 (2013): 561–80; and Lester K. Spence, *Knocking the Hustle: Against the Neoliberal Turn in Black Politics* (New York: Punctum Books, 2015).

economic governance. The ways white, progressive, advantaged parents assign value to schools entails not only symbolic effects but material ones as well, like perpetuating or disrupting patterns of segregation and influencing school funding tied to student enrollment. As such, this chapter nuances scholarly understandings of whiteness as a rhetorical identity through focused attention on how advantaged white parents negotiate structural power and privilege within the institution of K–12 education. In what follows, I summarize my methodology and provide local context on Madison, Wisconsin, as it relates to the position of white progressive parents and school choice. Next, I theorize white identities as privileged, embodied, and operating as if outside identity before describing my analytic frame of self-reflexivity. I then analyze the varying degrees of self-reflexivity through themes of white identity formation in parents' discourse: ambiguity, ease and comfort, and relationality. I conclude with reflections about what this chapter demonstrates in terms of a broader ethic of responsibility as it relates to the position of progressive white parents and school choice.

Methods

The parent discourse I examine in this chapter emerged out of rhetorical field work I conducted in the summer of 2021. Field methods augment our methodological toolbox, affording critics the ability to engage otherwise inaccessible texts among vernacular publics.[6] Rhetorical field methods enabled me to construct a text to interrogate the localized discursive phenomenon of how progressive white parents with privilege perform varying degrees of racial reflexivity in their school choice discourse. Moreover, the participatory nature of field methods creates opportunities for in situ rhetorical study, immersing the critic into the cultural context in which discourse circulates.[7] This methodological approach allowed me to capture the nuance, texture, and complexity in how this local, shared culture rhetorically constructs their racial identities amid broader discourses.

Through interviews and focus groups, I engaged with the unique perspectives of forty-three socioeconomically advantaged K–12 parents in Dane County, Wisconsin, that racially identify as white and politically identify as left

---

6. Sara L. McKinnon, Robert Asen, Karma R. Chávez, and Robert Glenn Howard, eds., *Text + Field: Innovations in Rhetorical Method* (University Park: Pennsylvania State University Press, 2016).

7. Michael K. Middleton, Samantha Senda-Cook, and Danielle Endres, "Articulating Rhetorical Field Methods: Challenges and Tensions," *Western Journal of Communication* 75, no. 4 (2011): 386–406.

of center.[8] Of the parents I met with, thirty-nine identified as female and four as identified as male. They worked in a range of careers such as attorneys, librarians, software engineers, social workers, researchers, educators, small-business owners, and stay-at-home moms. In addition to these roles, many parents assumed leadership positions at their children's schools, serving as classroom volunteers, afterschool club facilitators, members of parent leadership groups like the parent teacher organization (PTO) or parent equity groups, leaders of school fundraising efforts, or regular attendees of parent assemblies.

To recruit participants, I conducted snowball sampling through contacts in my personal network, including Madison-area parents and PTO leaders. They shared the details of my study on their neighborhood association listservs, school PTO listservs, social media pages, and directly with friends and neighbors in their social networks. I also asked study participants at the conclusion of their interview for recommendations of people that might be interested in participating. I followed up with some but not all as to ensure I recruited a representative sample of parents from a wide variety of neighborhoods across the Madison area. Prior to their interview or focus group, participants completed an eight-question demographic survey from which I determined their socioeconomically advantaged designation and confirmed their political identity.[9] This survey asked participants to classify themselves on a political identity scale. Although some classified themselves as "far left," "liberal," "Democrat," or "progressive," all participants collectively identified as left of center.[10] Therefore, throughout this chapter, I employ "progressive" as an umbrella term to refer to participants' collective left-of-center political identities despite scaled differences within their classifications. With approval from the University of Wisconsin-Madison Institutional Review Board and the consent of each participant, the interviews and focus groups were recorded and transcribed. They were semi-structured and followed an interview protocol that covered five main themes: school attendance background, political

---

8. I conducted twenty-nine interviews, lasting between thirty-nine minutes to one hour and thirty-five minutes. Twenty-six of these were one-on-one with an individual parent, and three were two-on-one with a married couple, totaling thirty-two interview participants. I also conducted three seventy-five-minute focus groups with three to four participants in each, totaling eleven focus group participants. The interviews and focus groups met either over Zoom or in-person. Participants received a monetary incentive in recognition of their time.

9. All participants earned at or above the median household income for Dane County and all participants held a BA/BS degree, with more than two-thirds holding advanced degrees.

10. The survey included a 9-point political identity scale: 1-Far Left; 2-Liberal; 3-Democrat; 4-Progressive; 5-Independent; 6-Moderate; 7-Republican; 8-Conservative; and 9-Far Right. All participants (100%) identified as left of center: 14 percent identified as 1-Far Left, 56 percent identified as 2-Liberal, 21 percent identified as 3-Democrat, and 9 percent identified as 4-Progressive. I employ "progressive" given how all participants identified as a 4 or less.

identity and values, definitions of school choice, race and difference, and the position of white parents in school choice.

The Progressive, Advantaged, and Segregated City of Madison

As Wisconsin's capital city and home to the state's flagship university, Madison's current population hovers around 269,840. Consistently ranked as one of America's "best places to live," Madison is nationally recognized as eco-friendly, physically fit, bike-friendly, family-friendly, and of course as a college football town.[11] Madison is also nationally well-known for its more liberal and progressive politics. In the 2020 Presidential election, over 75 percent of Dane County, where Madison is located, voted for President Biden, and over 76 percent of Madison voted in favor of two local school district referenda that would raise property taxes in support of the city's schools.[12] The city is steeped in a rich history of taking an active role in progressive causes. Protests regularly gather in front of the Wisconsin State Capitol building to advocate for abortion rights, gun control reform, marijuana legalization, or climate change policies. In the summer of 2020, after the murder of George Floyd by Minneapolis police, Madison-area residents participated in racial justice protests in downtown Madison for nearly eleven consecutive days. Dane County's population demographics also skew highly educated and socioeconomically advantaged. In 2022, 53 percent of Dane County residents held a bachelor's degree compared to only 31.5 percent of Wisconsin residents statewide. Moreover, the county's median household income in 2022 was $78,452 compared to $67,080 statewide.[13] These socioeconomic levels cater to class privilege, making Madison a comfortable city to live in for those who are white and middle class.

Accounting for Madison's racial segregation and educational disparities paints a less bright picture of the city. A 2020 report ranked Wisconsin the most segregated state in America, reflecting the significant disparities between the state's white and Black residents in areas such as income gaps and labor

---

11. US Census Bureau, 2020 Decennial Census, Table P1, https://data.census.gov/cedsci/profile?g=1600000US5548000 (accessed July 5, 2022); and "Rankings and Accolades," Destination Madison, https://www.visitmadison.com/media/rankings/ (accessed July 5, 2022).

12. "Election and Voting Information 2020 General Election," County of Dane Wisconsin, December 15, 2020, https://elections.countyofdane.com/Election-Result/124#race0041.

13. US Census Bureau, 2022 American Community Survey 5-Year Estimates, QuickFacts, https://www.census.gov/quickfacts/fact/table/WI,danecountywisconsin/PST045222 (accessed November 3, 2022).

force participation.[14] Historical patterns of residential segregation, which reveal the city's alignment with national trends of exclusionary housing and zoning practices dating back to the 1930s, continue to shape a racially segregated city.[15] Madison is an overwhelming white city with a population nearly 73 percent white, about 9 percent Asian, 7 percent Hispanic/Latino, 7 percent Black/African American, 5 percent two or more races, and less than 1 percent American Indian/Alaskan Native and Native Hawaiian/Pacific Islander.[16] Despite its majority white population, Madison Metropolitan School District (MMSD) is what is known as a "majority-minority" school district. More than half of MMSD's students are students of color, and white students comprise 43 percent of the district's enrollment.[17] Within the district, white students consistently outperform their Black and Brown peers on a variety of academic measures.[18]

Madison's school choice context made it a salient site for this study. All Madison-area students are assigned a default public school based on their designated attendance areas. There is a lottery system in MMSD for three middle schools and for the Dual Language Immersion program. MMSD offers an internal transfer program, and the Wisconsin Department of Public Instruction provides an interdistrict public school open enrollment program. Parents can also choose among the handful of charter school options in the area. Additionally, there are a variety of private schools around Madison as well as a statewide private school voucher program available for qualifying families. Within my sample, 67 percent of families chose among only public school options, and the other 33 percent choose among mixed public and private options.[19]

---

14. Adam McCann, "States with the Most Racial Progress," WalletHub, January 11, 2022, https://wallethub.com/edu/states-with-the-most-and-least-racial-progress/18428.

15. Jamie Perez, "Redlining Madison: Expert Describes How Cities Were Designed to Put People of Color at Disadvantage," Channel 3000, June 19, 2020, https://www.channel3000.com/redlining-madison-expert-describes-how-cities-were-designed-to-put-people-of-color-at-disadvantage/; and "City of Madison Analysis of Impediments to Fair Housing Choice," City of Madison Community Development Division, April 22, 2019, https://www.cityofmadison.com/cdbg/documents/DRAFTFullReport-ImpedimentstoFairHousingChoice4.22.19.pdf.

16. US Census Bureau, Quick Facts Madison city, Wisconsin, https://www.census.gov/quickfacts/fact/table/madisoncitywisconsin,US/PST045221 (accessed July 5, 2022).

17. Black/African American 18 percent, Asian 9 percent, Latino 21 percent, white 43 percent, two or more races 9 percent. "About," Madison Metropolitan School District, https://www.madison.k12.wi.us/about (accessed July 5, 2022).

18. "Accountability Report Cards—Madison Metropolitan District Report Card 2020–21," Wisconsin Department of Public Instruction, https://apps2.dpi.wi.gov/reportcards/home (accessed July 5, 2022).

19. Public options included staying at their default public school in the city of Madison proper or in a neighboring suburb, open enrolling to another public school in Madison's school district or neighboring school district, entering the lottery for a public magnet school, or enrolling in a publicly funded charter school. Private options included enrolling in religious, gifted, specialty, and secular private schools.

Theorizing White Social Identities and Levels of Self-Reflexivity

While rhetorical scholars and whiteness studies scholars have demonstrated the particularities of whiteness as a social identity in myriad ways, I wish to emphasize three key aspects: whiteness as privileged, embodied, and operating as if outside identity. Foregrounding whiteness as a privileged social identity illuminates necessary attention to the ways white individuals historically benefit from structural privileges that inform contemporary unfair racial positioning. Cheryl Harris historicizes white racial identity to forward her conceptualization of whiteness as property, which considers how various legal channels function to inscribe whiteness as a "valuable asset" in US society.[20] Likewise, George Lipsitz suggests how whiteness functions as a "possessive investment" that encourages white individuals' ongoing investment into an unjust system through rewarding them with resources, privileges, and opportunities.[21] Attention to the embodied aspects of whiteness focuses on how racial ideologies unevenly map onto bodies to bestow a symbolic value onto white bodies through their privilege to remain unmarked. Karma Chávez identifies how a failure to mark white bodies as such reinforces whiteness's normative identity.[22] Sara Ahmed similarly considers this dynamic, maintaining that spaces are oriented around whiteness through whiteness's ability to remain unseen, a privilege that nonwhite bodies do not equally enjoy.[23] White bodies thus move with a sense of comfort and ease in a majority of spaces they occupy. Finally, whiteness as outside identity refers to how whiteness often functions without needing to be explicitly named. Linda Martín Alcoff theorizes how white ideology operates simultaneously as both universal and absent.[24] She describes universality as the ways whiteness stands in as representative of all perspectives and absence as how whiteness exists outside of the color spectrum or as nonracialized.[25] In both cases, whiteness operates as nonmarked while nonwhite perspectives are distinctly marked. Thomas Nakayama and Robert Krizek observe how whiteness amasses its power through its unnamed positioning and that a nominalist rhetoric

---

20. Cheryl I. Harris, "Whiteness as Property," *Harvard Law Review* 106, no. 8 (1993): 1713.

21. George Lipsitz, *The Possessive Investment in Whiteness: How White People Profit from Identity Politics*, 20th anniversary edition (Philadelphia: Temple University Press, 2018), vii.

22. Karma R. Chávez, "The Body: An Abstract and Actual Rhetorical Concept," *Rhetoric Society Quarterly* 48, no. 3 (2018): 242–50.

23. Sara Ahmed, "A Phenomenology of Whiteness," *Feminist Theory* 8, no. 2 (2007): 157.

24. Linda Martín Alcoff, *The Future of Whiteness* (Malden, MA: Polity Press, 2015): 100–101.

25. Alcoff, *Future of Whiteness*, 100–101.

exposes whiteness as the "locus from which Other differences are calculated and organized."[26] The practice of recognizing and naming white racial identities disrupts whiteness's assumed normality as outside of a social identity. Yet, because whiteness functions materially and symbolically as an asset that grants privileges to individuals who protect its interests, those that attempt to engage such nominalist rhetorics do so with varying degrees of difficulty.

Despite operating as a rhetorical construct, whiteness's social force is not equally understood among white individuals. In attending to these three qualities of whiteness, it is necessary to examine the degree to which people are critically aware of their privilege. Self-reflexivity provides an analytic lens to observe the varying degrees of social awareness of white privilege that white people demonstrate. Dreama Moon and Lisa Flores define critical self-reflexivity as the "holding up of our own practices to question and critique."[27] Nakayama and Krizek observe how reflexivity directs attention to "that which has been silenced or invisible" through an individual's awareness of speaking from their social position.[28] Attention to differences in self-reflexivity need to be understood in a range of degrees to account for the gradations in how individuals understand and articulate their whiteness in relation to systems of privilege.

In the analysis that follows, I examine differing levels of self-reflexivity in terms of low, medium, and high levels of critical awareness. I characterize low reflexivity as having patterns of a refusal to come to terms with one's white privilege, a sense of denial, and/or rhetorical silences around the topic. I categorize medium levels of reflexivity as nominal recognitions of privilege without fully reckoning with the implications of one's white privilege. I define high critical self-reflexivity as not only critically reconciling with one's privilege but also describing a felt sense of responsibility based on that awareness and expressing a desire to change the status quo. I examine these varying degrees of self-reflexivity through three analytical themes of white identity formation in parents' discourse: ambiguity in articulating white identity, ease and comfort in school spaces, and relationality to other white people. Participants generally exhibited consistency in their reflexivity levels across these three themes. However, given that humans are nuanced and complicated, not all participants fell neatly into these classifications. Around 40 percent exhibited

---

26. Thomas K. Nakayama and Robert L. Krizek, "Whiteness: A Strategic Rhetoric," *Quarterly Journal of Speech* 81, no. 3 (1995): 297.

27. Dreama Moon and Lisa A. Flores, "Antiracism and the Abolition of Whiteness: Rhetorical Strategies of Domination among 'Race Traitors,'" *Communication Studies* 51, no. 2 (2000): 111.

28. Nakayama and Krizek, "Whiteness," 303–4.

some variation across these themes: some demonstrated high self-reflexivity in articulating their white identity but then medium levels of ease and comfort in school spaces and relating to other white people; some did not articulate their white identity with high levels of self-reflexivity but then expressed greater reflexivity around how they took up space and related to other white people; and a few exhibited varying levels across all three themes.

Through the analytic lens of self-reflexivity, I reveal how these differences have key implications for the rhetorical economies of whiteness. These varied levels of reflexivity provide insight into the range of degrees in which white parents with privilege demonstrate an awareness of the material and symbolic benefits associated with their identity. Because K–12 education is an institution organized by economic and class structures designed to benefit whiteness, it functions as an asset for folks to adhere to a white identity within these spaces. White parents with privilege enjoy the combination of material and symbolic processes that confer their identity and interests as the assumed norm, provide increased access to entitlements, and enable social and class mobility. Their differing levels of reflexivity reveal how parents engage the tenacity of whiteness within these spaces in ways that repudiate, defend, question, or interrupt a status quo that denies racial and economic justice. The more highly reflexive discourses of whiteness illuminate the difficulty in parents' attempts to detach from this unjust system designed to reward their investment and to intentionally act in counter ways.

Ambiguity in Articulating White Identity

Low Reflexivity

The theme ambiguity in articulating white identity considers the lack of clarity parents provided when describing how they racially identify and what their racial identity means to them. Rhetorical silences and equivocation emerged as one low-level reflexivity pattern from a very small number of parents. These individuals found themselves unable to articulate their racial identity and what it means to them beyond stating "Caucasian." To illustrate, one mother responded: "So just Caucasian. Um. I don't know [*laughs*]. What. Yeah." Her laughter and pauses indicated a discomfort with the question and an unfamiliarity with having to reflect on the assumed normality of her whiteness with me, a white researcher. Her lack of fluency in describing her whiteness demonstrated her privileged ability to inhabit an unmarked, unnamed racial position. Denial functioned as another low-level reflexivity pattern. Participants explained their whiteness in terms of their ethnic background absent of any consideration of power structures. One father told me, "I would say I'm white. Non-Latin.... What does that mean to me, uh most of my grandparents came from Western Europe. Western Europe ancestors." His answer ended there with no further elaboration, suggesting an understanding of his whiteness akin to the boxes checked on a Census form. He denied any association of his racial identity with white privilege through his silence on historical power relations that would inform his European ethnic heritage. A refusal to engage with the broader implications of one's racial identity marked a third pattern among low-level reflexivity discourses. When prompted to describe her racial identity, one mother articulated: "I am freckled [*laughs*]. I am sunburned and freckled. Um, I am white, um, you know as is often the case with white, we don't have to describe our racial identity, we're just the top check box, so yes, I am white, Caucasian ... with a period after that." Her unwillingness to immediately answer the question in terms of her racial identity and instead describe herself first by other physical traits demonstrated how whiteness functions as absent of identity. Although she recognized whiteness's privileged ability to remain unstated, she refused to elaborate any further on these privileges, suggesting that "white, Caucasian" provided a sufficient answer.

Medium Reflexivity

Parents that exhibited mid-levels of self-reflexivity nominally recognized their whiteness and complicated it through relating it to other aspects of their social identities to create ambiguity around its meaning. Sharing "European" references with low-reflexive discourses, mid-level discourses elaborated further to characterize whiteness by its absence of cultural identity markers, or as one participant told me, "white is kind of like the meaningless default." In the following quote, a mother racially identified as white and then muddled her response through elaborating on her European ethnic heritage:

> I mean just white, lots of mix of like Western and Eastern European, there's a whole bunch of different things in there.... I don't have a very strong ethnic identity in any way.... Like on my mom's side, I guess they're Swedish and something else.... My dad is a mix of Alsatian and Polish, and I say Alsatian because some people call it French and some people call it German. But it's not like we all were like these [are] the foods that we eat and these are the traditions we have, it was just sort of like, we're just white people, you know, so it's not very specific.

Like the low-reflexive pattern of denial, she described her ethnic heritage absent of any consideration of historical power relations, denying whiteness's privileged status. Language such as "meaningless default" and "just white" denotes white as nonspecific and without cultural identity markers, demonstrating how whiteness operates as both a universal and an absence. Such rhetorical moves minimize whiteness's privileged status and secures its position as unmarked and nonracialized.

Parents also referenced how their whiteness intersected with their other identities to inform their positionality. Doing so acknowledged their white privilege but then dampened its significance through highlighting other social identities. One participant employed the term intersectionality to reflect on her white racial identity in relation to her identity as a woman[29]: "I spend my time reading and thinking about intersectionality and how my story doesn't get to be the story. And, as a woman . . . I feel like my story hasn't been told or like I feel like I have stuff to say that men haven't let me say, but I need to make room at the table for other people and it's not just my story." She employed the frame of intersectionality to consider the power differential between her identity as a woman and her privileged identity as white. She indirectly referenced, without explicitly naming, how her whiteness unequally positions her in relation to women of color, thus recognizing her privileged positioning, albeit in an ambiguous manner. Other participants articulated their whiteness through observing how it intersected with their Jewish identity. As one participant described, "I identify as white . . . and Jewish, which, I think for lots of my family sort of feels like a pass, which I think is interesting, like, oh no we didn't do anything wrong because were discriminated against too. Like we get a free pass because somebody burned our village. . . . I don't know that it really works that way." She nuanced her white identity through identifying with the history of oppression that Jewish people have experienced. Although she wondered how this intersection informs her understanding of her white identity, she failed to fully account for the impact of her white privilege within a white supremacist system.

---

29. The term *intersectionality* originated in Black feminist theory to describe the multiple axes of domination unique to the social location of Black women. Scholars have criticized white co-optation of the term, suggesting that intersectionality's original focus does not translate in the same way onto whiteness. See Bernadette Marie Calafell, Shinsuke Eguchi, and Shadee Abdi, "Introduction: De-Whitening Intersectionality in Intercultural Communication," in *De-Whitening Intersectionality: Race, Intercultural Communication, and Politics*, ed. Shinsuke Eguchi, Bernadette Marie Calafell, and Shadee Abdi (Lanham, MD: Lexington Books, 2020), xvii–xxvii.

High Reflexivity

High-level critical self-reflexivity discourses went beyond identifying privilege to articulate a sense of responsibility. These parents explicitly named the relationship between whiteness and systems of power. One mother made this connection explicit: "I'm working on learning what my whiteness means, as far as my contribution to a system that has subjugated other races over time and . . . being a white woman, what my role is in either counteracting that or trying to live differently so that system doesn't keep working in the same way." She reflected a critical understanding of her white identity as part of a broader hegemonic system that unfairly distributes power. Her ability to position herself within a white supremacist system and name her responsibility to seek ways to interrupt it evidences a high level of critical self-reflexivity. These participants enumerated the various privileges their white positionality afforded them and expressed intentions to disrupt such patterns. After describing how some of her unearned privileges manifested, one mother reflected on "how to kind of muddle through that and . . . find a path that that can help pull others out of their white focus, including a lot of my family members and friends." Her desire to educate others in her white circles about their similarly unearned white privileges reflects a broader sense of responsibility. This marks a high level of critical self-awareness through her recognition of an unfair status quo and desire to change it.

Although these more reflexive parents clearly articulated a critical understanding of their whiteness in relation to systems of power, they expressed ambiguity around how to take action accordingly. Discussions around responsibility often generated more questions than specific answers. The following quote from a mother illustrates this sense of responsibility coupled with ambiguity around concrete action steps: "I grapple with the fact that what [my whiteness] means is that I have been granted privileges . . . that I don't deserve. And I don't know what to do with, and I have been trying to figure out that second piece . . . what to do with them and how to use them in a way to help those who unfortunately have not been granted that for no good reason other than not being white." To be sure, the logic of the responsibility of whiteness risks falling into a white savior mentality. While even the most self-reflexive participants did not use that exact language, some did express understanding this sense of responsibility in ways that would not enact further harm and the need to be conscious of their whiteness in various interactions.

The desire of wanting to raise their children in race-conscious ways emerged as one concrete way highly reflexive participants discussed the responsibility associated with their unearned racial privileges. Parents described their intent to take actions as a family to help cultivate a critical awareness of whiteness within their children. For instance, one mother critically recognized her white privilege and then wondered, "How am I bringing my kids up into the world in a way that they are recognizing that as well and . . . how do we walk with that and help bring other people up to that same place?" Although the desire to raise their children in race-conscious ways emerged as one of the more concrete actions parents could take to disrupt patterns of white privilege, ambiguity remained in terms of specific ways this type of parenting could look.

Ease and Comfort in School Spaces

Low Reflexivity

The theme ease and comfort in school spaces encompasses the ways white parents related their whiteness to their children's schools. Participants that exhibited low levels of reflexivity expressed uncertainty around how their white identity influenced their school choice process. They confessed that they had not previously given the relationship between their whiteness and choosing schools much consideration. Some remarked that they supposed their whiteness influenced their school choice decisions, but they refused to specifically indicate how. One father stated: "Hmm. I guess I haven't thought about it too much. You know, it's easy to say it doesn't but, you know, it's easy for a fish to say they don't know what water is either. [*pauses*] Yeah, I don't know. Hard to say." This participant's lack of reflection illustrates how whiteness operates as if beyond identity, allowing it to remain hidden or unnamed. Another participant admitted:

> I haven't thought about [my daughter's] whiteness . . . and how it moves her through the world. But I have thought about that I did want her in a school where there was going to be more diversity so that when she was in her peer groups . . . she was seeing people that have different . . . racial identities, have different racial skin tones, have different family heritages and traditions. And so I wanted her in that mix. So that it seemed like whiteness was just a part of that and not above it or below it, but it was just all on the same playing field.

Her perspective illustrates that although she had not reflected on her own daughter's whiteness, she had indeed racialized others in seeking a "diverse" school, as her use of "different racial identities" suggests nonwhite racial identities. A failure to reflect on her own identity maintains whiteness as a universal position from which she racialized others to guide her school choice decisions. Her "same playing field" language denies any understanding of her whiteness as implicated within power structures.

Entitlement in terms of expectations of schools and administrators also illustrated a lack of parents' reflection on their privileged positionality. Parents' comfort in making demands of school administrators' time demonstrated how they occupy space in school settings. In addition to participating in multiple school tours, many parents individually met with school principals to receive additional assurance that the school would be a good fit for their family. Indeed, several participants indicated that if other white parents felt unsure about their assigned neighborhood school, they should simply reach out to schedule a meeting with the principal, suggesting the normalcy of this behavior. Such comfort in making individualized demands of school administration reflects a history of white parents respected in public school systems and a confidence that breeds a contemporary sense of entitlement. Parents also discussed with me instances where school leadership failed to meet their expectations. These participants described some sort of disagreement they had with the principal or the district superintendent and told me how they expected more or felt like they were "owed" something. One mother recounted a disagreement with the school principal and reflected: "I'm selfishly hoping that by reaching out and letting . . . the principal know . . . that she's going to give me a good teacher. That feels really selfish but also . . . you owe me, lady . . . you totally failed us . . . big time." Her reflection suggests an absence of reflexivity around her privileged positioning in school spaces. She felt confident waging individualized demands for her child rather than broadly considering the principal's multiple obligations to the entire student population. Her white entitlement manifested through her level of expectations as a consumer, and when those were not individually met, the expressed feeling that the school then "owes" her something.

Medium Reflexivity

Participants with medium levels of self-reflexivity readily indicated how their white racial identity afforded them a sense of ease in the school choice process and a felt sense of comfort among many school options. Their perspectives reveal the embodied nature of whiteness and the luxury to make choices without fear; parents could rest assured that they possess many options from which to choose. Parents described a sense of "belongingness" as they characterized their comfort levels with a variety of the area districts and schools. One mother exhibited mid-levels of self-reflexivity as she reflected on the relationship between her whiteness and school choice, naming the connection between comfort and her whiteness but not going so far as to challenge it: "I feel comfortable everywhere. . . . There's no part of the city where I would be like oh, I can't go to that part of the city, I'm not welcomed in that part of the city." Her embodied whiteness grants her an increased mobility around the Madison area and its schools, privileging her with a sense of freedom in her choices. In contrast, families marginalized by race and class need to consider the circumstances that constrain their capacity to engage school choice so freely, such as material and social adversities like poverty, community instability, and family contexts.[30] The ease with which participants described exercising school choice illustrates how neoliberal logics reinforce such contexts as designed for white benefit and how schools have historically been comfortable spaces for white families with class privilege. Parents that identify as such thus reap the benefits of the ways that K–12 education as an institution is economically designed to secure their interests.

Parents' sense of comfort and ease in the school choice process extended to their relationships with school administrators. The institutional history of white parents possessing authority in school spaces enabled white parents to speak from a positionality that has traditionally been respected in the school system. To illustrate, one mother associated her whiteness with comfort: "I'm always speaking up for my son because of his ADHD . . . and I think . . . if I wasn't white would I be as fearless as I've been in telling [administration] what they need to do rather than like walking around it?" Although she recognized the connection between her whiteness and her confidence advocating for her son, she did not indicate a willingness to change her behavior in any way. Her language "telling them what they need to do" expressed a sense of authority in confronting school leadership. Unlike more highly reflexive participants, these parents did not express any reflection around learning to sit back quietly and not demand. Rather, they instead identified with the label of an "obnoxious" or an "annoying" white parent. One mother who identified herself as such described her attempts to work with the school to advocate for gifted services for her daughter: "The vibe from the school was that I was asking for something that was totally, like, unacceptable, and that only an annoying white par—of course, they didn't say that. But that was definitely how I felt, like, who do you think you are, asking for this? . . . Why should we give it to your

---

30. Derrick Darby and Argun Saatcioglu, "Race, Inequality of Opportunity, and School Choice," *Theory and Research in Education* 13, no. 1 (2015): 56–86.

kid when no other kids get this?" She stopped herself here from fully saying "annoying white parent," but eventually identified with this label more openly later in our interview. These parents qualified their outspokenness and willingness to make demands through recognizing their white positionality; however, this reflexivity was directed toward advocating for additional resources for their individual child as opposed to reflexivity around a broader responsibility in the service of equity.

High Reflexivity

In contrast, parents that exhibited high levels of self-reflexivity discussed their school choice behaviors in terms of the responsibility of white parents. One mother indicated how she understood her choice behaviors within broader patterns of white parent choice as connected to power structures, observing that because "resources follow whiteness ... there ... is the possibility that if enough white parents make choices to send their kids to diverse schools ... that there's a way of ... spreading resources.... Education in America is ... so ingrained with property and funding and wealth that something does need to change." Albeit well-intentioned, enacting one's white identity through associating it with material resources illuminates the material economy of whiteness through the ways white parents' choices direct the flow of taxpayer dollars to influence the education marketplace. Collectively, parents leverage these structural advantages to influence the quality of schools, and perhaps could even, as this mother indicated, wield this power to promote the value of integrated schools.

Parents described their intentional efforts to interrupt well-worn patterns of white comfort through challenging themselves to practice finding comfort in their discomfort. They noted their attempts to retrain automatic behaviors, like learning how to not demand and instead stepping back to listen. One mother reflected this higher awareness of her white positionality, expressing her intentionality around "just taking a backseat to not saying a whole lot.... I try really, really, really hard ... if there's going to be a complaint, it's going to come from a place of like, help me understand. Not you need to do these things because I'm demanding it, or because my kid deserves it." Although her white identity activates the material economy of whiteness that grants her increased access to the time and attention of administrators, she indicated how she actively chooses not to just willingly accept these privileges. In contrast to mid-level self-reflexivity discourses where parents expressed high levels of entitlement through the belief that the school "owes" them, this mother desires to take up less space through behaving as a less demanding customer.

Parents described working to reorient their approach to education to interrupt the attitude of needing to take advantage of every opportunity for their children. Recognizing how this mentality perpetuated unequal power dynamics, some participants discussed reframing their expectations from "what can I gain?" to "what can I contribute?" This shift from an individual-driven mindset to one that embraces a broader ethic of responsibility indicates a desire to resist further accumulation of the unearned material and symbolic economic benefits enacted by their whiteness. One participant described moving away from the mindset of "what I can take . . . if I choose to be an active perpetuator of racial inequity," elaborating:

> One way to do that is to . . . pull my kids out of the public school or . . . get them in the Spanish Immersion program because I want it. So I'm going to take that spot because I can get them there and I know how to put pressure on a school administrator, because I do know how to do that, but I'm not going to. . . . It's not just the privilege, but it's also . . . how I can tap that to take things away from others. . . . I do think when white folks do this on a bigger level . . . this is how we would get to, I don't know Philadelphia's schools or Chicago's or New York's.

Her perspective indicated an awareness around how whiteness functions as an asset within the institution of education. It suggested how privileged, white parents enjoy the structural advantage to behave as individual market consumers through a logic of neoliberalism, which minimizes the ways their choices affect broader systems. The result of which, as she identified, can produce underresourced public school systems. She expressed a desire to interrupt the automatic behaviors ingrained in white parents to willingly accept the rewards bestowed upon them for their continued investment in these systems to instead consider ways to undo such behaviors and disrupt white supremacy. This retraining of behavior she described asks white families to experience discomfort in spaces that have traditionally provided comfort and ease.

Relationality to Other White People

Low Reflexivity

This final theme considers how parents reflect their white identity through variously positioning other white people in relation to themselves. In low-level self-reflexive discourses, parents positioned themselves in close proximity to other white people through indicating how they are embedded within white social networks. They refused to acknowledge how these networks further privilege them in relation to school choice, and they were silent on any critiques of other white parents or their white privilege. To illustrate, parents described the ways their networks provided them increased access-to-choice opportunities. One mother told me that she found out about her children's private school for gifted students through a personal connection. She explained how the school does not engage in any external marketing strategies, instead relying on promotion through "word of mouth": "I knew a lot about the school because my friend's kids went there. And she and her husband were both professors . . . so I have that connection with other people." She was silent on any critique of the private school's reliance on insular, privileged parent networks to attract new pupils and how she personally benefited from her white, highly educated social network.

Parents described how their white social networks function to circulate and maintain various reputations of area schools and districts. Yet, they refused to acknowledge the possibility of bias in the circulation of these reputations, instead they actively engaged and maintained them. Participants told me about hearing "good reports" of a school from neighbors, believing stories of their middle school being a "slightly rougher school," friends telling them that they are "so lucky" to live in a particular school zone, or how coworkers would fearmonger about the quality of the public schools. One mother described the importance of these reputations in guiding her choice to move to one of the most sought-after suburban school districts, known for its "notoriety" and "ranking." After characterizing the high demand for the district, she shared how "people are trying to work through friends to get in before [houses] are listed because they want their kids in the school district." She described this behavior matter-of-factly, without a critical tone and without considering her own implication in these patterns. She was silent around any critiques of how these reputations circulate and who maintains them, as well as any mention of her privileged ability to move into that district.

Medium Reflexivity

Distancing from other white people characterized mid-level self-reflexivity discourses. Through contrast, parents demonstrated how they are different from what they identified as the problematic behaviors of other white people. This pattern suggests some reflexivity as participants named white privilege, but they waged their critique through projecting it onto other white people rather than critically interrogating their own positionality. For instance, participants juxtaposed themselves to other white people to cast a reflection of themselves as actually committed to living out their progressive values through their school choice decisions. Although participants recognized the political similarities between themselves and other white people, they differentiated themselves as further left than other people that they believe acted in ways that contradict progressive values. One father illustrated this through discursively distancing himself from a group of his friends:

> They all live in a suburb of some sort . . . politically, we're very well aligned, but it's like, this is a realm that they just are able to like compartmentalize and set aside and not see that . . . this part of their life is also a part of their politics. [They] just say like, well, no this is just me choosing a school for my kid that has nothing to do with whether I think schools should be segregated or integrated like, for certain I think they should be integrated, I just think my kid should go to an all-white school.

He observed how his friends can "compartmentalize" their political views and their school choices, suggesting that not only does he value integration, but he also sees himself living out his value through his school choices. Scholars observe that one pitfall white individuals often employ to manifest a positive white racial identity is distancing oneself from other white folks as if to suggest *I* am a better white person than *them*.[31] Timothy Lensmire observes of this problematic dynamic: "Instead of [mobilizing] other white people for anti-racist action, we use them, scapegoat them, to create our own anti-racist identities."[32] Participants employed contrast to cast an identity of themselves as antiracist and committed to equity, at the expense of scapegoating the school choices of other white people.

Several participants employed the historically loaded phrase "white flight" to critique trends of white parents moving out of Madison proper to its suburbs or out of the public schools to the private schools. Through this language, they associated other white people with the nearly century-long trend of white families moving out of integrating US cities or schools and into majority white

---

31. Pauli Badenhorst, "Predatory White Antiracism," *Psychoanalysis, Culture & Society* 26, no. 3 (2021): 284–303; Timothy J. Lensmire, "White Anti-Racists and Belonging," *Whiteness and Education* 2, no. 1 (2017): 4–14; Sharon Sullivan, *Good White People: The Problem with Middle-Class White Anti-Racism* (Albany: State University of New York Press, 2014); and Audrey Thompson, "Tiffany, Friend of People of Color: White Investments in Antiracism," *International Journal of Qualitative Studies in Education* 16, no. 1 (2003): 7–29.

32. Lensmire, "White Anti-Racists," 12.

suburban neighborhoods. As one participant described, "I do see that there's a lot of this white flight happening to . . . the neighboring districts. And you know what, I'm just not concerned about it. Like, I don't really care to lose white people in our district that . . . aren't here to be part of this community anyway, that don't see the value in what Madison offers." This participant implied that Madison's school district is more racially diverse than neighboring suburban districts and that she was able to appreciate the value in Madison's racially diverse student population whereas the other white people she dismissed were not. Contrast functioned to cast her own school choices on the historically correct side of "white flight" patterns. Although recognizing the racially problematic ways that other white individuals engaged choice to maintain unequal racial privilege within the school system, this participant scapegoated these white people to cast her own actions as superior rather than, say, take action to engage in critical dialogues with these acquaintances about the effects of their racially problematic behaviors. Despite positioning themselves as distant from the problematic actions of other white parents, these participants must contend with how one of the advantages of their positionality is the privilege to be able to talk about how they are a "good" white progressive without always engaging in direct, antiracist actions themselves.

High Reflexivity

In highly reflexive discourses parents placed themselves in close proximity to other white people, but in ways that suggested a critical stance of their positionality. They moved beyond scapegoating other people to taking accountability for their white privilege through working in coalitions to change the status quo. These parents engaged in modes of advocacy such as holding conversations with other white parents around reasons for staying in public schools. One mother characterized these conversations as "helping" and "educating." Another mother described the discussions she had with white parents in the fall of 2020 in response to concerns about virtual schooling and whether to remain in the public schools: "There were some conversations with people about like, let's balance your kid and, the school, the district. Let's at least have that conversation. . . . That's an example of how . . . we can keep schools as a public good, and make it a better public good, for everyone and, in a way that ideally would advance social justice and give families, and people an opportunity to thrive." Rather than simply dismiss these families, this participant engaged them in conversation, indicating her broader sense of responsibility around equity and the well-being of public schools for all families.

Highly reflexive parents positioned themselves in close proximity with other white parents with the critical mission to engage in challenging, equity-based conversations, rather than leverage parent networks to obtain more resources for their individual child, as less reflexive parents did. To illustrate, one mother who worked on a parent team tasked to expand out grade levels at her children's charter school described her experience of being called out by another community member from the neighboring public middle school about the possible ways fear of Blackness informed the charter school's expansion. She recounted, "It was a *really* important statement that needed to be said to us and . . . we need to keep reminding ourselves . . . who are we including and excluding. The parents that I know and who identify as white are . . . trying to understand . . . what does racism look like in their neighborhoods? . . . Those people are trying to do better and using their whiteness in a way that's valuable." Her proximity to the other white parents on the team enabled her to engage in challenging conversations around how their implicit biases may have informed school design. In such collectives, white supremacy is not denied, but critically examined. Likewise, one group of mothers told me about the "parent equity group" they formed to have a space to work through race-related issues at their children's school. They described the group as "very committed to trying to build an antiracist school environment" and working to critically understand various district-level policies that reinforce white supremacy. Through these networks, white parents uncover their privileges and work to change the status quo as a result of critical conversations they hold in close proximity with other white parents.

Conclusion

This examination of the force of white identity as a rhetorical construct within the context of K–12 education has emphasized the ways whiteness is privileged, embodied, and operates as if outside of identity. Employing critical self-reflexivity as an analytic, I demonstrated the distinctions between low, medium, and high levels of social awareness of whiteness as an identity associated with privilege through the themes of ambiguity, ease and comfort, and relationality. I have argued that low self-reflexive discourse reinforced whiteness's privileged position as unmarked and unnamed through how it is articulated, occupies space, and its proximity to other white folks. Medium levels indicated an awareness of structural privilege and perhaps a hopefulness for change, yet an absence of any action. High reflexivity demonstrated reconciliation with whiteness's privileged position through expressing a broader sense of responsibility to change the status quo. Through relating the impact of their individual school choices as part of patterns white parents enact on a broader scale, the more highly reflexive participants expressed an understanding of how their individual white identity relates to broader power structures and a desire to disrupt these patterns.

This chapter nuances scholarly understandings of whiteness as a rhetorical identity through turning our attention to the ways progressive, white, advantaged parents negotiate structural power and privilege through school choice discourse. My analysis reveals the varied positions progressive white parents occupy along a continuum of critical awareness of their white identities. These gradations of self-reflexivity demonstrate the different ways that whiteness as a rhetorical identity can operate to sustain, question, and challenge the status quo. The low self-reflexive discourses demonstrate the all-too-familiar rhetorical maneuvers of whiteness to defend a status quo that upholds racist neoliberal logics and the ways whiteness functions as an asset in the institution of K–12 education. The distinction between the middle and high levels reveals the difference between a nominalist rhetoric, or simply naming one's awareness, and a nominalist rhetoric coupled with action to change the status quo, or an ethic of responsibility. Whereas a nominalist rhetoric simply *recognizes* the status quo, highly reflexive discourses expressed the desire to *change* it.

Although this chapter provided sustained focus on white identity formation within the context of K–12 education, it would be a worthy endeavor to consider how this ethic of responsibility associated with whiteness as a rhetorical identity extends into other areas of economic governance, such as housing, urban planning, social services, or health care. The linking of white identity with an ethic of responsibility certainly poses risks of further harm, given whiteness's privileged position to organize racial disparities within institutions of economic governance. Yet, there is the potential that a nominalist rhetoric coupled with an ethic of responsibility can perhaps disrupt entrenched relations of power and move us closer toward empowering practices that envision agentic, multiracial communities and publics.

CHAPTER 4

Rhetorical Economies of Whiteness through Citizenship Excess in Higher Education

GODFRIED ASANTE, PAULAMI BANERJEE,
ADEDOYIN OGUNFEYIMI, AND STACEY K. SOWARDS

Introduction

Students who come from other countries to study at US universities are desirable recruits for a number of reasons. Such students represent linguistic, cultural, racial, and national diversity, bringing different perspectives to the college classroom. Designated as "international" students, they often pay higher (international) tuition rates, representing lucrative "markets." Indeed, a 2022 forum on international education trends hosted by the *Chronicle of Higher Education* calls attention to potential student markets in India, China, Bangladesh, Malaysia, Vietnam, and elsewhere, with explicit discussion about the "return on investment" of marketing and recruiting students from such countries.[1] Such language and motivation reflect a broader university agenda rooted in hollow neoliberal economics and discourses, in which international students offer greater tuition revenue plus the benefit of added diversity to oftentimes white majority institutions. For the students themselves, the promise of a US education can be a dream come true and a pathway to a better job, and possibly, a better life.

---

1. Karin Fischer, Jeong Powell, Adam Sapp, and Robert Summers, "Shifting International-Student Trends: Key Takeaways," *Chronicle of Higher Education*, November 15, 2022, https://connect.chronicle.com/rs/931-EKA-218/images/ShiftingInternationalTrends_Keytakeaway.pdf.

Students coming from outside of the US to study in US American institutions of higher education have long experienced the challenges, benefits, and privileges of such education, while also facing discrimination, racism, and differential treatment. For students coming from Global South countries in particular, the initial entry into the US and into university life can be a very challenging time, in part because of the extensive visa and travel red tape coupled with cultural and language differences as well as the pressures of assimilation and adaptation; expectations from universities, professors, families, and friends; and overt and covert forms of discrimination, along with aspects related to the materialities of whiteness and neoliberal rhetorics. For these students, many universities offer little support and frustrating bureaucratic structures and rules that must be followed to ensure legal student visa status, in addition to all the pressures of cultural adaptation and assimilation. For example, the *Chronicle of Higher Education* reported the following story, which is emblematic of the many problems "international" students face:[2]

> When Anson Tan got the call offering him an internship with a major airline, the junior business and finance major at the University of San Francisco was ecstatic that he'd managed to beat out other candidates for the sought-after position. But when his new employer sent over the offer letter, there was no mention anywhere in the paperwork about his student-visa status, said Tan, who is from Singapore. International students are allowed to work or do internships in the United States only under narrow conditions, when the work is related to their studies, and Tan said he had disclosed his visa status to recruiters during interviews.[3]

As Anson Tan experienced, students are offered opportunities, such as internships, assistantships, research experiences, and so forth without their professors or employers really understanding the legal paperwork situation related to their visa status. Students coming to the US for study might be allowed to work, but under very strict rules, usually only on campus in approved work-study or graduate assistantships. Since most of these positions do not fully support students over the course of the twelve-month year, students can reside

---

2. Here, we use "international" students as a way to problematize how higher education institutions call students "international." We have not been able to develop an alternative term, such as "students coming to the US to study," that isn't so clunky. Additionally, "international" assumes all students migrating to the US to study come from similar socioeconomic backgrounds.

3. Karin Fischer, "A Passport to Work," *Chronicle of Higher Education,* June 13, 2022, https://www.chronicle.com/article/a-passport-to-work.

in great financial and often mental duress, especially in the summer months when funding is often not available. Since all internships must relate to students' studies, they cannot accept jobs like working in a restaurant or paid internships that are unrelated to their program of study. Students also face the stresses of language issues and cultural differences in adapting to a new city, country, ways of thinking, not to mention differences in work, research, writing, and classroom settings with expectations for participation, reflecting many materialities of whiteness. Such confusion can lead to overpromising of such experiences and dismissal of students' concerns about how these opportunities will work out.

Supposing our undergraduate and graduate students make it through their programs does not mean that they continue in their success, whether it be a tenure-track job, industry position, or even the ability to return to their home country. Tenure-track jobs can be even more elusive for students without legal work authorization. Some institutions refuse to hire PhDs into adjunct, lecturer, or tenure-track positions, because they will not pay for visa expenses that can cost thousands of dollars; potential employees are not allowed to cover such expenses themselves, as the cost must be covered by the university or other hiring organization. Many new PhDs also have better chances at tenure-track jobs and later, successful tenure bids, if they can start as a postdoctoral fellow or visiting professor; however, these positions are even less likely to come with visa sponsorship. Some institutions allow visa expenses, but then pass the burden onto budget-tight departments, in which visa expenses may have to be covered through other faculty members' research or travel allocations. In other cases, the visa process can take so long that a newly minted PhD does not have time to get an H-1B visa in order to start working by a designated start date.

Professors who have secured tenure-track and/or lecturer positions may struggle to obtain the accompanying and appropriate visa. The Optional Training Program (OPT) only allows folks to stay in the US to work for one to three years, depending on the type of degree they have. Other visas (e.g., H-1B) have to be renewed frequently and are employer-based, causing stress on the applicant rather than a financial burden on an employer, travel to get the new visa if it needs to be done in person, and the mental/emotional worry of what happens if a visa is not approved or not approved in time for the start of the semester. These visas are tied to the specific employing department, so changing jobs is not easy and requires a great deal of expense and time. These scholars also may need to decide if they want to pursue permanent residency (green card status) and/or citizenship, which are more arduous, stressful, and expensive processes. Institutions may not want to support scholars who are not tenured or may not want to support scholars at all, given the expense. These are just a few examples of what we have seen and/or experienced first-hand as a collection of scholars who range from non-US citizens holding employment-based visas to a permanent resident (green card holder) to a US citizen working with "international" students and faculty both in and outside the US. The neoliberal aspects of how higher education institutions recruit "international" students for undergraduate and graduate programs perpetuates the individualistic, bootstrapping US American dream rhetorics that are infused with continued privileging of whiteness (even among "international" students, that is, white European or Australian students may be given preference over students from the Global South).

As such, in the rest of this essay, we explore how Hector Amaya's concept of citizenship excess,[4] the acquired surplus value of citizenship that grows over time, plays out in these rhetorical economies of whiteness, in which whiteness is reinforced through the privilege of US citizenship in higher education. The promise of degrees and employment in the US becomes a form of what Lauren Berlant calls cruel optimism,[5] which we illustrate in three narrative parts: temporal existence, ostracized denizenship, and baited optimism. Before we move to these stories, we first unpack citizenship excess as a theoretical framework. Using this concept of citizenship, we explore our three narratives through a process that we might align with Jo Hsu's concept of diasporic listening.[6] Using metaphors of constellating and homing, Hsu describes such diasporic listening as a way in which we find new possibilities, make connections, foreground the forgotten, and highlight nonnormative epistemologies within a critical orientation. While here we present stories in written form, we envision them as part of this approach of diasporic listening/reading/understanding/remembering/learning.

Defining Citizenship Excess in Higher Education

The very idea of defining citizenship as connected to nationhood, nationalism, national identity, and/or national belonging is rooted in Western rhetorical, political, and legal traditions. While on the one hand citizenship can create a sense of inclusion in the formation of a "we," that very same "we" also

---

    4. Hector Amaya, *Citizenship Excess: Latinas/os, Media, and the Nation* (New York: New York University Press, 2013).

    5. Lauren Berlant, *Cruel Optimism* (Durham, NC: Duke University Press, 2011).

    6. V. Jo Hsu, *Constellating Home: Trans and Queer Asian American Rhetorics* (Columbus: The Ohio State University Press, 2022), 11.

excludes those who are not part of "we"—those who are "they" or "them." As Hsin-I Cheng explains, citizenship as a concept originated in Europe as a Western construct and "has traditionally been approached from a legal perspective, with allusion to the process of 'othering' individuals separate from those who belong to a certain political community."[7]

The exclusionary forces of legal citizenship are well established in US American history, particularly for people who were enslaved, Indigenous communities, migrants from Asia, and Mexicans who after the 1846–48 war with the US suddenly found themselves living in US territory (the Southwest, Texas, and California). While US citizenship was forced onto certain populations (e.g., Mexicans living in the Southwest), they were treated as second-class citizens with restricted and racialized access to certain privileges. Other groups (e.g., Indigenous and Black folks) were enslaved and/or denied US citizenship outright based on their skin color or were seen to not be eligible at all for any kind of citizenship. In other words, full enjoyment of the privileges appended to US citizenship was accessible only to able-bodied, Christian, white cismen who had property. As Christa Olson notes in her book, *American Magnitude*, "American" came to be understood as rooted in whiteness and class privilege: "US Americanness may be officially codified in constitutional language and the various 'papers' of citizenship, immigration, and naturalization law, but its everyday life is largely a matter of feeling (even if sometimes feelings about papers and looking)."[8] Mae Ngai's book, *Impossible Subjects*, outlines in detail how legal/illegal statuses have been defined in the making of the "illegal alien," particularly starting in the 1920s with the Johnson-Reed Immigration Act of 1924. This Act set up literacy tests, national origin quotas, and bans to limit the number of immigrants from certain countries, including many Asian countries (although laws were passed before then, such as the Chinese Exclusion Act in 1882, which banned Chinese citizens from migrating to the US).[9] Both Ngai and Olson document how immigration processes became racialized and whitened. As Ngai argues:

> American historical writing and political culture have a long and entrenched tradition of exceptionalism, including the idea that the United States was built upon the principle and practice of immigrant inclusion. Even if

---

7. Hsin-I Cheng, *Cultivating Membership in Taiwan and Beyond: Relational Citizenship* (Lanham, MD: Lexington Books, 2021), xii.

8. Christa Olson, *American Magnitude: Hemispheric Vision and Public Feeling in the United States* (Columbus: The Ohio State University Press, 2021), 19.

9. Mae M. Ngai, *Impossible Subjects: Illegal Aliens and the Making of Modern America* (Princeton, NJ: Princeton University Press, 2014).

immigrants face obstacles along the way, it is believed that these obstacles are eventually overcome; Americans consider the path to full inclusion normative and evidence of the nation's democratic nature.[10]

The individualized nature of responsibility mentioned here reflects bootstrapping and US American dream metaphors rooted in neoliberalism and economies of whiteness: if one works hard enough, it is possible to be successful. However, nonwhite immigrants encounter forces of discrimination, racism, and related ideologies. They face pressures for assimilation, calls to renounce home cultures, experiences of financial disparities, and more. The resulting precarity makes overcoming such obstacles extremely difficult or impossible.

To explain further how immigration is racialized in contemporary academia, we turn to citizenship excess. Hector Amaya's book, *Citizenship Excess,* theorizes this concept, examining the underlying privileges of US citizenship and connections to race. He explains: "Citizenship excess theorizes that citizenship is inherently a process of uneven political capital accumulation and that the unevenness follows ethno-racial lines. . . . The accumulation of such surplus political value, over time, becomes the basis for more and for easier accumulation" and "therefore citizenship and its excess is how we express ethno-racial supremacy."[11] This form of supremacy results from what Amaya identifies as discrimination and balkanization: "Both the discrimination (pushing down) and balkanization (pushing away) of Latina/os secure the supremacy of ethno-racially white interests in political cultures and over the state."[12] Amaya writes that "there is something intrinsically poisonous in citizenship, a quality that cannot be fully contained, an excess that feeds the power hungry and that convinces otherwise good people that oppression is just."[13] Moving away from Western perspectives of citizenship rooted in rights, individualism, and political participation, Cheng offers the notion of relational citizenship to explore the ways in which citizenship and borders reflect power through discipline as well as agency. Relational citizenship can also disrupt patriotic and entitled membership in recognition of how value, worth, inclusion/exclusion, and distance are mapped onto peoples across societies. Yet such an approach to citizenship is elusive legally, politically, and culturally.[14]

The ideological positioning of citizenship excess also applies to non-US citizens in different ways, such as demands for assimilation. Catherine

---

10. Ngai, *Impossible Subjects,* xxiii.
11. Amaya, *Citizenship Excess,* 2–3.
12. Amaya, *Citizenship Excess,* 3.
13. Amaya, *Citizenship Excess,* 4.
14. Cheng, *Cultivating Membership.*

Ramírez describes the process of assimilation as one of inclusion/exclusion: that is, we invite "international" students in to achieve their dreams, and yet we exclude them from US jobs, internships, and even livable conditions.[15] People who are Othered experience an incomplete inclusion that also perpetuates and naturalizes whiteness. Students coming from outside the US become denizens, in which they are included or allowed to be, live, and work (with a lot of restrictions), but remain on the outside of normative "Americanness" and privileges/freedoms of US legal citizenship. Again, Mae Ngai argues that "undocumented immigrants are at once welcome and unwelcome; they are woven into the economic fabric of the nation, but as labor that is cheap and disposable."[16]

Undocumented immigrants might find access to cultural citizenship, but legal citizenship often remains impossible, as Ngai contends.[17] Indeed, the 1917 Immigration Act (banning immigrants from the barred zone across South Asia and implementing literacy tests to reduce "uneducated" immigrants) and the 1924 Johnson-Reed Act legislated that Asians "were racially ineligible for naturalized citizenship. . . . [and] solidified the legal boundaries of the 'white race'" as well as defined national origin as an identity marker.[18] The 1965 Immigration Act and subsequent efforts alleviated some of these issues and created different problems. The connection between race/ethnicity and immigration reform are intricately woven together. In higher education, the push to "internationalize" and recruit "international" students who often pay higher rates of tuition have shaped cultural landscapes for those who end up staying in the US (short or long term). However, we argue that "international" students face significant and racialized forces related to rhetorical economies of whiteness in citizenship excess. As Lisa Flores contends, "Politics of whiteness pollute *and* sustain our intellectual labor,"[19] and most certainly that is true for citizenship excess in higher education. To follow Lauren Berlant's cruel optimism, the US government and institutions of higher education construct a hope, an optimism, a dream that employment will be available, possible, even probable. Academic labor, through neoliberalism and whiteness, circulates the same old patterns of white privilege and social capital, a form of cruel optimism that individualizes crushing responsibilities. Systemically then, these material discourses fuse together as a form of white supremacy.

---

15. Catherine S. Ramírez, *Assimilation: An Alternative History* (Berkeley: University of California Press, 2020).
16. Ngai, *Impossible Subjects*, 2.
17. Ngai, *Impossible Subjects*, 3.
18. Ngai, *Impossible Subjects*, 7.
19. Lisa Flores, "Towards an Insistent and Transformative Racial Rhetorical Criticism," *Communication and Critical/Cultural Studies* 15, no. 4 (2018): 350.

Scholars and students whose legal citizenship and residency status exist outside of the US, and particularly those who are from the Global South, often live precariously in the US in a world of highly regulated visa and work status regulations. Problems and precarity abound in so many different ways, but because of space, we will share three stories (from three of the coauthors of this chapter), based on our respective work and student status in and outside of the US, as well as the mentoring and advising we all do to many students living in these precarious, frustrating, time consuming, and emotionally fraught situations. We identify these narratives through three themes in the following sections: temporal existence (by Ogunfeyimi), ostracized denizenship (by Asante), and baited optimism (by Banerjee)—followed by a brief vignette (by Sowards).

Temporal Existence (Ogunfeyimi)

Hector Amaya uses the term "citizenship excess" to frame the predictable, normative binary relation between citizens and noncitizens, but he also troubles such a relation by exploring citizenship in a hierarchical fashion, that is, in ways that organize and recognize citizens according to their racial categories and cultural and political capital.[20] While citizenship grants certain rights and privileges, Amaya notes that the term also constitutes a system of control or what he calls the "technology of power."[21] He identifies the dominant actors in this system as the Caucasian race—and sometimes others of non-European descent—with political, cultural, and legal capital. Forms of legal, cultural, and relational citizenship—viewed through citizenship excess—are therefore systems of power and whiteness that regulate, control, restrain, and discipline citizens and noncitizens without cultural and political capital through the instrument of law. In addition, these forms of citizenship are upheld, reinforced, and perpetuated within the neoliberal institutions of higher education. Law, in this case, underscores the common immigration vocabulary: "in/out-of-status," which suggests that noncitizens with nonpermanent visas can only exist within a permissible period and duration. And once they are "out-of-status," that is, out of the time allocated to them, they are considered illegal. So, legal citizenship operates through a temporal orientation within the bounds of law. Thinking through the relation of temporality and technology of control, how does the term "technology of power" not only produce and regulate noncitizens' time but also distribute and commodify such time? This relation

---

20. Amaya, *Citizenship Excess*, 2–4.
21. Amaya, *Citizenship Excess*, 15–16.

presupposes that how much or less time is given to or withdrawn from noncitizens to live depends on how much or less time is allocated to them by the state. In other words, the extent to which noncitizens can live is contingent on the amount of time that is granted to them. This is the basis of rhetorical economies of whiteness that relies on the demand of time by noncitizens and the regulated supply of such time by the United States Citizenship and Immigration Services (USCIS).

I demonstrate, through my immigration experience, that time is a rhetorical commonplace of power and economy, a contractual relation into which noncitizens enter with the United States, one that is renewable on sound evidentiary ground but that is also disposable when/if it contends or conflates with the permissible will of the state sovereign ethos. I have, in the last fifteen years, noticed that time—as duration, expiration, production, commodification—is one of the most significant commonplaces of the immigration service. So common that it appears in all (my) immigration documents, including my I-94 form, visa stamps, DS 2019 form (J-1 exchange visa), I-20 form (F-1 student visa), and I-129 form (O-1 extraordinary ability or temporary work visa). Immigration service deploys time to regulate my visa applications and statuses: when I should enter, stay, exit, and/or reenter the United States. I can't outlive it, erase it, or ignore it without consequence. So, as a good alien customer (it is funny, but it is true to describe myself that way), I have to conform to this temporal contractual directive to live. Despite the temporary statuses of my visas with their regulatory holds on me, I have to always justify, with sufficient evidence, why I deserve a visa type and a visa stamp that grants me a share of a temporary time. It does not matter how many times that I have shown up, gotten my passports stamped, and received approvals for my petitions at the US Consulate and USCIS, they still treat my visa interviews and visa petitions in a case-by-case fashion. And in each case, I must find and iterate evidence that appeals and attunes to each interview and petition and that persuades the state's technology of power to approve my visa application and grant me access to the temporary time. So, evidentiary demands have become, for me and other nonimmigrants, perennial burdens of being in and accessing the regulated time, but they have also reattuned us to the terms and conditions of the USCIS and the US Consulates. Richard Lanham's "the economics of attention," a deficit of attention and attunement to the high supply of the "information economy," underscores my immigration experience.[22] This is because it reclaims attention as a rhetorical way of attuning to existing,

---

22. Richard A. Lanham, *The Economics of Attention: Style and Substance in the Age of Information* (Chicago: University of Chicago Press, 2007), 1–39.

constantly changing, immigration rules/laws. Because the demands for the existing times by noncitizens are high, I must also find undoubtedly reasonable evidence to attune to the short, competitive supply of the times controlled by the USCIS and other immigration bodies.

My recent O-1 visa application underscores this rhetorical economy—the ways in which I adapted my attention to the expectations of the USCIS. For instance, when I was applying for the visa in the O-1A category (sciences, education, arts, business, or athletics), which requires applicants to demonstrate an extraordinary ability in their disciplinary areas, my first concern was how I could find and gather persuasive evidence to not just justify my "extraordinary" ability in the field of rhetoric but, more importantly, to justify the reason to *exist* here and now by purchasing another time. The term "extraordinary" means that you are just one of the very few who has made an "outstanding" impact in your field (and in a specific area), whose work has added "exceptional" contributions to the disciplinary conversation, and that you have made innovative/new findings in your research. The challenges here are twofold: First, how to at least meet three of the eight criteria of the visa category:

a. author journal articles
b. receive national/international awards or comparable awards
c. judge peers' works in the form of peer-reviewers/including editorial board members (mostly journals)
d. hold a critical position in a renowned institution (university or college) that must be justified
e. publish scientific/scholarly discovery
f. receive a salary way higher than your peers (see the other criteria at USCIS's website).[23]

Meeting any of these criteria requires a significant investment of time and labor in gathering, preparing, organizing, and formalizing documents and letters of support, which has been described by many going through this process as more arduous, critical, and time consuming than the tenure and promotion process.

Second, how to offer reasonable quality and quantity evidence to support the criteria, which required me to document my research and service work and acquire letters of support from other scholars in the field who have had notable contributions in the field of rhetoric. This body of evidence is

---

23. US Citizenship and Immigration Services, O-1 Visa: Individuals with Extraordinary Ability or Achievement, https://www.uscis.gov/policy-manual/volume-2-part-m-chapter-4. (accessed April 10, 2024).

twofold: I had to summarize my work using a disciplinary vocabulary as well as in plain language to help my attorney and petition assessor understand my scholarship. To meet these requirements, I requested seven to ten letters of support from my peers in the field who are advanced tenure-stream faculty, tenured associate professors, and endowed and full professors. In the end, I submitted more than two hundred pages of petition. These pages included my diplomas, transcripts, conference abstracts, peer/editorial board review email invites, the abstracts of the journal articles and book chapters, marriage certificate, and the petition itself.

I must admit, following my O-1 visa application experience, that evidence not only constitutes our ways of survival/being, but it also figures as a rhetorical means with which we access, negotiate, purchase, and maintain a fraction of time: to be, to live, and to stay. For us to be and to live is through and by evidence, to leave a trace of evidence in and through papers, to become a body of evidence, and to become evidence—and a sufficient one indeed. So, when I think about this way of being, I worry that my academic pursuit isn't always about offering a compelling body of evidence for faculty job search committee members or building my body of work for positive annual tenure reviews, but it is often more about how to be or live—how to find sufficient evidence to be granted that freedom to live or be, albeit temporarily so. Evidence, to me, is a rhetorical economy of being, even if the means to access such being is traumatic and exhausting.

Even though time has a visible presence in all (my) immigration documents, immigration offices in higher education still configure time as autogenerated emails that serve as the rituals of reminders—a different kind of control. These rituals, to invoke Michel Foucault, constitute the "panopticons," that is, the surveillance machine upon our presence,[24] not just as mere reminders but also as warning signals against overstays, for visa renewals/alternative visa decisions, or as calls to exit from the United States. The reminders are, no doubt, legitimate, but the anxieties such reminders trigger in some of the international students and faculty who lack (financial) supports in their visa renewals or changes, visa options, and continuity in their faculty jobs are tellingly frustrating and, most times, traumatic. This is especially so when the lack of financial and social support often disrupts their education and employment. Many students, particularly from the so-called "third world" countries, have resorted to crowdfunding sources including Gofundme, Hubbub, and Indiegogo to raise funds and complete their studies. Some minority

---

24. Michel Foucault, "'Panopticism' from 'Discipline & Punish: The Birth of the Prison,'" *Race/Ethnicity: Multidisciplinary Global Contexts* 2, no. 1 (2008): 1–12.

faculty on H-1B visas have also had to reapply for their positions. These tasks take time that is not counted in any professional way—not on review forms or CVs—constituting a form of invisible additional labor. As a graduate student, I panicked after my fifth year of funding was ending, but my department was generous enough to extend my funding beyond the initial five-year funding. In this case, I was lucky; many other graduate students are probably not.

More terrifying, however, was my first faculty position with a J-1 visa. As a J-1 visiting scholar, I got my position renewed in one to three months, in most cases, before the expiration date of my visa (DS 2019) every year after my first year. I also recognized my temporal limit in my visa status. While I could transfer my visa from one employer to another, I could not do that if my new job did not begin the day after my current position ended. This transfer also came with a contractual agreement between my current employer and the new one: the former must sign and release the transfer form; the new school must accept the release form within a specific time frame. The challenge for me was that I had to apply for most positions that I could transfer to without any temporal gap. This *transactional* and *contractual* clause also limited my chances for multiple faculty job prospects. Luckily for me, my current employer satisfied these criteria and moved my start date to July 1 since my end date at my previous institution (Dartmouth College) was June 30. However, in another situation, it was more challenging. In 2019, I received an offer for a full-time lecturing position at Stanford University, and I requested that my start date be moved forward to July 1, 2019, instead of the typical September start date to satisfy the time clause in my J-1 visa contract and to avoid any time gap. In the process of negotiating a new date, a new conversation emerged: My job title, "academic staff," required an H-1B visa, whereas I had a J-1 visa (for scholars, researchers, and/or professors). I lost the position because my J-1 visa did not fit with the job category, which originated in the time gap between the Dartmouth and Stanford jobs. I was lucky to get my job renewed at Dartmouth; otherwise, I would have been asked to exit the country.

What then do the challenges of *temporal gap* and the anxiety about time mean for me and others? And how do they underscore the economies of the nation-state? Time, and temporal gap in particular, has often placed me and others in a constant precarious position that counts us in and at the same time forces us out; we are here but are not really in; we are therefore here-there, disposable at the slip of time. This precarious condition forces us to become regular clients who seek, rely on, and present evidence to access the regulated supply of time—and to earn our existence. Time as autogenerated emails echo the "technology of power" that re/enforces or complements our temporal consciousness about being in and out of time, as well as about what we already know; what is already familiar to us, what we have come to live by, and what has come to define us, or is ingrained in our memories: That our arrival is also our departure; that we arrive to return; that, in Jay Dolmage's view, we are already "disabled upon arrival" through what he (Dolmage) describes as a "disabling and racializing force of immigration rhetoric,"[25] labeled as aliens, sometimes for tax purposes, other times for our noncitizen statuses, and are cast with suspicion as parasitic beings from a third-world nation. The email reminders are parts of the "technology of power" in their autogenerative forms or the programming of our time by the immigration services to respond to the directives of the USCIS and the Department of Homeland Security. While we may negotiate the extension and flexibility of time by resorting to the law or hiring an attorney to do so for us, we cannot transcend it or produce it or even erase it. It determines how much or less we live or is left for us to live; it is the legality and rhetorical economy of power that produces and regulates the basis of our being.

It is perhaps justifiable, given my experiences of visa renewals and changes, to seek a more permanent visa status that can lessen or end my anxiety about the continuum or the disruption of time that is almost always temporary. But even if I eventually *make* such a transition to become a permanent resident or even a citizen, that permanency or citizenship, I think, will still be temporary as my temporary identity will always be permanent. No doubt, I will, in a narrow sense of legal *citizenship,* as Amaya notes, gain access to certain privileges such as the symbolic power of the US passport and voting rights; but in a deeper sense of the term *citizenship excess,* my African accent, my Black body, my third-world place, and my Black racial identity are not admissible into such an ethno-racial privileged position of citizenship—of Caucasian descent and the few others who possess the cultural and political capital—that regulates the economy of time to sustain the nation-state. This is because my identity is always already marked as different, as outside of the common bodies, and as rhetorically unwhite. On that note, I will always be out-of-status even when I am permanently in-status. This is the essence of *citizenship excess*—a supremacist logic of othering: a rhetorical double. The neoliberal higher education landscape reinforces economies of whiteness and individuality, as each individual becomes responsible for the time invested in securing legal work status. These rhetorical economies of temporality illustrate citizenship excess in how US citizens (and especially those who obtain citizenship through birth and/ or whiteness) do not have to invest their time in legal, cultural, or relational

---

25. Jay Dolmage, *Disabled upon Arrival: Eugenics, Immigration, and the Construction of Race and Disability* (Columbus: The Ohio State University Press, 2018), 4.

statuses of residency. That excess overflows as these forms of citizenship are rooted in whiteness and historical and contemporary practices in which US American societies and systems have never fully allowed Indigenous, Black, Asian, and Mexican folks, who lived and were born in US states or territories, to be afforded cultural or relational citizenship.

Ostracized Denizenship (Asante)

Michael Walzer and Eduardo Mendieta, among others, have argued that the myth of the US as a nation of immigrants contradicts itself and falls apart when people who are considered outside of the white European norm migrate to this country.[26] Even for those who have attained legal status, Sundstrom and Kim identified "civic ostracism" as a kind of boundary maintenance between normative whiteness and the *other*, affording them a sort of insideness that could be legal, yet socially still bordered as an outsider.[27] The experiences of being included in the nation-state while ostracized as political and cultural subjects speaks varyingly to what Amaya describes as how citizenship excess can be marshaled against people and bodies who do not fit the nation's ethno-racial imaginations. As Catherine Ramírez explains, denizens reside in the borders of citizenship, as failed or alien citizens, often nonwhite, and never afforded the full privileges of cultural and legal citizenship and the excesses of whiteness that are attached to such citizenship. She argues that such experiences become a paradox of assimilation, in which one is invited in, but not regarded in the same way as white US citizens. In the neoliberal academy, we invite students/faculty into the system of US higher education, but the bureaucracies of legal status mean that the denizen remains ostracized and individually responsible for their status.[28]

In this section, I describe my immigration experiences through my time as an undergraduate, a graduate student, and a faculty member to explore structures of power marshaled though supposedly mundane migration policies that have the tendency to produce racialized effects. Importantly, this section reinforces the notion that citizenship excess is in fact transnationally

---

26. Michael Walzer, *What It Means to Be an American* (New York: Marsilio, 1992), 206–24; and Eduardo Mendieta, "Racial Justice, Latinos, and the Supreme Court: The Role of Law and Affect in Social Change," in *Race or Ethnicity? On Black and Latino Identity*, ed. Jorge J. E. Gracia (Ithaca, NY: Cornell University Press, 2007), 206–24.

27. Ronald R. Sundstrom and David Haekwon Kim, "Xenophobia and Racism," *Critical Philosophy of Race* 2, no. 1 (2014): 20–45.

28. Ramírez, *Assimilation*, 11–17.

mediated and is used in conjunction with institutions of power such as education to reinforce whiteness (and heteronormativity) by legitimizing the unfair distribution of social and legal resources to racialized and sexualized subjects. As Eithne Luibhéid and Karma R. Chávez have documented in their edited collection, queer and trans orientations add another complication to migration processes and legal statuses in the US.[29]

As a queer Ghanaian, my desire to migrate to the United States was ignited by the lure of liberal freedom that dominates US American movies and TV shows. Same-sex sexual relations remain criminalized in the Ghanaian constitution—which is a remnant of British colonial times. Additionally, my desire to move to the United States was also due to an economic issue. Given the dwindling numbers of job prospects for college-level graduates, migration was not only about the desire to be free from sexual persecution but also a desire for financial security. Yet, it is this desire for sexual liberation and financial security—sites sutured to US citizenship—where racialized structures, policies, and institutions collaborated to produce differential racial effects. As Adedoyin Ogunfeyimi described in the previous section, rhetorical economies of legal and/or cultural citizenship structure our thinking related to race and nationality, but they also form thinking related to queer identities and these forms of citizenship.

Citizens of most African countries, demarcated with the unsavory term "third world," have the least opportunities of movement around the world. Specific institutional barriers have been put in place mostly in the US and Western European countries, denying them the opportunity to migrate and seek similar economic opportunities that are guaranteed to US and European citizens who seek economic opportunities in other countries. Barriers instituted through the visa application process are used to deny access under the sheen of protecting the citizens of US and European countries in the homeland. For instance, the first time I applied for a US visa, I was asked by the visa consular if I owned property in Ghana. I said no because I was nineteen years old at the time and barely starting college. Subsequently, I was denied a US visitor's visa because I could not establish strong connections to Ghana such as property ownership. Property ownership in this context is an indication that one intends to return *and* that one has middle- to upper-class standing, that is, the financial ability to attend school and return to one's home country. That I wanted to visit a brother I had not seen in seven years did not matter. The fact that I was not a property-owning citizen was grounds for visa denial.

---

29. Eithne Luibhéid and Karma R. Chávez, eds., *Queer and Trans Migrations: Dynamics of Illegalization, Detention, and Deportation* (Champaign: University of Illinois Press, 2020).

Other friends also had similar experiences at the US embassy, effectively barring us from traveling abroad even if we have the financial capabilities to do so. Here, "property-owning" as the benchmark for global travel is embedded in US heteronormative capitalist logics where cultural citizenship and the benefits thereof were and are still reserved for propertied white men.[30] We might also think of whiteness as a form of property, one that prevents most (nonwhite) Africans from obtaining travel visas. Indeed, as Aileen Moreton-Robinson has written in her book, *The White Possessive,* the very notions of property ownership, the colonial state, and nation making are rooted in whiteness and colonial enterprises.[31]

When I decided to move to the United States eventually for my undergraduate education at the University of Minnesota, I experienced similar barriers and hurdles that have been instituted to "protect" US citizens. For instance, US students had the opportunity to work both on campus and off campus. However, international students were not allowed to work off campus even though not that many internship-related opportunities existed on campus. This meant most of the students were confined to working in the university dining services, which had its benefits but also was limiting in the sense that international students only received very narrow job-related skills. Noting how such confinement could jeopardize our job prospects both in the US and in our respective countries, I reached out to the chancellor of the University of Minnesota to ask for additional opportunities. During the meeting, she asked if I thought I was coming to the US to work and not to go to school. Surprised by that question, I responded that international students' tuition is higher than what US students pay, and yet, we are unable to get work experience beyond the campus dining services. I explained to her that I expected to get both an education and related work experience that many US citizens can receive in institutions of higher education. As a result of our conversation, three new positions were opened in the International Office and I was invited to apply. This individual action, as a result of this conversation, illustrates that circumstances can be different, and yet, structurally the rhetorical economies of citizenship mostly prevent institutional and systemic change not to mention material realities and disparate forms of compensation.

After September 11, 2001, international education in the US was transformed. Drawing on the rhetoric of national security, international students

---

30. For more details on how property ownership is a colonial construct in which lands are stolen essentially from Indigenous peoples around the world, see Aileen Moreton-Robinson, *The White Possessive: Property, Power, and Indigenous Sovereignty* (Minneapolis: University of Minnesota Press, 2015).

31. Moreton-Robinson, *White Possessive.*

were consistently surveilled through bureaucratic policies where international students' visa status were tied to their student status. In other words, if a student could not prove that they were consistently in school, they could be subjected to deportation and be denied reentry to the United States. This meant that international students could not take a mental break or be perceived as unable to complete their studies, as their ability to stay in the US was strictly tied to their consistent and uninterrupted status as a student. The inability to take a break presents several challenges, especially to international students' mental health, and even more so for students grappling with the sudden salience of their racial, gender, and sexual identities. For example, moving to the US was supposed to present opportunities to explore my same-sex attraction. However, residing in a small town in south Minnesota made it difficult to come to terms with my same-sex desires. Even though the University had an LGBTQ center, there was no person of color at the center. Furthermore, their programs at the time were primarily geared toward US white students, effectively leaving out several nonwhite and non-US queer students, forcing them to seek a sense of belonging elsewhere. In order to mitigate the effects of such loneliness, I joined the African Students Association (ASA). However, the ASA reproduced particular African Christian heteronormative expectations in a way that made it necessary that I recoil into the proverbial closet again. Consequently, while I thought moving to the US might create the space for self-exploration, the conditions attached to my visa status and the lack of outreach of LGBTQ centers to racial minorities and international students forced me to maintain a sense of heteronormativity with my ASA friends. Ironically, the "closet" felt safer for my mental health so that I could continue my education uninterrupted. Here, the possibilities, opportunities, challenges, and dangers of exploring queer identities are complicated within the contours of race, nationality, continent, and related rhetorical economies of whiteness, as well as how advances for LGBTQ rights have been made, but many of those rights attained reside within contexts of whiteness.

Amaya explains that "citizenship had to be codified in law in such a way as to simultaneously acknowledge the promise of legal equality and the justification for inequality."[32] It is the justification for inequality to which I now turn my attention. As an international faculty member with relative financial stability, my employment at a US university has largely been what has made it relatively easier to apply for visas to travel internationally for conferences and collaborate with international colleagues. Even though I am currently a permanent resident in the United States, there are still several barriers that are put in place when applying for visas to travel, mostly to European countries.

---

32. Amaya, *Citizenship Excess*, 26.

First of all, US citizens are not required to apply for a visa for most European countries if they plan to stay there for less than ninety days. In contrast, by being defined as a Ghanaian, I am automatically ascribed a judicial deficit that legitimizes my exclusion from legal and mobility privileges ascribed to US citizens. The ascription of judicial deficit through my Ghanaian citizenship means I am perceived as a suspicious potential Black immigrant and as such, can be treated unequally. Even though I have traveled to Europe several times, I am still required to travel to the nearest embassy or consulate to apply for a visa in person because a fingerprint needs to be taken. Additionally, I have to prove that I can sustain myself while in Europe by submitting all my checking and saving accounts. Furthermore, I have to answer invasive questions about everyone in my family—who and where they are—among several other queries. These processes and measures have been normalized as ways to protect European citizens from potential criminals, terrorists, and undocumented migrants. However, such processes concretize the excesses embedded in whiteness citizenship in that mainstream (white) US citizens do not have to undergo such procedures. US citizens of color face significant barriers related to racism and discrimination in traveling abroad as well as at home in the US; the citizenship excess of whiteness means that many such folks are treated as denizens even while holding legal citizenship. As Amaya describes, such is the process of political capital accumulation where citizenship becomes the avenue for the demarcation of who is human and who isn't; whose views get reinforced and whose views are erased; who deserves state protection and who citizens need to be protected from.

Baited Optimism (Banerjee)

Along the lines of Lauren Berlant's cruel optimism, the constant dream of a tenure-track job that will enable legal status stability becomes a form of baiting. Each bait/bite comes in the form of a cool job announcement (or any permanent job at all). As the job market moves into the academic year, the bait/bite becomes more of a desperate feeling caused by the stress of being willing to do anything for some kind of promise of stability. This feeling is likely experienced by anyone on the tenure-track job market, but it is particularly acute for those who need a job in order to obtain the legal status that will allow them to remain in the US. As Berlant explains, in our pursuit of "the good life," we may attach the notion of a job to "conventional good-life fantasies."[33]

---

33. Berlant, *Cruel Optimism*, 2.

In higher education, the pursuit of the tenure-track job with the attenuating legal status that comes with it (in most cases) isn't just the good life. It's what is right, what is fair, what is deserved, what is just. And yet, Berlant observes, "the fantasies that are fraying include, particularly, upward mobility, job security, political and social equality, and lively, durable intimacy. The set of dissolving assurances also includes meritocracy, the sense that liberal-capitalist society will reliably provide opportunities for individuals to carve out relations of reciprocity that seem fair and that foster life as a project of adding up to something and constructing cushions for enjoyment."[34] The elusiveness of tenure-track positions that might enable stability, a sense of self-worth, and so forth reflects the "impasse" in which there seems to be no exit or path forward from positions of precarity.[35] Cruel optimism, "as a relation of attachment to compromised conditions of possibility whose realization is discovered either to be impossible, sheer fantasy, or *too* possible, and toxic,"[36] manifests in doctoral programs, academic job markets, departments, and universities for non-US students or faculty trying to live up to the promise/dream/fantasy of the good life in the academy.

In what follows, I share my experiences on the academic job market (both as a tenure-track and postdoctoral candidate) trying to navigate the seemingly endless and treacherous pathway from a temporary postgraduate STEM F1-Optional Practical Training (OPT) employment to the "coveted" yet "elusive" H-1B visa. OPT is a program in which recent graduates are allowed to legally stay in the US for employment or internship possibilities related to their field of study to gain relevant research or work experience. OPT participants cannot get any job, but rather it has to be related to their field of study. The precarious immigration status on OPT leads to "liminal belonging—always already belonging . . . but denied recognition of that belonging in the form of secure immigration status," which hinders immigrants' "ability to meet their needs and sustain themselves, materially, emotionally, and socially."[37]

---

34. Berlant, *Cruel Optimism*, 3.
35. Berlant, *Cruel Optimism*, 4.
36. Berlant, *Cruel Optimism*, 24.
37. Kathryn Tomko Dennler, "Challenging Un-Belonging and Undesirability: How Acts of Autonomy Transform Everyday Realities of Living with Precarious Immigration Status in Toronto, Canada," *ACME* 19, no. 2 (2020): 502, 513. See also Anna C. Korteweg, "The Failures of 'Immigrant Integration': The Gendered Racialized Production of Non-Belonging," *Migration Studies* 5, no. 3 (2017): 428–44; and Stacey K. Sowards and Paulami Banerjee, "Paradox of Assimilation, Racialization, and the Rhetorical Canon," in *Handbook of Ethnicity and Race in Communication*, ed. Shinsuke Eguchi and Bernadette M. Calafell (New York: Routledge, 2024).

As my two-year postdoctoral fellowship while on OPT was nearing completion in June 2022, I was desperately seeking some kind of full-time academic employment that would allow me to extend my stay in the US as I continued my search for the elusive tenure-track position. Having consulted with several immigration lawyers about the visa options available (EB-1, EB-2 NIW, O-1) before my sixty-day grace period post-OPT expired, I was left with no choice but to look for departments that would be willing to sponsor my H-1B visa should I be hired. With the time clock ticking to not only land a prized tenure-track position but wherein my visa paperwork would be submitted on time before the expiration of my legal grace period, I started the job application process as early as August 2021. Between August 2021 and March 2022, I applied for seventeen tenure-track positions in the field of environmental studies, environmental science, geography, sustainability, and environmental communication (not to mention the jobs I applied for in the previous two years). During the same time period, there were several other tenure-track job openings that I could not apply for as H-1B visa sponsorship was not available for international candidates. During this job cycle, I obtained four first round interviews and one campus interview. While none of these interviews led to a tenure-track job, the lure of "finally making it" in this country while overcoming all hardships and obstacles pushed me into greater desperation to find "a job/any job" that would prove that I was not a quitter, tragically echoing the premises of Berlant's "cruel optimism." For me, the fear of shame and ridicule that I would potentially face upon returning home to India was equally humiliating and debilitating, constantly eating away at my self-esteem and my worth as an academic. In a weird twist of fate perhaps, this was also the period during which my publications saw a 59 percent increase in citations, often cited by academics in departments where I had interviewed. While I should have been ecstatic that my scholarship mattered, I was left with a numbing feeling that while my work was good enough to be cited, it was not good enough to get me hired; the citations and the politics of citations do not mean anything for one who does not have a job.

And yet, through rationalization of the self, I had to somehow find ways to pull myself out of this "self-shame spiral" to live up to the dream/fantasy of the "good life" in higher education, reflecting what Lauren Berlant terms as "slow death," or the "physical wearing out of a population and the deterioration of people in that population that is very nearly a defining condition of their experience and historical existence."[38] Through this concept of "slow death,"

---

38. Lauren Berlant, "Slow Death (Sovereignty, Obesity, Lateral Agency)," *Critical Inquiry* 33, no. 4 (2007): 574.

Berlant posits a "development in the ways we conceptualize contemporary historical experience, especially when that experience is simultaneously at an extreme and in a zone of ordinariness, where life building and the attrition of human life are indistinguishable, and where it is hard to distinguish modes of incoherence, distractedness, and habituation from deliberate and deliberative activity, as they are all involved in the reproduction of predictable life."[39]

In tune with what Berlant terms "unconscious and explicit desires," my inability fueled by my stubbornness against letting go of my dream of obtaining a tenure-track position in the US and instead exploring other opportunities has not only manifested in low self-worth but also has taken a toll on my physical and mental health and, unbeknownst to me, affected the long-term friendships that I had built in this country—a country I considered my home away from home, a country that brought friends into my life, friends who became family. For someone who came to this country with big dreams of completing her PhD, leading the life of a successful academic, and cherishing and nourishing the friendships along the way, life has become an interplay between

> pragmatic (life-making) and accretive (life-building) gestures and tracks the relation of that activity to the attrition of the subject. It focuses on what's vague and gestural about the subject and episodic about the event. It presumes nothing about the meaning of a decision or the impact of an act. Without attending to the varieties of constraint and unconsciousness that condition ordinary activity we persist in an attachment to a fantasy that in the truly lived life emotions are always heightened and expressed in modes of effective agency that ought justly to be and are ultimately consequential or performatively sovereign.[40]

Agency in this sense is relegated to the individual as responsibility for doing extraordinary work (indeed, the language of USCIS!) beyond what (white) US citizens have to prove in their tenure and promotion packets at their institutions. There is little, if any, accountability, responsibility, or ethic of care within the system of US higher education and the US immigration process. As such, individuals take on the burdens of proving themselves, not always recognizing the rhetorical economies of whiteness within neoliberal university and immigration systems.

---

39. Berlant, "Slow Death," 574.
40. Berlant, "Slow Death," 757.

Vignette: Family Separation and Higher Education (Sowards)

In working with my coauthors on this essay, I had intended only to highlight their direct experiences with US immigration. In reading their stories, I realized that my own father faced similar circumstances as an international student, which also affected me and my upbringing. While interacting with USCIS, other parts of the US immigration system, and US higher education systems is difficult and traumatic as Ogunfeyimi, Asante, and Banerjee have documented, these experiences also affect families and future generations, as my own story illustrates. I was born in the United States (with US citizenship), and I have white skin, brown straight hair, and brown eyes. I speak English with a US American standard accent, and my name is a typical sounding US American name. In other words, I have phenotypic markers of whiteness and all their accompanying privileges.[41] And yet, my own life story is also complicated by US immigration politics and the neoliberalism of US higher education systems. My biological father was born and raised in Chile; he came to the US as an international student in the 1960s on a scholarship. He earned a bachelor's degree, and then a master's degree. In 1972/73, after he finished school, he could not find a job that would sponsor him to stay in the United States. Chile was in political turmoil at the time, with president Salvador Allende in power. Allende either shot himself upon the advent of a military coup or was assassinated (there are conflicting reports) on September 11, 1973, about six months after I was born. Unable or not wanting to return to Chile, my biological father went to France and then Mexico for the rest of his life, even while he traveled to Chile where his parents still lived. Recruited into the US system of higher education, with the promise of a US American college experience, my biological father never returned to the US to live. I grew up in rural Colorado; I was adopted by my nonbiological father when I was in sixth grade. Family separations have dominated news stories on immigration, a story that is partly my own, even though mine is rooted in much more class, racial, and citizenship status privilege. These are not new stories; many families have experienced forced separations of all kinds for decades and centuries. Also not new: family separation by "choice." That is, so many who have legal status to live and work in the US may also be allowed to travel outside the US but may "choose" not to because of problems Asante outlined, among many others. Expired passports, travel expenses, long-distance relationships,

---

41. Stacey K. Sowards, "Rhetoricity of Borders: Whiteness in Latinidad and Beyond," *Communication and Critical/Cultural Studies*, 18, no. 1 (2021): 41–49.

time zones, and many other factors all contribute to a form of "chosen" separation from families. In that sense, rhetorical economies of whiteness through the lens of citizenship excess represent historical and contemporary forms of family separation, even when such paths are "chosen" in pursuit of the US American dream of making it in academia.

Conclusion

Through our narrativized themes presented here, we hope to engage in a little diasporic listening/reading/learning to unpack just a few examples and experiences of how citizenship excess operates as a rhetorical economy of whiteness in university systems through temporal existences, ostracized denizenship, and baited optimism. Through Hsu's concept of diasporic listening/reading, we offer stories here to concretize the problematic neoliberal institutions of higher education in the US. Media stories abound about family separation and the plight of desperate immigrants clustered along the border, waiting in Mexico. As Hsu argues, "Homing enables diasporic subjects to deconstruct, co-construct, and maneuver among sites of (un)belonging. It exposes the narrative and structural forces that constrain and expand the possibilities for intimacy, security, and kinship."[42] Yet, citizenship excess infiltrates places like neoliberal structures within higher education institutions without recognition, perpetuating whiteness regimes and power structures. These stories help US American students, faculty, staff, and administrators see the real impact of decisions that often result in the precarity of international students in these forms of inclusion/exclusion and the pursuit of the US American dream that becomes cruel optimism. Citizenship excess in higher education, then, reflects the privileges and rhetorical economies of whiteness. The privilege is in part to not have to think about the financial burdens and bureaucracies of living in the US, with the constant changes in rules, regulations, and the different applications of such rules and regulations. There are constant anxieties, worries, and stresses related to ensuring "model minority" status, being the right kind of immigrant, and knowing that racism, discrimination, nationalism, anti-immigrant and antiqueer sentiments are in full force throughout US American society and in higher education, even among our most well-meaning and intentioned colleagues, students, and friends. As individuals, noncitizens in higher education apparatuses take on the brunt of emotional and material labor in following bureaucratic rules and regulations. Existing in such systems

---

42. Hsu, *Constellating Home*, 9–10.

makes it hard to see beyond the difficulties of one's own experiences and that it is these systemic rhetorical economies of whiteness that perpetuate feelings of inadequacy and/or inability to succeed in such structures. Adding racism, discrimination, xenophobia, linguistic differences, and intersections related to gender, ability, and queer identities create citizenship excess that resides in these economies of whiteness within neoliberal higher education systems.

What is to be done? Confronting these structures and systems that are bound up in neoliberal capitalist structures, bureaucracy, immigration, academia, racism, sexism, antiforeigner sentiment, and so forth is not an easy task, and these systems are hard to dismantle. Immediately, however, the practice in which universities require US citizenship status for employment and refuse to consider applicants who are not citizens for faculty positions must be resisted and challenged whenever possible. Human resources departments and hiring committees should and must consider how precarious "international" students and faculty might be in their visa statuses. Non-tenure-track positions could be open to anyone, including those who are not US citizens. Support services for both "international" students and faculty could help a great deal. But in the end, unless we move away from neoliberal, institutionalized thinking about what "international" students offer in terms of money, and the added benefit of "diversity," the best we can offer are the few piecemeal suggestions above.

CHAPTER 5

The *Master* Narrative

A Black Nihilistic Reading of Misogynoir, H(a)unting, and US Higher Education

RICO SELF

Institutions of higher learning in the United States have been unable to escape the impact of the racial reckoning that ensued after the horrific death of George Floyd. To be sure, community activists, students, scholars, and higher education professionals alike were working to address the role of institutions of higher learning in promoting and preserving systemic racism and other intersecting systems of oppression even before Floyd's untimely passing. In 2015, for instance, Washington, DC-based Georgetown University, the nation's first and largest Roman Catholic university, began efforts to reckon with its history of benefiting from slavery and segregation.[1] As COVID-19 decimated communities of color,[2] however, such activism for racial redress

---

1. "Georgetown Reflects on Slavery, Memory, and Reconciliation," Georgetown University, https://www.georgetown.edu/slavery (accessed December 4, 2022); Annalisa Merelli, "The Jesuits' Plan to Compensate Their Slaves' Descendants Gets Reparation Wrong," Quartz, June 3, 2021, https://qz.com/2010943/georgetown-and-the-jesuits-slavery-reparations-plan-falls-short; John Murauski and RealClearInvestigations, "Georgetown University's Road to Slavery Reparations Was Paved with Good Intentions, Leading to a Can of Worms," National African American Reparations Commission (NAARC), July 13, 2022, https://reparationscomm.org/reparations-news/georgetown-universitys-road-to-slavery-reparations-was-paved-with-good-intentions.

2. Lakisha D. Flagg and Lisa A. Campbell, "COVID-19 in Communities of Color: Structural Racism and Social Determinants of Health," *OJIN: The Online Journal of Issues in Nursing*, 26, no. 2 (2021); and Valerie Wilson, "Inequities Exposed: How COVID-19 Widened Racial Inequities in Education, Health, and the Workforce," Economic Policy Institute, June 22, 2020, https://www.epi.org/publication/covid-19-inequities-wilson-testimony/.

reached a fever pitch once the world bore witness to the horrible spectacle of now-convicted Minneapolis Police Department officer Derek Chauvin kneeling on Floyd's neck for more than nine minutes. Floyd's eventual death, in tandem with the murders of other unarmed Black people by law enforcement personnel, moved the world in such a way that its effects could not be denied. During a global pandemic, activists and protesters poured into the streets and flooded social media to declare in a way never seen before that Black lives do matter.

As part of this thrust for racial redress, activists placed increased attention on higher education.[3] They sought to make institutions of higher learning come to terms with their racist roots and commit to moving beyond mere lip service and other performative gestures of racist condemnation. Instead, these activists and organizers wanted to effect material and structural changes that would reflect higher education's promise of diversity and inclusion. The momentum brought in the wake of Floyd's death saw many higher education institutions rush to remove from their campuses long-standing symbols of the Confederacy and other relics of white supremacy, including monuments, building names, flags, and so forth. Additionally, many colleges and universities hired a cadre of diversity, equity, and inclusion (DEI) strategists and professionals; pledged to hire and retain larger cohorts of faculty and staff of color; endowed scholarships to help recruit and retain students of color and address barriers preventing access to even the most prestigious American colleges and universities; made curricular changes; and promoted people of color to prominent administrative positions, including college and university deanships, provostships, and presidencies. Lastly, several institutions created and/or devoted resources to already existing research centers and institutes, programs, and offices and departments designed to address systemic disparities. On the surface, higher education appeared to be committing itself to the work of DEI.

Years later, though, the follow-through on these promises has largely been woeful and the momentum has decreased. Funding priorities have shifted, DEI professionals have lost their jobs, and students and faculty of color still find that predominantly white institutions are hostile to their presence. As such, questions abound about the commitment of colleges and universities

---

3. Melissa Ezarik, "More Discussion than Action: Racial Justice on Campus," Inside Higher Education, May 5, 2021, https://www.insidehighered.com/news/2021/05/06/what-students-think-about-racial-justice-efforts-campus; and Jon Edleman, "Two Years after the Murder of George Floyd, Colleges Reflect," *Diverse: Issues in Higher Education*, May 25, 2022, https://www.diverseeducation.com/demographics/african-american/article/15292519/two-years-after-the-murder-of-george-floyd-colleges-remember-and-reflect.

to substantiating and sustaining material and systemic change in support of faculty, students, and staff of color. To illustrate, take the case of Uju Anya, a Nigerian American professor at Carnegie Mellon University. Anya, a direct descendent of Britain's colonial violence,[4] tweeted in celebration of Queen Elizabeth II's declining health and looming death. "I heard the chief monarch of a thieving raping genocidal empire is finally dying," she wrote. "May her pain be excruciating."[5] Amazon founder Jeff Bezos, one of the world's wealthiest people and a Carnegie Mellon benefactor, responded via quote tweet: "This [Anya] is someone supposedly working to make the world better? I don't think so. Wow."[6] Bezos's response ignited an even larger firestorm. Amid the increasing onslaught of tweets of condemnation directed at Anya, Twitter deleted Anya's initial tweet, claiming that it violated the social media platform's policies.[7] Carnegie Mellon released a statement similarly condemning Anya's "offensive and objectionable" language, stating that her views "absolutely do not represent the values of the institution, nor the standards of discourse we seek to foster."[8] Interestingly, Anya was recruited by Carnegie Mellon during the hiring wave that followed Floyd's murder, a direct result of activism calling for racial redress in higher education.[9]

How might these acts of discipline against Anya function as exemplars of the rhetorical economy of whiteness? In other words, how do the above-mentioned moments demonstrate how whiteness works as a rhetorical construct alongside economic signifiers so that discourses of whiteness come to dictate universal standards of decorous behavior and wield economic impact when people of color violate their benevolent norms and expectations? Uju Anya's censure and other moments like it provide ideal opportunities to think through the limits and even the im/possibility of higher education's commitment to DEI, particularly as neoliberalism—the framework of the capitalist

---

4. Rich Lord, "CMU Professor Offers Context for Tweet Wishing Pain on Dying Queen," PublicSource, September 9, 2022, https://www.publicsource.org/queen-elizabeth-excruciating-pain-professor-tweet-carnegie-mellon-university.

5. Jack Dutton, "Carnegie Mellon Refuses to Condone Uju Anya over Queen's Death Remarks," *Newsweek*, September 9, 2022, https://www.newsweek.com/carnegie-mellon-refuse-condone-uju-anya-over-queens-death-remarks-1741404.

6. Dutton, "Carnegie Mellon Refuses."

7. Bruce T. Wright, "Twitter Deletes Black Professor's Tweet about Queen Elizabeth's 'Excruciating' Death," NewsOne, September 8, 2022, https://newsone.com/4404943/uju-anya-queen-elizabeth-tweet/.

8. Dutton, "Carnegie Mellon Refuses."

9. Marcela Rodrigues, "Jeff Bezos Criticized a Professor's Tweet about the Queen. Then the University Condemned Her Comments," *Chronicle of Higher Education*, September 11, 2022, https://www.chronicle.com/article/jeff-bezos-criticized-a-professors-tweet-about-the-queen-then-the-university-condemned-her-comments.

market and extension of this framework (including defining characteristics like competition, rugged individualism, customer satisfaction, profit) to all domains of life—continues as the dominant model in higher education.

The 2022 psychological horror *Master* represents in many ways the ambivalence surrounding higher education's ability to foster a truly inclusive environment for people of color as racism continues to structure institutional norms and values. The film, which was written and directed by Mariama Diallo, premiered during the Sundance Film Festival in January 2022. It was screened at South by Southwest (SXSW) the following March and was released via Prime Video shortly thereafter. The film follows three Black women who embark upon separate but intertwined journeys at Ancaster College, a prestigious university in New England: Professor Gail Bishop (Regina Hall) is appointed the college's first Black master, a position synonymous with dean; Jasmine Moore (Zoe Renee) begins her college matriculation; and biracial professor Liv Beckman (Amber Gray) is up for tenure. Ancaster College signifies the best of higher education in the United States. It has historical cachet, a presumably large endowment, premier faculty and graduates, and a prominent location near other "high-quality" institutions of higher learning. Ancaster also counts people of color, especially Black women, as students, professors, and administrators in its ranks. Upon first glance, Ancaster is democracy's ideal depiction of inclusivity, yet this depiction obscures the commonplace, insidious, and deadly workings of the rhetorical economy of whiteness within the context of the neoliberal university. Ultimately, *Master* responds to the call for racial redress by looking beyond policing as the primary institution of analysis and centering the multidimensional experiences of Black women in higher education as necessary components of these discussions. Indeed, universities function as a sort of diversity experiment, seeking ways to catalog and incorporate difference.[10]

Given this volume's emphasis on how discourses of whiteness organize economic vocabularies, I argue that rhetorical economies of whiteness, buttressed as they are by neoliberal tendencies and impulses, establish whiteness as the ideal medium of exchange in higher education. In this supposedly "postracial" and colorblind epoch brought presumably by the election of Barack Obama to the US presidency,[11] this exchange requires and enacts Black social

---

10. Roderick A. Ferguson, *The Reorder of Things: The University and Its Pedagogies of Minority Difference* (Minneapolis: University of Minnesota Press, 2012).

11. Kimberlè Williams Crenshaw, "How Colorblindness Flourished in the Age of Obama," in *Seeing Race Again: Countering Colorblindness across the Disciplines*, ed. Kimberlè Williams Crenshaw, Luke Charles Harris, Daniel Martinez HoSang, and George Lipsitz (Berkeley: University of California Press, 2019).

death to the extent that the integration of Black people into relations structured by neoliberalism is nearly futile precisely because neoliberalism instrumentalizes Blackness as the primary means by which whiteness reasserts and recenters itself. To demonstrate these claims, I focus primarily on Gail Bishop and Jasmine Moore to show how Gail's appointment as the first Black master of Ancaster College and Jasmine's simultaneous matriculation as a student set off a macabre series of events that result in what I call the exorcism of Blackness from Ancaster. In this way, *Master* functions as a critical and necessary intervention in public discourse and cultural politics that names and transcodes the particularity of Black women's experiences in academia to provide important insights into how misogynoir—defined by Moya Bailey as "the uniquely co-constitutive racialized and sexist violence that befalls Black women as a result of their simultaneous and interlocking oppression at the intersection of racial and gender marginalization"[12]—shapes experiences of institutional racism and how those experiences are represented in US visual and digital culture. In the next section, I lay out an overview of whiteness studies in the field of communication and then introduce Black nihilism as a critical intervention that will help construct what I propose as a practice of reading or uncovering rhetorical economies of whiteness.

Critiquing the Communicative Power of Whiteness via a Black Nihilistic Lens

According to Ronald L. Jackson II, "The crucible of race and racism in the United States continues to plague our society, and the sheer force of hegemonic whiteness is at the epicenter."[13] By *hegemonic whiteness*, Jackson calls forth ideas related to the discursively dominant and idealized versions of bourgeois whiteness against which all other racialized constructs are judged and toward which all other racial groups are expected to aspire. This chapter takes the relationship between race and racism and hegemonic whiteness—normal and normalizing as it is—as a generative starting point for understanding how *Master* calls attention to rhetorical economies of whiteness by means of neoliberal social and economic arrangements in higher education. To begin, I situate this conversation in what McIntosh, Moon, and Nakayama

---

12. Moya Bailey, *Misogynoir Transformed: Black Women's Digital Resistance* (New York University Press, 2021), 1.

13. Ronald L. Jackson II, forward to *Interrogating the Communicative Power of Whiteness*, ed. Dawn Marie D. McIntosh, Dreama G. Moon, and Thomas Nakayama (New York: Routledge, 2019), viii.

refer to as the *communicative power of whiteness*, which, for these scholars, refers to the "shifting strategic moves of whiteness as manifested in the current cultural climate."[14] Considering how communication engenders whiteness as a racial category, identity marker, and institutional norm, it is imperative to attend to the ways whiteness finds its power and continuity by drawing on and (re)circulating older visions and versions of itself during times of social and cultural unrest. Whiteness then materially and symbolically concretizes these logics and longings in the present. This diachronic maneuvering, or the ever-changing same, is also strategic:[15] its purpose is to continually extend, recenter, and extol the virtuosity of whiteness through processes of communication by which it tautologically justifies its hegemony. In this zeitgeist of diversity and inclusion, critical assessments of whiteness's communicative power are necessary, especially as demographic shifts suggest that white people will eventually occupy a minority status in the United States by 2044.[16]

Since the 1990s, scholars in communication have been leveraging the resources of the field to contribute to conversations in the field of whiteness studies. This critical trajectory arguably began with Nakayama and Krizek's "Whiteness: A Strategic Rhetoric" in which the authors consider the discursive (and therefore strategic) functions of whiteness. In particular, they consider how the term *white* signifies "relatively unchartered territory that has remained invisible as it continues to influence the identities of those both within and without its domain."[17] Similarly, Shome writes that

> whiteness, as an institutionalized and systemic problem, is maintained and produced not by overt rhetorics of whiteness, but rather, by its 'everydayness,' by the ordinary unquestioned racialized social relations that have acquired a seeming normativity and through that normativity function to make invisible the ways white people participate in, and derive protection and benefits from, a system whose rules and organizational relations work to their advantage.[18]

---

14. Dawn Marie D. McIntosh, Dreama G. Moon, and Thomas Nakayama, introduction to *Interrogating the Communicative Power of Whiteness*, ed. Dawn Marie D. McIntosh, Dreama G. Moon, and Thomas Nakayama (New York: Routledge, 2019), 3.

15. Thomas K. Nakayama and Robert L. Krizek, "Whiteness: A Strategic Rhetoric," *Quarterly Journal of Speech*, 81, no. 4 (1995): 291–309.

16. Justin Gest, "What the 'Majority Minority' Shift Really Means for America," *New York Times*, August 24, 2021, https://www.nytimes.com/2021/08/24/opinion/us-census-majority-minority.html.

17. Nakayama and Krizek, "Whiteness," 291.

18. Raka Shome, "Outing Whiteness," *Critical Studies in Media Communication* 17, no. 3 (2000): 366.

Thus, whiteness's symbolic power lies in its stealthy ordinariness, universalization, and taken-for-grantedness.

Moreover, Nakayama and Krizek elucidate in their essay how communication scholars have rarely interrogated the cultural center, the hold of privilege or what Jackson might call the "sociopolitical habitat of whiteness,"[19] from a critical perspective. As such, the field has consequently left the "everydayness" of whiteness (including its economic logics and arrangements) unmarked and undefined in its theoretical and critical pursuits even as whiteness itself has continued to evolve. Nakayama and Krizek seek therefore to "expose whiteness as a cultural construction as well as the strategies that embed its centrality."[20] They advocate for whiteness's decentering and denaturalization, a move that removes its protective cover and opens avenues for the critical assessment of its racialized power dynamics. Other scholars in communication have followed this trajectory by contending with the ideological/strategic, discursive, institutional, disciplinary, representational, intercultural/global, and intersectional wages of whiteness.[21] Taken together, these and other scholars have worked to interrogate critically the way whiteness functions as a—or perhaps the—primary organizing principle of Western modernity.

Since the communicative power of whiteness lies in its ordinariness—how it goes unquestioned and thus remains fundamentally unchallenged and functionally unchanged—the daily functioning of whiteness is found in its institutional and symbolic proliferation as commonsense. Put simply, we can find

---

19. Jackson, forward to *Interrogating the Communicative Power of Whiteness*, xii.

20. Nakayama and Krizek, "Whiteness," 297.

21. See Megan Morrissey, "Under (Y)our Skin: Rachel Dolezal and the Elasticity of Whiteness," *Communication and Critical/Cultural Studies* 18, no. 3 (2021): 229–45; Shome, "Outing Whiteness"; Stephanie L. Hartzell, "Whiteness Feels Good Here: Interrogating White Nationalist Rhetoric on Stormfront," *Communication and Critical/Cultural Studies* 17, no. 2 (2000): 129–48; Myra Washington, "Woke Skin, White Masks: Race and Communication Studies," *Communication and Critical/Cultural Studies* 17, no. 2 (2020): 261–66; Lisa M. Corrigan and Anjali Vats, "The Structural Whiteness of Academic Patronage," *Communication and Critical/Cultural Studies* 17, no. 2 (2020): 220–27; Bryan J. McCann, Ashley Noel Mack, and Rico Self, "Communication's Quest for Whiteness: The Racial Politics of Disciplinary Legitimacy," *Communication and Critical/Cultural Studies* 17, no. 2 (2020): 243–52; Linsay M. Cramer, "Whiteness and the Postracial Imaginary in Disney's *Zootopia*," *Howard Journal of Communications* 31, no. 3 (2019): 246–81; David C. Oh, "Black-Yellow Fences: Multiracial Boundaries and Whiteness in the *Rush Hour* Franchise," *Critical Studies in Media Communication* 29, no. 5 (2012): 349–66; Mohan J. Dutta, "Whiteness, Internalization, and Erasure: Decolonizing Futures from the Global South," *Communication and Critical/Cultural Studies* 17, no. 2 (2020): 228–35; Stacey K. Sowards, "Rhetoricity of Borders: Whiteness in Latinidad and Beyond," *Communication and Critical/Cultural Studies* 18, no. 1 (2021): 41–49; and Rachel E. Dubrofsky and Emily D. Ryalls, "*The Hunger Games*: Performing Not-Performing to Authenticate Femininity and Whiteness," *Critical Studies in Media Communication* 31, no. 5 (2014): 395–409.

whiteness in overlapping neoliberal structures and institutional domains such as housing, medicine, education, law, biology, economics, and the like that structure social relations while rearticulating and co-constituting whiteness's hegemony. While this present period of shifting demographics and culture wars has been dubiously dubbed a postracial and colorblind America, such neoliberal fantasies are characterized by the ability to disregard race or refuse to "see" its import and/or impact. On the other hand, these fantasies also refer to the enactment of policies or the passage of laws without regard to race in an effort to promote racial equality and secure social equity. As a result, circulating the logics of whiteness as commonsense via social institutions and cultural discourse effectively recenters whiteness as normative through the refusal to recognize or critically interrogate the specificity of cultural location. Rather, neoliberalism depends upon the elision of difference and places concentrated attention on the individual rather than prevailing systems of privilege and inequality. This elision of difference is consequential; it is one of neoliberalism's defining assumptions. It operates from the belief that the norms and structures created by and mostly beneficial to white people can account for all people through processes of assimilation—that is, if any person simply works hard enough. Moving from race-conscious social justice approaches to those that are colorblind demonstrates whiteness's stealthy "everydayness," that is, its communicative power, and the relationship of that everydayness to the ways the rhetorical economies of whiteness reify and justify anti-Black capitalist logics. In another sense, we may even speculate that as white people move closer to minority status, whiteness's ordinariness will discursively continue as a defining feature of the neoliberalist project.

To augment the critical study of whiteness in communication scholarship, I advocate for a treatment of rhetorical economies of whiteness—or how whiteness exists as a rhetorical construct in a direct and mutually constitutive relationship with economic signifiers—by employing what I call a *Black nihilistic lens*. Black nihilism seeks to "expose the unbridgeable rift between Being and function for blackness"[22] as Blackness in the metaphysical world gives form to nothingness, which justifies continuous efforts to expel it. As a critical practice of literacy (e.g., reading media), viewing texts through the lens of Black nihilism works to recognize and engage how rhetorical economies of whiteness lend themselves to the "horrifying meaninglessness, hopelessness, and lovelessness" that have come to characterize Black ontology in Western modernity.[23] For if one accepts the well-argued position that slavery did not

---

22. Calvin L. Warren, *Ontological Terror: Blackness, Nihilism, and Emancipation* (Durham, NC: Duke University Press, 2018), 6.

23. Cornel West, *Race Matters* (Boston: Beacon Press, 1993), 14.

end in 1865 but was sustained as a "relational dynamic"[24] that has continued to impact the lives of Black people postslavery, then a Black nihilistic lens reads Blackness and whiteness as racial antagonisms. By suggesting that Blackness and whiteness exist in an antagonistic relationship, I follow the position, articulated by Frank B. Wilderson, that whiteness and Blackness are structurally irreconcilable.[25] This irreconcilability withstands precisely because whiteness is the realm of the Human and Blackness is the realm of nothingness[26]—a nothingness demarcated primarily by a social death that creates the conditions of abjection, subjugation, pathology, and gratuitous violence in capitalist relations.

Black people, according to Calvin Warren, "have function but not Being [in civil society]—the function of black(ness) is to give form to a terrifying formlessness (nothing)."[27] This formlessness characterizes Black ontology and demonstrates the ways whiteness recreates in the present its older forms to help (re)secure and (re)justify its position of privilege through its constant exorcism of Blackness. Taking Calvin Warren's understanding of nihilism at face value, a Black nihilistic view is invested in, among other things, interrogating the social construction of whiteness over and against Black people—those who occupy nothingness and who exist outside the structure but are subject to its strictures. In other words, the structural arrangements of civil society require Blackness to maintain themselves. Hegemonic whiteness, ensconced in the realm of the normalizing, normative, and natural, is anti-Black by its very nature. It is through its anti-Blackness that whiteness enacts, maintains, and exacts its stability and coherency. Whiteness does not exist simply for or independently of whiteness's sake. Rather, whiteness's very definition depends upon the violent expulsion of Blackness through a concerted attempt by whiteness to reposition itself as/at the cultural center (e.g., through discourses of colorblindness). Social death is always already physical, economic, representational, spiritual, and corporeal. So, too, are rhetorical economies of whiteness.

There is also an economic and discursive drive to this ontological problem. Wilderson repudiates radical discourses for their overreliance on the Human. For Marxism, in particular, Wilderson notes that the assumptive logic of exploitation and alienation are endemic to the worker vis-à-vis Slaveness or Blackness, which are coterminous. For it is not work or forced labor that

---

24. Frank B. Wilderson III, *Red, White and Black: Cinema and the Structure of U.S. Antagonisms* (Durham, NC: Duke University Press, 2010).
25. Wilderson, *Red, White and Black.*
26. Warren, *Ontological Terror.*
27. Warren, *Ontological Terror*, 5.

defines the condition of (anti-)Blackness; rather it is exclusion itself. In other words, Black people are excluded from civil society for no other reason than that they are Black people, not simply because they are exploited workers. It is this exclusion that gives civil society its shape and defines social relations in modernity. Drawing from the position that slavery continued after the conclusion of the Civil War as a material and metaphysical relational dynamic, a Black nihilistic viewing practice also pays particular attention to the libidinal economy that undergirds capitalist relations, including neoliberalism. Put differently, rhetorical economies of whiteness are at the same time undergirded by libidinous desires and impulses of anti-Blackness that describe, according to Jared Sexton, "the fantasies of murderous hatred and unlimited destruction, of sexual consumption and social availability that animate the realization of such violence."[28] Black nihilistic practices of seeing then consider how rhetorical economies of whiteness manifest discursively as routine enactments of violence against Black bodies, minds, and spirits.

To consider rhetorical economies of whiteness through the lens of Black nihilism challenges the pervasiveness of liberal humanist tendencies often found in communication scholarship since Black people are the antithesis of whiteness, that is, the Human. Since whiteness functions discursively, materially, economically, and strategically, and in ways that mask its insidiousness, a Black nihilistic reading practice interrogates whiteness's contours at the levels of discourse and representation. As a socially engaged film—or, according to Wilderson, a "Slave" film in which the director is Black and the main character who carries the narrative and its ethical dilemmas is Black[29]—*Master* highlights the ontological and representational contradiction of emplotting a Black character paradigmatically or structurally into a film.[30] This ontological impossibility is exactly because, as Wilderson argues, "No Slave, no world."[31] In other words, the structures of modernity owe themselves to the Middle Passage that constructed the Slave as an anti-Human against which the races of humanity, including whites and Asians, have defined themselves. *Master* comments on the communicative power of whiteness in higher education and particularly how Black women must navigate its everydayness. The film also catalogs the economic contours of the communicative power of whiteness to reveal both its "stability and coherence" and demonstrate how "it maneuvers based on past communicative patterns and, in response, to changing social

---

28. Jared Sexton, "Afro-Pessimism: The Unclear Word," *Rhizomes: Cultural Studies in Emerging Knowledge*, 29 (2016): para. 14.
29. Wilderson, *Red, White and Black*.
30. Wilderson, *Red, White and Black*.
31. Wilderson, *Red, White and Black*, 11.

conditions."[32] Consequently, a Black nihilistic viewing practice exposes, denaturalizes, and interrogates the communicative power of whiteness's rhetorical economy that is fueled by the violent exorcism, rather than assimilation, of Blackness. Below, I enact a Black nihilistic reading of *Master* to demonstrate how connections to the past and the unrestrained gratuitous violence inherent in rhetorical economies of whiteness inevitably result in the violent exorcism of Blackness.

Cleaning Up the Master's House: On the Limits of Black Assimilation

A Black nihilistic lens is invested in critiquing the roles Black people—Black women, for our purposes here—perform in predominantly or historically white spaces. This reading practice moves beyond liberal notions of diversity, inclusivity, and rainbow coalitions to a critical assessment of the strategic functions of whiteness. In this way, understanding the rhetorical economies of whiteness requires a consideration of the ways Black people's labor is utilized by whiteness and how and toward what ends this exploitation is taken up in discourse and representation. For example, during enslavement and Jim Crow, Black people were allowed in white spaces primarily as servants or entertainers. Through their labor and/or (often sexual) exploitation, Black women were granted access to, yet still marginalized in, intimate and institutional domains of whiteness. Black feminists have attended to the particularity of Black women's labor, including the circumstances of their employment and their experiences of ostracism within such spaces.[33] Collins writes that Black women's labor benefited their enslavers and employers such that Black women were reduced to "economically exploited, politically powerless units of slavery."[34] To chart the shifting dynamics of whiteness's strategic and economic power, it is important to understand how Black women's labor is used in this assumed postracial moment as a necessary component of whiteness's shifting dynamics. In the film, one of Gail's primary functions as master is analogous to Black women's historical role as domestic servants: that is, Gail's charge is attending

---

32. McIntosh, Moon, and Nakayama, *Interrogating the Communicative Power of Whiteness*, 2.

33. See Patricia Hill Collins, *Black Feminist Thought: Knowledge, Consciousness, and the Politics of Empowerment* (New York: Routledge, 2000); bell hooks, *Yearning: Race, Gender, and Cultural Politics* (Boston: South End Press, 1990); and Brittany C. Cooper, *Beyond Respectability: The Intellectual Thought of Race Women* (Urbana: University of Illinois Press, 2017).

34. Collins, *Black Feminist Thought*, 49.

to and cleaning up after white people. Consequently, her title of "master" is ironic, if not wholly inappropriate.

At her own reception as Ancaster's newest master, Gail simultaneously acts as guest of honor, hostess, and symbolic domestic worker. In welcoming two former masters to the reception, Gail is bombarded with microaggressive congratulatory remarks about how "amazing" her appointment is. Brian, one of the former masters, says assuredly that Gail will be president next. Diandra, another former master replies, "Should we call her Barack?" Diandra's gesture of comparing Gail as first Black master of Ancaster College to the first Black president of the United States makes Gail visibly and audibly uncomfortable. Brian tries to soften the impact of Diandra's statement by clarifying that he was suggesting Gail would be president of the college and that Barack is clearly a man's name. Each of the masters laughs in an effort to shrug off the awkward moment, and Brian eventually welcomes Gail to "the club." His use of the term "club" suggests the heretofore racially exclusive and exclusionary nature of Ancaster's group of masters and rhetorically conjures images of the old boys' club. However, we are quickly reminded that Gail's invitation and integration into the club are "not quite the same," as Diandra points out earlier in the conversation. In the next short scene, Gail goes to the kitchen to refill Diandra's drink. She spills the wine and, while searching for paper towels to clean up the spill, finds a mammy figurine on a kitchen shelf. As Gail studies the figurine (likely in disbelief that the racist relic is in the home), Diandra calls her name and breaks her concentration. This call—inflected with a question mark as if inquiring about why Gail is taking so long, beckons the new master the same way one would a servant. The call startles Gail, who quickly places the figurine on the shelf and responds, "I'm coming." That Gail deals with conversational microaggressions from Brian and Diandra, refills Diandra's drink, finds a mammy figurine, and responds to Diandra's call seems to imply her proximity to domestic servitude even as she holds one of Ancaster's most exalted positions.

In addition to refilling drinks for white colleagues and cleaning up spills, Gail also addresses and sanitizes (i.e., cleans) racial atrocities and racist histories in Ancaster. Gail's first official duty is giving a welcome speech to first-year students in her home, Belleville House. In the speech, she associates Ancaster's history and pedigree with the political establishment of the United States: "Legends. Ancaster College is crowded with them. When you go to a school nearly as old as the country, you can expect to hear a few [legends]." She adds, "Like, maybe you've heard that FDR was rejected from Ancaster and had to settle for his safety school. . . . Harvard." The students chuckle and whoop, amused by the association between Ancaster and "safety school"

Harvard, the oldest and arguably most prestigious institution in the country. This tidbit is not inconsequential or by happenstance. In fact, Franklin Delano Roosevelt's New Deal comprised social programs designed to address the nation's epidemic of economic suffering caused by the Great Depression. Black Americans benefited greatly from these New Deal programs and subsequent social programs of the 1950s and 1960s that redistributed resources and shifted the US toward a more socialist democracy.[35] However, this redistribution essentially ushered in an era of probusiness activism that sought to undo the welfare state and enhance corporate profits, particularly under the concurrent administrations of Ronald Reagan and Margaret Thatcher. This probusiness response to social welfare programs, begun in the New Deal Era and expanded into the civil rights era of the 1960s, serves as the foundation of neoliberalism. Because Ancaster likely rejected FDR, it symbolically rejects the premises and promises of the New Deal and embraces neoliberalism—the development of which the politics of race, gender, and sexuality have been central[36]—as a guiding institutional framework. Though Gail admits that she cannot confirm if the rejection is true, it is true that "two U.S. presidents and 'an army' of senators count [Ancaster] as their alma mater." During this speech, Gail effectively cements Ancaster's association with the political establishment of the United States in a way that figures the association as a coconstitutive relationship.

This speech follows a scene transition in which white writing—"Can someone clean that up, please?"—appears over a black background. This visual representation indicates Black people's, especially Black women's, historical roles as servants in white homes, restaurants, and other venues. Additionally, what this scene also implies is that the link Gail, as the first Black master, relays between Ancaster's prestige and its relationship to the political establishment of the United States rhetorically places racism, the country's "original sin," as the driving engine of Ancaster. While Gail occupies a relative position of power in Ancaster's hallowed halls, her presence is better viewed as Ancaster's attempt to cleanse itself (and, by extension, the country) of the stain of racism. This exercise of cleansing is partly how the rhetorical economy of whiteness makes use of Black women in institutions structured by neoliberalism.

In addition to cleansing its racist history, Gail is also responsible for addressing—that is, attending to and cleaning up—institutional race-related issues at Ancaster. As master, for instance, Gail must help judge the tenure case of presumably Black professor Liv Beckman. The scene opens in a conference

---

35. Lisa Duggan, *The Twilight of Equality: Neoliberalism, Cultural Politics and the Attack on Democracy* (Boston: Beacon Press).

36. Duggan, *Twilight of Equality*.

room with each master engaged in discussing work-related issues. One colleague is being poached by an Ivy League institution. Another is taking a writing sabbatical. One colleague even had a heart attack in the lecture hall. Gail sits silently, likely because she knows how the conversation will transpire. It is not until Diandra makes eye contact with Gail sitting at the other end of the table and positioned as an opponent in a sports match that the meeting starts without prompting: "Honestly, I think she's [Liv's] the perfect candidate for tenure right now," Julianne says self-assuredly, indicating that Liv's tenure case responds to some exigence. Foremost among Julianne's reasons for supporting Liv's tenure case is that Liv is very popular among students, fifteen of whom write testimonials on her behalf. Julianne also believes that Liv's race should be taken into consideration regarding the professor's suitability for tenure. The camera pans to Gail, who sits silently, while other colleagues agree with Julianne's assessment. "That is the image that Ancaster should have," Liam states, though it remains unclear exactly what that image is. Gail's silence as the only Black person in the room during this conversation is telling.

Rhetorical economies of whiteness demonstrate how neoliberal impulses discursively motivate decisions to grant or deny opportunities to Black people. Diandra dismisses Julianne's support for Liv as irrelevant because Liv's tenure decision must be made on "the basis of what is in here [Liv's tenure file]. Does Professor Beckman deserve to be tenured? It's a privilege; it's not right." Diandra mentions the scarcity of Liv's publications as the main reason why she should not be granted tenure. Gail finally speaks, noting that, to be fair, Liv has published enough, even if not excessively. Gail's response reveals that Diandra's question of whether Liv *deserves* tenure is rooted in a sadomasochistic understanding that the goal of tenure should be achieved at whatever cost to the individual. Indeed, structural barriers that might have impinged upon Liv's productivity are not brought to the fore. The conversation belies the structural challenges Black women face when trying to achieve tenure. This is precisely why when Diandra mentions the privilege of tenure, Julianne quips, "You'd know something about privilege."

What is interesting here is that there is a clear inversion of the trope of the Black woman domestic worker mentioned above. Where the domestic's likeability was the most important factor in maintaining employment,[37] Liv's likeability factor among students is derailed as a consideration for tenure, which Diandra hinges on the number of publications. To further support her claims, Diandra uses Gail as a foil, the symbolic antithesis of Liv. What I mean here is that Diandra configures Gail as almost superhuman in her achievement of ten-

---

37. Collins, *Black Feminist Thought*.

ure and that Gail, therefore, should reject Liv's less-than-extraordinary tenure case. Diandra recalls that Gail had two books and several other publications by the time she was considered for tenure and is "surprised" for that reason that Gail is not in agreement with her. "We've all been through the process. We all know how grueling it is, but we earned it [hits table]! We can look each other in the face and know that we belong here. Imagine if that's brought into question," Diandra says, sharing a knowing glance with Gail.

The integrity of the process is rooted in neoliberalism; it inheres in rhetorical economies of whiteness. In other words, whiteness is embedded in neoliberal institutional policies and procedures (i.e., productivity, student satisfaction, etc.) such that a Black woman has to exhibit extraordinary qualities to receive basic consideration. Gail is heralded in this scene as a golden child, who, her race notwithstanding, has been able to achieve the prize of tenure. But at what cost? Gail, as Black master, functions in this scene as what João Costa Vargas and Joy James might call an integrated Black person. According to Vargas and James, Black people are irredeemable, and Blackness, as it were, is proof of the sin of enslavement. Given its irredeemability, Blackness can only be integrated at a cost. "For a [B]lack person to be integrated," they write, "s/he must either become non-[B]lack, or display superhuman and/or infrahuman qualities."[38] Gail's impressive tenure file is taken as the barometer from which to judge Liv's tenure case and suggests the implicit conditions of her own tenure appointment. As feminists of color have noted, the condition includes reflecting standards of whiteness.[39] Thus, strategic whiteness upholds only exceptional Blackness because only exceptional Blackness is worthy of integration. As a result, Gail seems forced to reveal her reservations about Liv's tenurability. She cites Jasmine's appeal of an F she, as one of the only Black students on campus, received in Liv's class. After the meeting, Diandra thanks Gail for using her "voice."

It is necessary to recognize that exceptional Blackness, or the Black cyborg, colludes with racist ideologies toward its own death.[40] It is a full embrace of whiteness at Blackness's own expense, by which I mean whiteness cannot be and ultimately is not held accountable in any capacity for its violence—

---

38. João Costa Vargas and Joy James, "Refusing Blackness-as-Victimization: Trayvon Martin and the Black Cyborgs," in *Pursuing Trayvon Martin: Historical Contexts and Contemporary Manifestations of Racial Dynamics*, ed. George Yancy and Janine Jones (New York: Lexington Books, 2014), 193–205.

39. Bernadette Marie Calafell, *Monstrosity, Performance, and Race in Contemporary Culture* (New York: Peter Lang, 2015), 19.

40. Vargas and James, "Refusing Blackness-as-Victimization," 198.

symbolic, material, or physical—against Black bodies. Rather, the systemic is individualized and Blackness bears the responsibility for the gratuitous violence visited upon it. Though Liv eventually is successful in her tenure bid at Ancaster, it is only after a slew of racist incidents and assaults that lead her to chastise Ancaster for not protecting its faculty and students of color. It appears that, since it cannot engage in truly radical and systemic change, Ancaster grants Liv tenure to rid itself from the charges of racism levied against it. Gail is central to these efforts, left to attend to both Jasmine and Liv as she and they navigate institutional misogynoir. It is once Jasmine dies, a point to which I will return in the next section, that Gail recognizes the impossibilities of the cyborg. "I was never a master!" She tearfully says to her colleagues. "I'm the maid. You brought me here to clean up. I didn't change anything." This realization causes a shift in Gail, who decides to leave Ancaster. Thus, Jasmine's death and Gail's decision to leave represent the rhetorical economy of whiteness's mandatory exorcism of Blackness.

A Black nihilistic lens charts the movement of discourses from history to the present to establish a spatiotemporal relationship between whiteness, its rhetorical economy, and its necessary exorcism of Blackness. *Master* demonstrates this spatiotemporal relationship in how Gail is expected to physically and symbolically clean up the school's issues of racism as a necessary precondition for her position at Ancaster. As the Black cyborg, however, Gail fails at the ontological and political game of whiteness. In the next section, I will demonstrate how a Black nihilistic lens charts material and symbolic violence to which Black people are subjected within domains of whiteness.

H(a)unting Blackness; or, the Ghosts of Racist Pasts, Presents, and Futures

In addition to a concern about how rhetorical economies of whiteness are supported by, draw upon, and (re)circulate stereotypical and one-dimensional archetypes of Blackness, a Black nihilistic lens is also interested in uncovering how rhetorical economies of whiteness expose Black people to gratuitous violence as a necessary precondition and effect of their presence in predominantly white institutions. Put another way, this lens seeks to expose how whiteness functions as an asset of protection from and permission to engage in and subject Black people to such undue violence. This ontological position of exclusion and derision distinguishes Blackness from whiteness in civil society, where Black people are reduced to non-Humans or even anti-Humans—that is, "a position against which Humanity establishes, maintains, and renews its coherence, its corporeal integrity."[41] In *Master*, what I term the "h(a)unting of Blackness" instantiates the physical and psychic symptoms of gratuitous violence. Following from this assumption of the Black as non/anti-Human, Wilderson argues that Blackness is constantly open to violence for which there is no acceptable reason. The authorization and varied permutation of this violence manifest themselves as a h(a)unting of Blackness that at once signifies a symbolic return of the past in the contemporary moment—a haunting via the legacies or afterlife of enslavement—and the consequential production and enactment of violence on Black bodies via this return—hunting of Black bodies. This h(a)unting is central to rhetorical economies of whiteness, and I will spend some time below unpacking the relationship.

One of the ways Gail is h(a)unted by the past is through subtle reminders of ancestral proximity that function similar to the ways described above. While posing for her official portrait, Gail hears a faint ringing sound. "That sound," she says, barely above a whisper, to herself. The painter responds, "It's a good time to stop anyway. We can pick back up next week." Just as Diandra did when Gail was in the kitchen examining the mammy figurines, the ringing calls for Gail's immediate attention. After the painter's departure, Gail decides to inspect the sound because the bell continues to ring intermittently in the distance. The sound's trail leads her to a doorway behind which is a staircase leading to a door in the attic of Belleville House. Gail cautiously climbs the stairwell, her footsteps steady and near rhythmic against the creaking stairs, ominous music, and the eerie sound of wind. She opens the door and enters what appears to have been a bedroom. The door to the small room closes gently behind her—a suggestion she should be there, that this is a private moment. There is a twin-size white iron bed with a dirty mattress rolled up on top against the wall. Across from the foot of the bed is a wall of hanging bells, each bell corresponding with a different room in the house. The wall of bells indicates that this was once a servant's room. The bell indicating PARLOR is easiest to discern, and, when Gail flicks the bell's clapper, it sounds identical to the bell she heard ringing as she was being painted in the parlor. While she inspects the room further, the foreboding music seems to guide her anticipation of what will come. Gail finds a box containing random content, including a photo of what appears to be a former master, his wife, and their son, sitting on the floor. Gail studies the photo and notices an anomaly: the servant, a Black woman in a black-and-white uniform, is captured in the background. The domestic worker stares intently, even defiantly, into the lens

---

41. Wilderson, *Red, White and Black*, 11.

of the camera and, therefore, back at Gail. Because they are employed in different capacities—that is, the nature of their different versions of employment at Ancaster—we might even say the servant looks knowingly into Gail's soul as if to say she, too, knows something about the rhetorical economies of whiteness and their undercurrents of misogynoir.

In *Black Looks: Race and Representation*, bell hooks theorizes what she calls the oppositional gaze. This gaze, or practice of looking, extends from slavery. "The politics of slavery, of racialized power relations," hooks writes, "were such that slaves were denied their right to gaze."[42] She adds that even though slaves were denied this right, they looked anyway: "By courageously looking, we defiantly declared: 'Not only will I stare. I want my look to change reality.'"[43] This change, hooks argues, is where we can find agency in Black relations of looking, or where "we can both interrogate the gaze of the Other but also look back, and at one another, naming what we see."[44] It is in this looking back at one another—Gail and the nameless Black domestic worker; one interrogating, the other defiant—that metaphorically cements and critiques Ancaster's asymmetrical relations of racial dominance through the similarities between the master and the servant. This h(a)unting reminds Gail of Ancaster's racist past and her contemporary connection to it.

These relations of Black looking between the past and the present become evident in Jasmine's violent h(a)unting, as well. While visiting the cafeteria, Jasmine notices that one of the portraits of a white man—likely a former president or master—hanging in the cafeteria is disfigured. The face is reduced to a skeleton with red cheeks, its mouth gaping and front teeth missing. The portraits face then quickly changes back to normal. While Jasmine is transfixed on the portrait, the white students move throughout the cafeteria without a second thought. Their movement and chatter signify the normal hustle and bustle of a college cafeteria. Clearly, no one but Jasmine sees the horrific changes in the portrait, and it also appears that the students do not see Jasmine. As she stares in horror at the portrait, this encounter—one of presumably looking too long—is the beginning of Jasmine's h(a)unting. Moreover, this encounter, which immediately follows her awkward interaction with the Black dining worker, symbolically opens her to that which represents structural violence and social death.

According to Jeffrey McCune, "To be a 'death-bound subject' is to be a queer subject, always in danger of being destroyed. Physically. Spiritually.

---

42. bell hooks, *Black Looks: Race and Representation* (Boston: South End Press, 1992), 115.
43. hooks, *Black Looks*, 116.
44. hooks, *Black Looks*, 116.

Representationally."⁴⁵ Thus, life-threats that Black people experience are the gratuitous forms of violence that come to characterize the ontological status of Blackness. Put differently, Black death, from a perspective of Black nihilism, is not a position from which Black bodies can escape. It is undue and, in fact, a priori, prior to any transgression. As Warren reminds, Black people "must assume the function of nothing in a metaphysical world. The world needs this labor. This obsession, however, also transforms into hatred, since nothing [i.e., Blackness] is incorrigible."⁴⁶ Thus, I read Jasmine and Gail's h(a)untings in *Master* as discursive representations of rhetorical economies of whiteness that in their neoliberal impulses seek to exorcize Blackness from social institutions and civil society. Since Blackness is already prone to social death, its h(a)unting is evitable. Both Gail and Jasmine have encounters with spirits from Ancaster's past almost immediately after they are introduced. Though differently inflected, the specters remind them they have no place at Ancaster.

Once Jasmine learns that her room is cursed, she is almost immediately exposed to a host of spectral forms of violence. One morning at 3:33 a.m., a ghoul under Jasmine's bed rubs her arm. When she looks to inspect, Jasmine is awakened by her white roommate Amelia, who informs her that she has been sleepwalking. Another night, while walking home alone as the leaves are rustling and the wind is blowing through Ancaster's campus, Jasmine looks into one of the dormitory windows to find a young white woman watching her. A big shadow is immediately cast onto the wall behind Jasmine as she notices another shadowy figure simultaneously growing in the window of her dorm room. The figure takes hold of her from behind, and she is immediately awakened by Gail knocking to reveal the word "LEAVE" carved into the door and a noose hanging on the doorknob. Thus, the goal of the h(a)unting is to banish Blackness from Ancaster's campus—an exorcism that supports its neoliberal compulsions and their racist underpinnings.

Later one night, Jasmine enters her dormitory to find one of the counselors conducting a tour. The hallways, however, are dark with only dim red lights to provide some illumination. As the guide informs the presumably white parents about the dormitory and the surrounding community, the tourists stare ominously at Jasmine. When the tour reaches room 302, which is the room Jasmine shares with Amelia, the tour guide opens the door and all the tourists file inside. "What's this?" One of the parents asks. "It's a Black student sleeping," the tour guide answers as Jasmine looks through the tourists at her sleeping Black body caught in the white gaze's objectification. Another tourist

---

45. Jeffrey Q. McCune Jr., "The Queerness of Blackness," *QED: A Journal in GLTBQ Worldmaking* 2, no. 2 (2015): 174.

46. Warren, *Black Nihilism*, 6.

casually asks about the gruesome figure slowly raising the window to Jasmine's room to place a noose, an ostensible symbol of white supremacy, around Jasmine's neck. "That's what's coming," the guide responds. The tourists obstruct Jasmine as she attempts to break the line to wake herself up. When she gets through them, the figure pulls on the noose, which immediately pulls Jasmine from the dream by awakening her. Amelia is standing over her, claiming to only be checking to see if Jasmine is okay after frighteningly talking in her sleep. Jasmine's neck, however, is scarred by the noose. "What's coming," or, more aptly, who's coming, is Margaret Millet. According to Gail in a previous scene, Millet was a white woman who was hanged near the campus for practicing witchcraft. As Jasmine learns, Millet haunts Black students assigned to room 302 and, according to word of mouth, killed another student named Treasure most recently. Millet ultimately represents the exorcism of Blackness through unrestrained violence as a function of rhetorical economies of whiteness. This racialized dynamic is likely why Amelia is present each time Millet assails Jasmine. Likewise, Jasmine's assignment to room 302 indicates her proximity to the Black women who walked Ancaster's campus before her.

Within the context of media representation, bell hooks writes, "critical, interrogating [B]lack looks were mainly concerned with race and racism, the way racial domination of Blacks by whites overdetermined representation."[47] However, in another sense, we may make the argument that these Black interrogating looks, especially by way of a Black nihilistic lens, also concern themselves with the way racial domination overdetermines experience. It is because of her h(a)unting that Jasmine is led to search the archives where she symbolically comes face-to-face with another young Black woman, Louisa Weeks, who attended Ancaster in 1965. In the archives, Louisa, across time and space, speaks to Jasmine from her journal in much the same way the Black maid speaks to Gail through her photograph. This connection is another form of ancestral proximity, a vexing reminder. Looking through Louisa's journal, Jasmine learns information about Louisa's experiences—for example, what she ate for lunch and her positive views of the campus scenery. But continuing to flip through the journal, Jasmine finds that Louisa had issues contacting her family: "No news from home. Called all day. Nothing." She also learns that Louisa had trouble with her schoolmates at Ancaster: "V̶i̶v̶i̶a̶n̶'̶s̶ ̶B̶i̶r̶t̶h̶d̶a̶y̶ ̶d̶i̶n̶n̶e̶r̶ Uninvited." And she also learns that Louisa was hunted by Millet: "Strange noises all night," "Someone has been in the room," and, finally, "Knock on the door past midnight. Margaret?" This spatiotemporal relationship between two Black women demonstrates the permanence of misogynoir,

---

47. hooks, *Black Looks*, 117–18.

its enduring qualities and stealthy shifting that come to demonstrate the institutional workings of whiteness.

When Jasmine visits the library again, she stays late to read Louisa's diary. "Another migraine," she writes. "Can't make it." When the security guard calls for the library to close at 3:28 a.m., Jasmine does not immediately move and is left in the building after the lights are turned off. On December 2, 1965, the day before the anniversary of Margaret Millet's hanging, Louisa writes, "She comes dragging her rope." The words appear on the screen as Jasmine exits the library to briskly walk back to her dormitory. On the short walk, she encounters a hooded figure as the phrase, "She will take me with her," words from Louisa's diary, appear on the screen. Jasmine runs to Gail's house, but is unable to get an answer. Still terrified and breathing heavily, she runs to her room and locks the door. A few moments later, someone walks past the door and eventually tries to break into the room. Jasmine makes a beeline for the window, opening it at 3:32 a.m. She waits, unsure of what to do, on the icy roof of the building. Before the door to the room opens, the scene flashes to Louisa's diary entry, which reads, "3:33 MARGARET." The entry is dated December 3, the same date of the scene. The viewer is afforded a flashback of Margaret Millet's hanging, quickly after which the door opens and Jasmine falls from the roof. Margaret comes to represent the parasitic nature of whiteness—always seeking to feed off Blackness.

Jasmine wakes up in a hospital with Gail sitting at her side, suggesting clearly that what happens to Jasmine implicates Gail through ancestral proximity. When Jasmine explains that she tried to get away from the witch, Gail responds that the witch isn't real. Jasmine protests that she won't go back to Ancaster, but it is a protest Gail also refuses to hear. "Jasmine, you can't quit. It's not ghosts. It's not supernatural. It's America. And it's everywhere. I went through it. I went through it, and I understand. I was one of three Black women," Gail says, her voice breaking, "and they couldn't even tell us apart. It was humiliating. But I stuck in there, and I didn't let them push me out." She continues to tell Jasmine that she won't be able to get away from "it"—the gratuitous hatred and libidinal violence that stems from rhetorical economies of whiteness—which leaves Jasmine in tears. In the following scene, Jasmine is again awakened in her hospital room by a sobbing elderly white woman asking for help. Her shadow looms largely behind the partition that separates her bed from Jasmine's. When Jasmine pulls back the partition, the white woman, whose head is bandaged, refers to her as Vergie and says, "We're too late. They're almost here."

This episode of seeming white delirium suggests that the woman is likely the wife of the master in the photograph Gail finds and that Vergie may have been their live-in domestic. Jasmine touches the woman's shoulders and says she will get assistance. The white woman recoils, "Get your Black hand off me. You think you can touch me?! Ooh, I let you get too comfortable. Gary warned me about this. This is my house!" The phrase "This is my house!" continues to echo into the next scene in which Jasmine is shown back in her dormitory—the house of white supremacy. The cloaked figure is in the hallway contorting itself to the echoes as if it were speaking them to Jasmine. The next morning, Jasmine returns to campus and runs into Liv. Liv senses that Jasmine is distressed and says Jasmine should not be on campus. However, Jasmine is resolute, saying that she "understands" what she has to do now. Gail, the Black cyborg, eventually finds Jasmine dead in her dorm room from an apparent suicide by hanging. That Jasmine dies by suicide in the same way as Louisa Weeks and Treasure demonstrates how rhetorical economies of whiteness collude with Black social death.

In with the Old: Future Directions of the Black Nihilistic Lens

Jasmine dies, and Gail resigns. And it is revealed that Liv, à la Rachel Dolezal, is likely a white woman appropriating Blackness to counterbalance her less-than-stellar record. Each of these narrative destinations points to how whiteness is recentered at the expense of Black people (i.e., those who occupy the ontological position of nothingness) in social institutions structured by neoliberalism. This recentering is part of the strategic work of rhetorical economies of whiteness. Thus, a Black nihilistic view moves beyond the liberal humanism found in communication studies by concerning itself with the wanton nature of anti-Blackness in relations framed through neoliberalism and how whiteness is particularly interested in exorcizing the Blackness that it both needs and abhors. A Black nihilistic reading of *Master* allows us to see how whiteness functions as an asset in higher education—that is, as something that both protects one from gratuitous violence and gives one license to engage in submitting another to such violence through simultaneous h(a)untings that reveal Blackness's incapacity for assimilation into whiteness—or liberal humanism for that matter.

On December 15, 2021, Florida Governor Ron DeSantis introduced legislation that built on the outrage levied against the 1619 Project and critical race theory. The Stop Wrongs Against Our Kids and Employees Act, commonly known as the Stop WOKE Act, claims partially to (1) prohibit the teaching of critical race theory in K–12 schools and (2) bar school districts, colleges, and universities from hiring consultants who specialize in critical race theory. Additionally, the Florida Department of Education rejected the College

Board's Advanced Placement African American Studies course, claiming that the course violated Florida law and had no educational value. These acts show how neoliberalism devolves into compulsory whiteness, especially since relations in modernity are structured through anti-Blackness. Thus, the legislation that DeSantis introduces is rooted in age-old tropes that demonstrate how whiteness needs Blackness to constitute its hegemony. A Black nihilistic lens is a version of looking, a practice of literacy, that demonstrates how the old order of things has not yet passed away. In fact, the old never subsides; it persists into the contemporary in ways that continue to define the lives of those outside civil society. Thus, even in an era of neoliberalism, whiteness still takes center stage at the expense of Blackness. This is the master narrative of modernity. Therefore, neoliberal tenets like individuality and colorblindness work in tandem as racist ideology for they do not endeavor to challenge whiteness as much as they allow for whiteness to go unchecked, a strategic function for sure. Higher education is a place where rhetorical economies of whiteness proliferate unabated and consequently call for the constant exorcism of Blackness.

Lastly, a Black nihilistic practice of viewing thinks through the hardship of imagining freedom in relations structured by Western modernity. Thus, a Black nihilistic reading of rhetorical economies of whiteness exposes what McCune calls whiteness's "canonical prejudice," or the ways whiteness reverts to "historically racialized phantasmagoria which evokes fear and often requires defense."[48] More importantly, a Black nihilistic lens reveals our dire need to create and center new worlds, new relations, that undo the anti-Blackness of modernity as our nihilistic responsibility.[49] It also recognizes the agency Black people enact—especially when they refuse to allow their deaths at the hands of systems meant to take their lives. Though in very different ways, Jasmine and Gail both leave Ancaster on their own accord. We must turn our attention to the ways Black visual and cultural production unravels anti-Blackness toward an implosion of the world. A Black nihilistic lens seeks to uncover sites of what Ferguson might call "critical possibilities," or the ways Black cultural forms "offer accounts of institutional modes—not simply the disenfranchisements and betrayals of institutions, but also the rules of inclusion and the anatomies of recognition and legitimacy; not simply how we are entrapped, but also how we might achieve provisional forms of freedom and insurgency."[50] In other words, a Black nihilistic lens seeks insights into possibilities that demonstrate how this world is not the end.

---

48. McCune, "Queerness of Blackness," 173–76.
49. Warren, *Ontological Terror*.
50. Ferguson, *Reorder of Things*, 15.

CHAPTER 6

Jeremy Lin and the Global Rhetorical Economy of Whiteness

LINSAY M. CRAMER

Between March 19, 2020, and December 31, 2021, a total of 10,905 hate incidents against Asian American and Pacific Islander (AAPI) people were reported in the United States.[1] Of the AAPI hate crimes reported, 4,632 of those incidents happened in 2020 after the COVID-19 pandemic began, while 6,273 occurred in 2021, an increase of more than 35 percent.[2] As hate crimes against AAPI people increased, Jeremy Lin, a former National Basketball Association (NBA) player, was featured in numerous media for sharing his experiences on social media with stereotypes and racial hate during his basketball career, including a player calling him "Coronavirus" while playing in the NBA G-League, the NBA's official minor league. As the first NBA player of Taiwanese descent, and one of few AAPI people to have played in the NBA, Lin has since 2011 been a symbol of hope and progress for the AAPI community.[3] In February 2021, he shared on social media that "being an Asian American doesn't mean we don't experience poverty and racism," and "being a 9-year NBA veteran doesn't protect me from being called 'coronavirus' on

---

1. "Stop AAPI Hate," https://stopaapihate.org/wp-content/uploads/2022/07/Stop-AAPI-Hate-Year-2-Report.pdf (accessed September 20, 2022).
2. "Stop AAPI Hate."
3. Dave Zirin, "Jeremy Lin Inspires a Nation," *The Nation*, June 29, 2015, https://www.thenation.com/article/archive/jeremy-lin-inspires-nation/.

the court."[4] Since then, he has been an advocate for the humane and equitable treatment of the AAPI community. He has been interviewed on ABC News, CNN, podcasts like *Takeline,* major YouTube channels like the NBA, and Bleacher Report.[5] He has done substantial community work with his foundation, the Jeremy Lin Foundation. Lin's celebrity also has bolstered his economic position, as he serves as a global brand ambassador for LingoAce, a Singapore-based global technology company that provides second-language education for K–12 children, and his celebrity has promoted the NBA's international brand.[6]

My analysis in this chapter addresses Lin's activist rhetoric for the AAPI community from February 2021 through July 2022 as well as his economic role as a global brand ambassador. In prior scholarship, Michael Park critically examines how US news media covered the rise of Lin's fame, a time called "Linsanity," in ways that sustained white hegemonic masculinity while drawing upon common cultural stereotypes of Asian American men as effeminate and "the model minority."[7] Chiaoning Su offers a comparative analysis of the coverage of "Linsanity" in US and Taiwanese media, revealing different perceptions of Lin's public persona across national borders.[8] Building upon these projects, and others, like the work of Cramer and Donofrio, Grano, and Khan, who have rhetorically examined racial constructions and activism in sport and capitalistic contexts, I examine Lin's public rhetoric as a case study in

---

4. Marlene Lenthang, "Basketball Star Jeremy Lin Says He Was Called 'Coronavirus' on Court, Denounces Racism against Asians," ABC News, February 27, 2021, https://abcnews.go.com/US/basketball-star-jeremy-lin-called-coronavirus-court-denounces/story?id=76152456.

5. Lenthang, "Basketball Star Jeremy"; Anderson Cooper and George Ramsay, "Violence towards Asian Americans Is 'Hitting Differently' amid the Pandemic, Says Former NBA Star Jeremy Lin," CNN, March 18, 2021, https://www.cnn.com/2021/03/18/sport/jeremy-lin-anti-asian-violence-spt-intl; Jeremy Lin, Jason Concepcion, and Renee Montgomery, "Jeremy Lin Opens Up about Anti-Asian Racism and His Rise to Fame," *Takeline,* March 16, 2021, https://www.youtube.com/watch?v=4A70BeF3S6Y; Caron Butler, Jeremy Lin, Vanita Gupta, and Andrew Yang, "Caron Butler, Jeremy Lin & Others Discuss Countering Anti-Asian Discrimination & Violence," NBA, May 12, 2020, https://www.youtube.com/watch?v=qPH3NbKsCZc; and Jeremy Lin, "Jeremy Lin Speaks on Rise of Racism against AAPI Communities," Bleacher Report, March 11, 2021, https://www.youtube.com/watch?v=yVRFseXxXtw.

6. "LingoAce Appoints Jeremy Lin as Global Brand Ambassador," *Business Wire,* May 19, 2022, https://www.businesswire.com/news/home/20220519005155/en/LingoAce-Appoints-Jeremy-Lin-as-Global-Brand-Ambassador-percentC2percentA0.

7. Michael K. Park, "Race, Hegemonic Masculinity, and the 'Linpossible!,'" *Communication & Sport* 3, no. 4 (2014): 367–89.

8. Su Chiaoning, "From Perpetual Foreigner to National Hero: A Narrative Analysis of US and Taiwanese News Coverage of Linsanity," *Asian Journal of Communication* 24, no. 5 (2014): 474–89.

the rhetorical economy of whiteness in two parts.[9] First, I focus on the social media, news, and public discourse of Lin himself from 2020 through 2022 in response to the Stop Asian Hate Movement and subsequent circulation of disempowering discourses of race and difference that sometimes have been referenced in scholarly and popular contexts as exhibiting an "Oppression Olympics." I regard this phrase as naming a rhetorical strategy of whiteness that positions historically marginalized groups against one another by casting their oppression as a contest over whose oppression is most severe, creating an illusion that they are in competition for resources.[10] It is essentially a conservative trope that maintains white supremacist structures by preventing productive coalition building and dismissing multiple and intersectional claims of oppression. This discourse also reinforces white supremacist logics by most commonly situating Black individuals as threats to the safety and progress of white and AAPI people. It is a rhetorical strategy that fosters anti-AAPI sentiments among Black people and anti-Black sentiments among AAPI people. In characterizing marginalized groups as behaving in ways that are counterproductive to coalition building, the term "Oppression Olympics" functions effectively as a rhetorical wedge that obfuscates potentially shared interests and concerns while reinforcing the hegemonic power of whiteness.

Second, answering the call of Colpean and Dingo, this chapter examines the rhetoric of Lin within a global economic context. It attends to Lin's positioning and agency amid the repair of the NBA and China's fractured relationship resulting from a 2019 tweet supporting Hong Kong protesters by the General Manager of the Houston Rockets (NBA team), Daryl Morey.[11] While Lin's advocacy work entails arguing for coalition building against white supremacist structures that seek to divide minority groups, in this case his economic role required subordinating his Taiwanese American identity to the economic interests of the mostly white ownership of the NBA and his corporate sponsors. Engaging these complex contextual dynamics, this chapter works to avoid "drive-by race scholarship," which Colpean and Dingo define

---

9. Linsay M. Cramer and Andrew Donofrio, "Threatening Whiteness: 'Angry Russell' and the Rhetoricity of Race," *Rhetoric Society Quarterly* 51, no. 2 (2021): 152–66; Daniel A. Grano, "Risky Dispositions: Thick Moral Description and Character-Talk in Sports Culture," *Southern Communication Journal* 75, no. 3 (2010): 255–76; Abraham Iqbal Khan, "A Rant Good for Business: Communicative Capitalism and the Capture of Anti-Racist Resistance," *Popular Communication* 14, no. 1 (2016): 39–48.

10. Angela Y. Davis and Elizabeth Martínez, "Coalition Building among People of Color," Center for Cultural Studies, University of California, Santa Cruz, May 12, 1993, https://culturalstudies.ucsc.edu/inscriptions/volume-7/angela-y-davis-elizabeth-martinez/.

11. Michelle Colpean and Rebecca Dingo, "Beyond Drive-by Race Scholarship: The Importance of Engaging Geopolitical Contexts," *Communication and Critical/Cultural Studies* 15, no. 4 (2018): 306–11.

as "a flattened articulation of race that is not sharply attuned to the nuances and/or the complex economic and geopolitical processes of racialization."[12] By examining both Lin's resistive discourse and representations of him within a neoliberal global context, a nuanced understanding can be cultivated concerning how geopolitical and economic interests contribute to and depend upon whiteness discourses and the obfuscation of differences among AAPI peoples under the umbrella term Asian American to maintain racial power hierarchies. Considering both his advocacy work and his brand ambassadorship demonstrate the tensions surrounding his participation in rhetorical economies of whiteness: Lin resists calls to engage in discourses of division, yet his economic role implicates him in global neoliberal structures.

I argue that, as the Black Lives Matter (BLM) and Stop Asian Hate movements both work to address racial violence and systemic racism unique to their own communities, Lin's emphasis on his personal journey to develop a standpoint with a focus on building mutual understanding and coalitions resists a false narrative of competition with the Black community. Through the sharing of counterstories, a tenant of critical race theory, Lin is able to achieve this aim. In a politically and socially polarized culture, Lin cultivates a welcoming space for education, growth, and mutual care among Black and AAPI peoples through his own standpoint and usage of counterstories. Such articulations advance the voices and concerns of the AAPI community, displace whiteness from its normative and powerful cultural center, and offer what Chávez calls a differential vision that values differential belonging for the sake of coalitional advances, rather than competition, with other marginalized groups.[13] I also examine the rhetorical positioning of Lin as "Asian American" rather than "Taiwanese American" in his media appearances specifically during the peak of the Stop Asian Hate movement in 2021 and more recently in 2022 in his position as a global brand ambassador for LingoAce within a global basketball and NBA marketplace that depends largely upon Chinese consumers. Lin works with LingoAce to promote language learning and cross-cultural understanding through education technology.[14] This chapter examines how Lin rhetorically challenges whiteness and its strategic divisiveness through his activism and coalition efforts within the AAPI community while concurrently his image is utilized by the sports media complex to maintain a

---

12. Colpean and Dingo, "Beyond Drive-by Race Scholarship," 306.

13. Karma R. Chávez, *Queer Migration Politics: Activist Rhetoric and Coalition Possibilities* (Urbana: University of Illinois Press, 2013), 27.

14. Janice Tan, "Edtech Firm Lingoace Names Ex-NBA Player Jeremy Lin as First Global Ambassador," *Marketing Interactive*, May 24, 2022, https://www.marketing-interactive.com/lingoace-jeremy-lin-global-brand-ambassador.

global rhetorical economy of whiteness through particular strategic representations and mediated constructions of him. I begin with a summary of Lin's career and rhetorical influence as a global professional basketball player and athlete activist.

Jeremy Lin: Global Professional Basketball Star and AAPI Activist

Jeremy Lin was the first Taiwanese American to play in the NBA, where he had a career from 2011 to 2019. In 2012, two years after going undrafted in the NBA Draft, Lin's performance for the New York Knicks made him an overnight NBA sensation and immediate source of hope, progress, and inspiration in the AAPI community.[15] He scored a historic 136 points in his first five career starts for the Knicks, becoming an instant celebrity. He subsequently played for the Warriors, Rockets, Lakers, Hornets, Nets, Hawks, and Raptors, and also played in the NBA G-League. He is the first Asian American to win an NBA championship.[16] Lin spent the 2021–22 season with the Beijing Ducks of the Chinese Basketball Association.[17]

In addition to his on-court success, Lin is an activist for the AAPI community. He founded the Jeremy Lin Foundation in 2011 with the mission to "love and serve overlooked AAPI (Asian American Pacific Islander) and cross-racial youth by supporting comprehensive programs through narrative change, community empowerment, and cross-racial solidarity."[18] In 2021, the foundation donated $1.4 million to COVID-19 relief efforts and responded to the increased hate crimes against the AAPI community. Namely, through activist-oriented community work and media appearances, Lin and the foundation work to educate people across various positionalities about the historical and present-day racism that the AAPI community experiences. In 2022, he became the global brand ambassador for LingoAce while continuing his career with the Chinese Basketball Association in Beijing. In total, Lin has been a global advocate for the AAPI community and intercultural solidarity during a very dangerous and fearful time for AAPI people in the US

---

15. Zirin, "Jeremy Lin Inspires a Nation."
16. Jeremy Lin Foundation, https://www.jeremylinfoundation.org/ (accessed September 20, 2022).
17. Brian Wacker, "Jeremy Lin Details 'Scary Things That Happened' during Linsanity: 'Lost My Humanity,'" *New York Post*, August 12, 2022, https://nypost.com/2022/08/11/jeremy-lin-details-scary-things-that-happened-with-knicks/.
18. Jeremy Lin Foundation.

while also continuing his career as a professional basketball player with brand endorsements.[19]

Violent Crimes against the AAPI Community in 2020 and 2021

On March 16, 2021, eight people, six of whom were AAPI women, were murdered by a white man in a series of spa shootings outside of Atlanta, Georgia.[20] The murders occurred amid the increased violence against AAPI people throughout the country during the COVID-19 global pandemic. Such violence was spurred by public officials, including then US president Donald Trump, who utilized inhumane rhetoric that wrongly scapegoated Chinese people as the exclusive cause and carriers of the virus by referring to the virus as the "China virus" and the "Kung flu."[21] For instance, then-President Trump publicly called COVID-19 the "Chinese virus" or "China virus" in tweets between March 16 and March 18, 2020, as well as in a White House press conference on March 19, 2020.[22] An image captured at the March 19, 2020, press conference shows Trump's notes with the "corona" in "coronavirus" crossed out and replaced with "Chinese."[23] He then repeatedly defended his use of these labels for the virus throughout March and early April of 2020.[24] As Gover, Harper,

---

19. Jeremy Lin Foundation.
20. Shaila Dewan, "How Racism and Sexism Intertwine to Torment Asian-American Women," *New York Times*, March 18, 2021, https://www.nytimes.com/2021/03/18/us/racism-sexism-atlanta-spa-shooting.html.
21. Tami Abdollah and Trevor Hughes, "Hate Crimes against Asian Americans Are on the Rise. Here's What Activists, Lawmakers and Police Are Doing to Stop the Violence," *USA Today*, March 4, 2021, https://www.usatoday.com/story/news/nation/2021/02/27/asian-hate-crimes-attacks-fueled-covid-19-racism-threaten-asians/4566376001/; Angela R. Gover, Shannon B. Harper, and Lynn Langton, "Anti-Asian Hate Crime during the COVID-19 Pandemic: Exploring the Reproduction of Inequality," *American Journal of Criminal Justice* 45, no. 4 (2020): 647–67; Li Zhou, "The Stop Asian Hate Movement Is at a Crossroads," Vox, March 15, 2022, https://www.vox.com/22820364/stop-asian-hate-movement-atlanta-shootings.
22. James Fallows, "Two Ominous Signs for U.S.-China Relations," *The Atlantic*, March 22, 2022, https://www.theatlantic.com/notes/2020/03/2020-time-capsule-5-the-chinese-virus/608260/; Brett Samuels, "Trump Expresses Support for Asian Americans after Repeatedly Using Term 'Chinese Virus,'" *The Hill*, March 23, 2020, https://thehill.com/homenews/administration/489107-trump-expresses-support-for-asian-americans-after-repeatedly-using/.
23. Allan Smith, "Photo of Trump Remarks Shows 'Corona' Crossed Out and Replaced With 'Chinese' Virus," NBC News, March 19, 2020, https://www.nbcnews.com/politics/donald-trump.
24. Allyson Chiu, "Trump Has No Qualms about Calling Coronavirus the 'Chinese Virus.' That's a Dangerous Attitude, Experts Say," *Washington Post*, March 20, 2020, https://www.washingtonpost.com/nation/2020/03/20/coronavirus-trump-chinese-virus/.

and Langton explain, this harmful rhetoric is a legacy and continuation of scapegoating AAPI people during times of US and international crisis.[25] They also explain, "Despite comprising a tapestry of diverse ethnicities, Asian Americans have been historically viewed as a monolith, othered by the myth of the model minority in times of peace and economic security, while othered as a scapegoat in times of economic adversity, wars, or pandemics."[26] Such rhetoric contributed to the violence targeted at the AAPI community during the COVID-19 pandemic.

Of the 11,467 hate crimes reported against AAPI people between March 19, 2020, and March 31, 2022, 68 percent of those reports were made by women, 17 percent of the reported incidents involved physical violence, 67 percent involved harassment or verbal abuse, and 40 percent of the incidents took place in public spaces like parks, streets, and sidewalks.[27] As a result of such violence and hate, in 2021, a nationwide survey found that only 49 percent of AAPI people felt safe going out, and 85 percent worried about the safety of their family members and elders. Stop AAPI Hate also found that 72 percent of AAPI people surveyed named discrimination against them as their greatest source of stress, ahead of the COVID-19 global pandemic and health concerns.[28]

In response to such violence, Zhou explains, "the devastation of the Atlanta shootings compelled many Asian Americans to speak out in a new way. In the weeks that followed, rallies erupted across more than 50 cities, and hundreds of thousands of people participated in trainings, petitions, and crowdfunding efforts to support victims and condemn anti-Asian violence."[29] Likewise, Lin, joining the nationwide Stop Asian Hate Movement, which stemmed from the online movement, #StopAsianHate, utilized his platform as a professional basketball player to educate local and global audiences about AAPI hate and advocated for intercultural knowledge and empathy among historically marginalized peoples. In what follows, I detail the connection between whiteness and "Oppression Olympics" before offering a discussion of how Lin's rhetoric challenged this idea during the Stop Asian Hate and BLM movements in 2021.

---

25. Gover, Harper, and Langton, "Anti-Asian Hate," 653.
26. Gover, Harper, and Langton, "Anti-Asian Hate," 653.
27. "Stop AAPI Hate."
28. "Stop AAIP Hate."
29. Zhou, "Stop Asian Hate."

Whiteness and the "Oppression Olympics"

Drawing from Nakayama and Krizek, I understand whiteness as a strategic rhetoric and cultural space of racial power and privilege.[30] The purpose of critically interrogating whiteness is to identify its social construction and unmarked location and to reveal its power, also known as "naming" whiteness.[31] As Flores and Villareal explain, "The logics of whiteness and white supremacy are premised on dichotomies of superiority and inferiority."[32] As divisive discourses of whiteness, represented in the derisive terminology of an "Oppression Olympics," frustrate coalition building, they also flatten differences among minority groups.[33] To build efficacious coalitions that can dismantle white supremacist structures maintained by whiteness, members of AAPI and Black communities need to understand their respective histories and experiences, especially experiences of power.[34] In the US, white advocates and institutions have complicated these efforts by depicting AAPI peoples as a model minority.[35] The model minority myth positions AAPI people as collectively having an unquestioned respect for authority, a strong work ethic, and an advanced capacity for academic success.[36] Not only does this depiction homogenize and understate the challenges that AAPI people face, but it rebukes other minorities for not "measuring up." According to the model minority myth, if AAPI people have succeeded, then others, especially Black people, only have themselves to blame.[37] Historian Ellen Wu has explained that the model minority myth historically was developed to further marginalize and blame Black people.[38] This myth underscores the need to consider

---

30. Thomas K. Nakayama and Robert L. Krizek, "Whiteness: A Strategic Rhetoric," *Quarterly Journal of Speech* 81, no. 3 (1995): 293.

31. Nakayama and Krizek, "Whiteness," 293.

32. Lisa A. Flores and Mary Ann Villareal, "Unmasking 'Ignorance,'" *Quarterly Journal of Speech* 106, no. 3 (2021): 312.

33. Tashi Copeland, "Oppression Olympics: The Game That Needs to End," Central Indiana Community Foundation, September 13, 2021, https://www.cicf.org/2021/08/02/oppression-olympics-the-game-that-needs-to-end/.

34. Davis and Martínez, "Coalition Building."

35. Madeline Y. Hsu, *The Good Immigrants: How the Yellow Peril Became the Model Minority* (Princeton: University Press, 2015).

36. Theresa Agovino, "Asian Americans Seek More Respect, Authority in the Workplace," SHRM, June 19, 2021, https://www.shrm.org/topics-tools/news/all-things-work/asian-americans-seek-respect-authority-workplace.

37. Hsu, *The Good Immigrants*.

38. Jeff Guo, "The Real Reasons the U.S. Became Less Racist Towards Asian Americans," *Washington Post*, November 29, 2016, https://www.washingtonpost.com/news/wonk/wp/2016/11/29/the-real-reason-americans-stopped-spitting-on-asian-americans-and-started-praising-them/.

relations of power that may complicate coalition building and promote actions by AAPI people as surrogates for structures of whiteness. Indeed, this myth of a model minority illuminates how the strategic invocation of an "Oppression Olympics" exerts its force as a wedge tactic.

The increase in anti-Asian violence and the focus on long-standing police brutality targeting Black communities in 2020 and 2021 (namely the Atlanta murders and the police murder of George Floyd, a Black man, on May 25, 2020) positioned the Stop Asian Hate and the BLM movements for coalition building.[39] Both communities experienced violence, murder, and subsequent trauma at the hands of white supremacy: one through institutionalized police violence and the other through institutionally sanctioned hate crimes. Both communities have been subject to a long US history of systemic racial discrimination, hate, and exclusion due to their social locations outside of whiteness and the motivations of white supremacy. Given that in 2020 and 2021 both movements were concerned with racial violence and shared unique histories of racial discrimination, violence, and maltreatment, many Black and AAPI activists wore "Black-Asian Unity" T-shirts and attended each other's rallies in major US cities.[40] Key leaders of the two movements promised to cooperate to reduce violence and discrimination against their communities.

While coalition building seemed possible, discourses of conflict on social media, online platforms, and news outlets emerged, reinforcing historical disagreements among Black and AAPI communities about violence aimed at their communities.[41] Divergent perspectives about the severity of particular issues, like policing and hate crimes, which impact each community distinctly due to each community's unique history, were circulated in news media.[42] For instance, an article by Browning and Chen focused on interviews with activists in the BLM and Stop Asian Hate movements in which disagreements about policing emerged.[43] Namely, BLM supporters wanted less policing, while Stop Asian Hate supporters wanted more policing to prevent attacks. Furthermore, on social media, supporters of the BLM movement and Stop Asian Hate movements disagreed about using #AsianLivesMatter, with some saying its co-option works to erase or encourage the forgetting of Black

---

39. Ivan Natividad, "How Can Black and Asian American Communities Build Power? Unity," *Berkeley News*, May 28, 2021, https://news.berkeley.edu/2021/05/28/how-can-black-and-asian-american-communities-build-power-unity.

40. Kellen Browning and Brian X. Chen, "In Fight against Violence, Asian and Black Activists Struggle to Agree," *New York Times*, December 19, 2021, https://www.nytimes.com/2021/12/19/us/black-asian-activists-policing-disagreement.html.

41. Zhou, "Stop Asian Hate"; and Browning and Chen, "In Fight against Violence."

42. Browning and Chen, "In Fight against Violence."

43. Browning and Chen, "In Fight against Violence."

oppression.⁴⁴ In such cases, white power and whiteness, the sources of the racial hate crimes and police violence that both groups were aiming to reform, were obviated through the rhetorical distraction that wrongly situated each community at odds with each other.

Jeremy Lin's response to such discourses of disagreement and distraction, however, displaces whiteness and challenges anti-Blackness by presenting a rhetoric of empathy and coalition building between Black and AAPI people, particularly through his expression of his standpoint and his use of counter-stories that emphasize the shared, yet very distinct, histories of oppression among Black and AAPI people. While calls for unity among historically marginalized peoples can elide differences in histories and oppressions, calls for empathy and education can move people into coalitions for change.⁴⁵ Lin invites a mutual advancement on and challenge to whiteness when he calls out and discourages whiteness discourses that situate Black and AAPI people as in competition for resources and instead encourages engagement in mutual listening and coalition building to instigate change. This strategy contradicts common media and political discursive strategies that effectively divide people and dichotomize complex issues, particularly when those issues involve race.⁴⁶ As such, he challenges whiteness rhetorics that encourage and/or construct a perceived disdain and competition among AAPI and Black communities. He does so by seeking dialogue that fosters empathy and knowledge, which can move communities into a shared space of activism that benefits both communities. While not necessarily considered a leading activist in the AAPI community during 2020, Lin has held a significant platform among AAPI and Black communities since the peak of Linsanity in 2012. His popularity among basketball fans and the AAPI community (which are not mutually exclusive), in which 74 percent of its players identify as Black, as well as his continued success as a professional player in China, positions him as not only a national but also a global icon with significant economic privilege and rhetorical power to influence society.⁴⁷

44. Serena Morris, "Should We Say 'Asian Lives Matter'? Atlanta Shootings Spark Debate," *Newsweek,* March 17, 2021, https://www.newsweek.com/should-we-say-asian-lives-matter-atlanta-shootings-spark-debate-1576764.

45. Michael Butterworth, "Sport and the Quest for Unity: How the Logic of Consensus Undermines Democratic Culture," *Communication & Sport* 8, nos. 4–5 (2020): 452.

46. John David Marquz, "Juan Crow: Progressive Mutations of the Black-White Binary," in *Critical Ethnic Studies: A Reader,* ed. Nada Elia, David M. Hernández, Jodi Kim, Shana L. Redmond, Dylan Rodríguez, and Sarita Enchavez See (Durham, NC: Duke University Press, 2016), 43–62.

47. Richard E. Lapchick, "The 2020 Racial and Gender Report Card: The National Basketball Association," The Institute for Diversity and Ethics in Sport, https://www.tidesport.org/racial-gender-report-card (accessed April 26, 2023).

Resisting Whiteness through an Expressed Standpoint and Counterstory

Through his public communication, Lin seized opportunities to advance the Stop Asian Hate Movement while also expressing care and concern for the Black community through his condemnation of divisive discourses as harmful distractions to actual coalition building and systemic change. To resist the "Oppression Olympics," Copeland suggests, "take people's lived experiences at face value and truly listen—instead of simply waiting for a pause to respond."[48] Lin supports this idea in an interview on ABC News when he says, "Listen to the voices that are teaching us how to be anti-racist towards ALL people. Hear other stories, expand your perspective. I believe this generation can be different. But we will need empathy and solidarity to get us there."[49] He also stated in an interview with ESPN, "There is a feeling that the world is really divisive right now. There's a lot of hostility and finger-pointing and name-calling. I just want to be able to create a more unified world built around empathy."[50] By focusing on empathy and listening, Lin seeks to build solidarity among groups to resist the hegemony of whiteness.

A close examination of Lin's rhetoric also shows how he details a current experience to highlight the significance of preventing hate through empathy and education. Namely, in an interview with Michelle Martin about a teammate calling him "Coronavirus" while playing in the NBA G-League in 2021, he says, "Me in sharing my own experience was not to compare it with what other people are going through, but to say that nobody is immune to this, and as Asian Americans we are all hurting and all being targeted."[51] In this response, Lin balances his calls for mutual advancement, or coalitions, with a recognition of power differentials, and thus avoids flattening difference. He continues, "The bedrock of what I am trying to say is that we need to have love, empathy, and compassion for one another."[52] Lin's reference to empathy, or the expressed effort to attempt to understand how another person feels, thinks about, or experiences something within a given context, positions an other-oriented, or community-based focus on dismantling systemic problems and ending violence toward people who may seem like a threat. He indicates that divisiveness, hostility, name-calling, and finger-pointing could

---

48. Copeland, "Oppression Olympics."
49. Lenthang, "Basketball Star."
50. Tan, "Having Tasted."
51. Christiane Amanpour, "NBA Veteran Jeremy Lin on Being Called 'Coronavirus' on the Court," March 17, 2021, https://www.youtube.com/watch?v=R7vTuIjO7DY.
52. "NBA Veteran Jeremy Lin."

be remedied with intentional attention to each other's experiences, or rather, relational attention to each other's humanity, allowing for a coalitional front against white supremacy and whiteness, rather than a war among each other. As such, he makes no attempts to flatten each community's experiences with violence under the guise of "unity," but instead welcomes a complex understanding of each other for the sake of coalition building to confront white supremacist structures.

Building upon this relational focus of listening and empathy, Lin offers a rhetorical invitation to people of differing social locations to listen to his own personal process of developing and vocalizing his standpoint. In turn, he invites others to develop their own standpoint as a means to work toward social justice progress and reform. Kinefuchi and Orbe, as well as Flores, explain that people are placed into racial or ethnic categories (or "raced") developed by those in power, or dominant systems, like people who occupy whiteness.[53] Flores explains that racial recognition occurs through racial excess and containment. When the body is read as excessive, or outside the bounds of whiteness, discursive containment works to discipline the body back into its preestablished racial category.[54] This in turn influences how people who are raced perceive and come to understand the world around them.[55] Understanding one's racial or ethnic identity, or social location, however, does not mean that someone has developed a standpoint. Instead, Kinefuchi and Orbe explain, "Racial standpoint, in short, refers to more than social location, experience, or perspective; it encompasses a critical, oppositional understanding of how one's life is shaped by larger social and political forces. Such understanding is only achieved dialogically."[56] Developing a standpoint, and thus understanding the complexities of how historical, social, and political forces influence one's agency and opportunities, allows for someone to engage in activist and advocacy efforts that advance the needs of their community in informed, and thus more effective, ways. Lin's discourse expresses and exemplifies this dialogic process and invites dialogue with others.

---

53. Etsuke Kinefuchi and Mark P. Orbe, "Situating Oneself in a Racialized World: Understanding Student Reactions to *Crash* through Standpoint Theory and Context-Positionality Frames," *Journal of International and Intercultural Communication* 1, no. 1 (2008): 74; Lisa A. Flores, *Deportable and Disposable: Public Rhetoric and the Making of the "Illegal" Immigrant* (University Park: Pennsylvania State University Press, 2020).

54. Lisa A. Flores, "Mobility, Containment, and the Racialized Spatio-Temporalities of Survival," Carroll C. Arnold Lecture, annual meeting of the National Communication Association, Baltimore, MD, November 2019, https://www.natcom.org/sites/default/files/publications/NCA_ArnoldLecture_2019.pdf; see also Flores and Villarreal, "Unmasking 'Ignorance,'" 314.

55. Kinefuchi and Orbe, "Situating Oneself in a Racialized World," 74.

56. Kinefuchi and Orbe, "Situating Oneself in a Racialized World," 74.

In his interviews, Lin communicates his educational and experiential evolution toward developing a standpoint as a means to assert a counterstory. Counterstories are narratives expressed by marginalized people to assert their own voices and value and challenge systems of power, like whiteness and the white racial hierarchy.[57] The retelling of one's process toward developing a standpoint, and then asserting one's own narrative and creating space for other narratives, is a form of counterstory. Lin's retelling of his personal growth toward developing a standpoint since Linsanity, as well as his retelling of his experiences with racial hate, invite both AAPI and non-AAPI people to engage in empathy, education, and coalition building as a means to fight systemic racism and violence fueled by whiteness. Counterstory operates here as a way to challenge white supremacy, particularly when it is utilized by someone with global rhetorical power, like Lin.

Following Lin's tweet in 2021 in which he shares his experience with being called "Coronavirus" by a teammate in the NBA G-League, he engaged in interviews on mainstream media to share his own experiences with racial hate, explain his evolution toward developing a standpoint, and advocate for mutual empathy, listening, and coalition building to stop violence against AAPI people. Lin's expression of his progression toward developing a standpoint is evident in an interview with Michelle Martin on *Amanpour and Company*, in which he reflects on who he was during an earlier interview with Martin during Linsanity, which was in 2012:

> I couldn't understand and articulate the underlying issue that we have seen, whether it's the model minority, or the bamboo ceiling, or all these different things about how Asian Americans and Asians in general have kind of just become whatever the people in power have wanted us to become and to stay silent over certain issues and to be, you know, good immigrants in other situations. So, what I have seen through the education process and my experiences and just life is that, man, there's a lot of things I didn't understand when I last spoke to you, and I definitely didn't understand during Linsanity . . . so I think it's just my evolution.[58]

In this quote, and in the overall interview, Lin's consciousness and embrace of his evolution toward developing a standpoint is a rhetorical strategy that invites others to also engage in such educational and reflective processes. Lin humbly expresses a vulnerability in sharing that in 2012, at the peak of

---

57. Richard Delgado, Jean Stefancic, and Angela P. Harris, *Critical Race Theory: An Introduction* (New York: New York University Press, 2017).
58. "NBA Veteran Jeremy Lin."

Linsanity, he did not have the knowledge or skills to understand how the history of AAPI oppression informs contemporary problems that he and others in the AAPI community face. Such vulnerability or acknowledgement of his shortcomings at the time not only invites others to reflect upon their own needed areas of growth, but his discourse also invites others, without shaming them, to reflect and learn themselves. This message is repeated in several of Lin's interviews in 2021. For instance, when speaking with NBC, he reflects on Linsanity and says, "I think I was so brainwashed into already being what society had pigeonholed me to be. I never grew up thinking I was attractive or manly. Even now, I still struggle with a lot of these things."[59] In various interviews, Lin describes how during Linsanity he had experienced so much hate, but he was unaware of how subtler comments and slights could be harmful. For example, when ESPN published a story about Lin entitled "Ch**k in the Armor," he says that it did not appear as racist to him, even though the article received backlash from Asian Americans. He said, "When they came out with a 'Ch**k in the Armor' headlines and, when I was playing, people would make fun of Asian genitals, these things to me were just jokes."[60] Reflecting on that time, Lin stated, "To me, racism was really simple. Racism was basically when people would look at me and call me 'Yao Ming, Go back to China' or 'Can you even open your eyes?' 'Beef chow mein, chicken fried rice'—what I had been called so many times."[61] Lin's disclosures express his development toward understanding racism as culturally and historically embedded, rather than surface-level comments made by ignorant people.

Further reflecting on that time, in an interview with NBC he said that during Linsanity "I was just so focused on playing well in the next game, I wasn't so tuned into what everybody else was saying." He continued, "There was a lack of understanding of what that moment meant and I feel like, because of that . . . I wasn't able to say more and do more with my platform off the court that I wish I could have done and should have done."[62] It is evident in these accounts of Lin's past that he expresses a move toward a critical consciousness of how these hateful treatments are actually part of a larger system that devalues AAPI people, which is part of developing a standpoint. In doing so, he expresses vulnerability and attention to his past shortcomings

---

59. Kimmy Yam, "Jeremy Lin Reflects on 'Linsanity' 10 Years Later, Gets Candid about 'Big Regret,'" NBC News, February 16, 2022, https://www.nbcnews.com/news/asian-america/jeremy-lin-reflects-linsanity-10-years-later-gets-candid-big-regret-rcna15364.

60. Yam, "Jeremy Lin Reflects."

61. Yam, "Jeremy Lin Reflects."

62. Kimmy Yam, "Jeremy Lin Launching Basketball School to Inspire Asian Diaspora Youth," NBC News, June 16, 2022, https://www.nbcnews.com/news/asian-america/jeremy-lin-launching-basketball-school-inspire-asian-diaspora-youth-rcna33928.

in understanding the societal forces that helped to shape him and the AAPI community; he articulates a self-reflection necessary to move into a standpoint. Furthermore, his explanation of history and contemporary discriminations demonstrate his newfound knowledge of racism that propels his activist work forward.

To further this point, Lin has been vocal about his past experiences with racial hate as a high schooler playing basketball. He shares these stories to demonstrate how as a young person, he did not understand the place of his experiences within a larger system of domination. He details an experience he had while playing in a tournament in Florida as a highschooler:

> I just remember as I was walking out, people were calling me "Yao Ming" and different names, and I was so embarrassed. My whole face turned red and I kept my head down and tried to walk as fast as I could. I was the only Asian there. I think back on that and I just wish I had held my head high. And when they called me "Yao Ming," I had told them "No, my name is Jeremy Lin." I wish I had stood up and just carried myself with pride, versus allowing everything from the outside to make me shrink and become small. I'm comfortable in my skin today but probably spent most of life not. The fact that everybody else has an opinion and narrative about who I am, and everybody wants to tell me who I am meant sometimes I don't even know who I am. Ultimately, where I am today, I know where my grandparents and parents were born and raised, I know where I was born and raised, and I'm proud of everything that makes me "me," and I don't try to hide from it.[63]

In this telling, Lin reinforces his growth in self-understanding, a key element of a standpoint, by pointing out how dominant narratives and opinions about him as a Taiwanese American boy influenced his personal agency. Such reflection expresses his move into a more confident and informed articulation of identity, arguably reclaiming of his personal agency, which bolsters his public statements.

Lin's confidence and expression of AAPI people's needs is further evident in his discussion of how discourses of whiteness pit people against each other. In the interview with Martin, Lin says, "How do I be more vocal or tell the stories that need to be told to show people my side of the story?" He continues, "One thing that I have seen through this whole thing is that everyone's so quick to compare your experience to person x, to person y, to person z, or

---

63. Gabriel Tan, "Having Tasted His Fair Share of Hate, Jeremy Lin Is Now on a Mission to Redefine Love," ESPN, June 29, 2022, https://www.espn.com/nba/story/_/id/34166452/having-tasted-fair-share-hate-jeremy-lin-now-mission-redefine-love.

this minority group or that minority group. And it's like, why are we comparing?" Martin then asks, "Do you feel like there's a competitive suffering contest going on?" Lin responds, "Yes. I think there's a lot of comparing. I think there's a lot of gaslighting. I think there's a lot of 'oh let me discount that.' . . . We are hearing about all different types of wrongs, stories of injustice, and we should be focusing on the root of the injustice, rather than focusing on which injustice was worse." In reference to people and/or media comparing injustices between the Black and AAPI communities, he responds: "We are all kind of missing the point if we go down that route." He closes with a call "to band together. We need to figure it out. We need to listen to each other and hear each other's stories and that can cause real change. Actually get to know people and have tough conversations."[64] In these statements, by urging people to listen to one another, Lin invites others to develop their standpoints. Lin also calls out the ways that rhetorical strategies of whiteness employ wedge tactics that distract people from discussing the "root of injustice"—problems of white supremacy and systemic racism—by promoting competitive assessments of who has suffered more.

Through Lin's discourse, he also advances a practice of differential belonging. Drawing from the work of Aimee Carrillo Rowe, Karma Chávez argues that differential belonging can lead to the formation of coalition subjectivities in which people understand their different oppressions and struggles as interconnected. Further, Chávez explains that differential belonging can lead to coalition building: "The resulting coalition subjectivities can provide the agency to resist in ways that are not bound by fixed identities as people learn to politicize their belongings and adopt impure stances that allow for further connection between individuals and groups who are very different."[65] In saying "we need to listen to each other and hear each other's stories," then, Lin recognizes the importance of differential belonging and offers a differential vision, which invites subjectivities into mutual care, empathy, and ultimately, mutual and coalitional resistance. Yet, as I have explained above, and as the very phrase "differential belonging" suggests, to form coalitions, advocates need to not only understand their potentially aligned interests, but their different experiences with power and violence. In calling for people to listen to one another, Lin articulates the need for openness to others. As scholars, we need to reiterate that this should be paired with a commitment to understanding histories and different experiences of oppression.

---

64. "NBA Veteran Jeremy Lin."
65. Chávez, *Queer Migration Politics*, 27.

Moreover, Lin's discourse functions to name or call out competitive claims to suffering as discourses of distraction and detraction from productive coalitional work, particularly with the Black community. Lin's rhetorical accounts of his own experiences with racist hate, his reflexive telling of growth toward becoming an advocate for social justice for the AAPI community, and his insistence on relationality through empathy and coalition building with the Black community, actively discount whiteness and the invidious discourses he critiques. His standpoint and expressions of counterstory, as well as his direct rebukes, are resistive to the distractions of wedge strategies and thus centralize issues of racial violence, thereby decentering whiteness and inviting others to join him in coalitional work. In doing so, he articulates possibilities for differential belonging and advances a differential vision, albeit one that does not fully account for the ways that relations of power impact AAPI and Black communities in distinct ways.

Even as Lin critiques disabling discourses of whiteness, his public persona as an elite athletic and global brand himself participate in wider neoliberal logics that sustain rhetorical economies of whiteness. Even as he tells his own story to articulate his personal growth and to invite others to develop their standpoints, Lin experiences the modulation of his identity globally to satisfy neoliberal dictates. This next section, then, seeks a way to understand the media framing and positioning of Lin's social location and standpoint as part of a rhetorical economy of whiteness that extends beyond the geographical boundaries of the US and constrains possibilities for identity expression and activism.

Asian American or Taiwanese American? The NBA, Jeremy Lin, and the Global Rhetorical Economy of Whiteness

On October 4, 2019, Daryl Morey, who at that time was the General Manager for the NBA's Houston Rockets, tweeted an image that read "Fight for Freedom, Stand with Hong Kong." Within an hour, Rockets owner Tilman Fertitta clarified with his own tweet that the team is "NOT a political organization."[66] NBA star James Harden also publicly praised the NBA's relationship with China. However, the NBA received significant backlash from China, resulting

---

66. Kurt Helin, "Daryl Morey on Hong Kong Tweet: 'I'm Very Comfortable with What I Did,'" NBC Sports, December 23, 2020, https://nba.nbcsports.com/2020/12/23/daryl-morey-on-hong-kong-tweet-im-very-comfortable-with-what-i-did/.

in China banning the NBA's games from state-run TV for three years, until the 2022 NBA playoffs. The tweet likely cost the NBA $400 million.[67]

During this ban, NBA team owners and the NBA remained quite silent, refraining from making further comments about China or Hong Kong in any mainstream media. Fainaru-Waida and Fainaru explain that "the owners had reason to stay quiet: In addition to the money their teams derive from the NBA's $5 billion business in China, many have significant personal stakes there through their other businesses."[68] ESPN analyzed the investments of forty NBA principal owners and uncovered that they collectively possess more than ten billion dollars in investments in China. This includes one owner, Miami Heat's Micky Arison, whose company has a joint venture with an entity that has been sanctioned by the US government. According to Strategy Risks, cited in Fainaru-Waida and Fainaru's 2022 article, NBA China is valued at approximately $5 billion, and the NBA owns 90 percent of the entity (ESPN owns a 5 percent stake, and several state-controlled banks collectively own the rest).[69] Furthermore, according Strategy Risks, several NBA owners have significant China exposure through their ownership of private equity or venture capital firms, including the following:

- Miami Heat owner Micky Arison has $375 million invested in China through the team and his business, Carnival Corp., the world's largest cruise operator. Before the pandemic, Chinese passengers represented 8 percent of the cruise industry's total volume.
- Houston Rockets owner Tilman Fertitta is president and CEO of Landry's, which operates 10 restaurants in China that earn $57 million annually.
- Memphis Grizzlies owner Robert Pera is the founder and majority shareholder of Ubiquiti, a wireless equipment manufacturer that earns 10 percent of its revenue in Asia. Ubiquiti's manufacturing and logistics operations are based primarily in southern China. Pera's total exposure in China is about $369 million.
- Joshua Harris, owner of the Philadelphia 76ers, has exposure through Apollo Global Management, a private equity firm he co-founded; Harris owns 20 percent of the company, which managed assets worth $481 billion. AGM has three subsidiaries in Hong Kong and one in Shanghai.

---

67. Helin, "Daryl Morey."
68. Mark Fainaru-Wada and Steve Fainaru, "ESPN Analysis: NBA Owners, Mum on China. Relationship, Have More than $10 Billion Invested There," ESPN, May 19, 2022, https://www.espn.com/nba/story/_/id/33938932/nba-owners-mum-china-relationship-more-10-billion-invested-there, para. 1.
69. Fainaru-Waida and Fainaru, "NBA Owners."

- Michael Jordan, owner of the Charlotte Hornets, has an estimated China exposure of approximately $85 million.
- Brooklyn Nets owner Joseph Tsai, the co-founder and chairman of Alibaba Group, has about 53.5 percent of their net worth tied to China.
- Sacramento Kings co-owner Paul Jacobs has more than 30 percent of his net worth linked to business there. Jacobs is heavily invested in wireless technology company Qualcomm, which had two-thirds of total annual revenues earned in China and Hong Kong in 2021. Jacobs, a former CEO at Qualcomm, owns shares in the company worth more than $200 million. Jacob's China exposure is worth about $140 million.[70]

These financial and capitalist relationships and dependencies that both the NBA as an organization and the NBA team owners individually have with companies in China illustrate a global economy dependent upon and supporting the interests of wealthy white men and neoliberal institutions and structures. As previously stated, the NBA has a $5 billion business in China. With the exception of Joseph Tsai, who is Taiwanese Canadian, and Michael Jordan, who is African American, the list of NBA owners with substantial investments in China occupy white masculine positionality. Furthermore, the leadership, and thus, those who profit the most financially from the NBA's success, also occupy whiteness. While 83.1 percent of the players in the NBA identify as Black, Indigenous, and People of Color (BIPOC; Black [74.2 percent], Asian [0.4 percent], Hispanic or Latino [4.2 percent], Other [6.3 percent]), 87 percent of majority owners of NBA teams are white, 89.1 percent of team presidents/CEO's are white, 76 percent of vice presidents are white, 72 percent of general managers are white, 70 percent of head coaches are white, and 60.6 percent of all office professionals are white. In total, the NBA, which is largely owned and operated by individuals who occupy white positionality, is dependent upon global consumption of its sport, which is predominantly played by BIPOC people.[71]

As the case of Daryl Morey's tweet shows, any support of political or humanitarian efforts that conflict with China's expressed political position, could result in further economic penalizations for the NBA, and possibly, its team owners. Therefore, how Lin, a Taiwanese American who played in the NBA until 2019 and in the NBA G-League in 2021, was and continues to be positioned within the media was/is important for this volatile yet profitable relationship between the NBA, its majority owners, and China. Furthermore,

---

70. Fainaru-Waida and Fainaru, "NBA Owners."
71. Lapchick, "The 2020 Racial and Gender Report Card."

how Lin positions himself is important, given that he played professionally in China (the Beijing Ducks) and has brand endorsements with companies located in China. These issues interact with the specific, portentous global context of ongoing China and Taiwan tensions: if Lin or others situate his social location as a Taiwanese American as an important ethnic identity, and if Lin extends his social justice effort to humanitarian issues in Taiwan, the rhetorical economy of whiteness dependent upon the Chinese economy could be challenged.

For background, Maizland explains, "Beijing asserts that there is only 'one China' and that Taiwan is part of it. It views the PRC [People's Republic of China] as the only legitimate government of China, an approach it calls the One-China principle, and seeks Taiwan's eventual 'unification' with the mainland."[72] Furthermore, Taiwan, officially known as the Republic of China (ROC), is an island separated from China by the Taiwan Strait. Taiwan has been governed independently of mainland China (PRC) since 1949. Maizland notes that "the PRC views the island as a renegade province and vows to eventually 'unify' Taiwan with the mainland. In Taiwan, which has its own democratically elected government and is home to twenty-three million people, political leaders have differing views on the island's status and relations with the mainland."[73] Tensions have escalated since the election of Taiwanese President Tsai Ing-wen in 2016. Beijing has also engaged in increasingly aggressive actions, including flying fighter jets near the island.[74] In September 2022, China began carrying out military drills near Taiwan after US House Speaker Nancy Pelosi visited Taipei, Taiwan, including firing missiles into waters near the island.[75]

Within this global context, if the NBA as an organization, and thus, by extension, its owners, rhetorically embrace Lin's Taiwanese American identity and familial connections to Taiwan, as with Morey's tweets, such expressions could have potential risky outcomes for NBA ownership and Lin's brand associations. These possibilities raise serious questions: does calling attention to Lin's Taiwanese heritage and current connections, particularly since he was the first Taiwanese American to play in the NBA, risk communicating

---

72. Lindsay Maizland, "Why China-Taiwan Relations Are so Tense," Council on Foreign Relations, https://www.cfr.org/backgrounder/china-taiwan-relations-tension-us-policy-biden. Maizland (accessed September 28, 2022).

73. Maizland, "Why China-Taiwan."

74. Maizland, "Why China-Taiwan."

75. Ben Blanchard and Martin Quinn Polard, "Taiwan Denounces China's Peaceful 'Reunification' Pledge," *Reuters*, September 21, 2022, https://www.reuters.com/world/asia-pacific/china-willing-make-utmost-effort-peaceful-reunification-with-taiwan-2022-09-21/.

that the NBA supports the sovereignty of Taiwan, and thus, does not support the "reunification" of China and Taiwan? Would this, in turn, be an insult to China and its politics, as the NBA and potentially its owners would be viewed as being on "the wrong side"? According to Fainaru-Waida and Fainaru, "The owners' myriad ties to the world's second-largest economy leave their businesses vulnerable if they get on the wrong side of the Chinese government or the public there."[76] Media positioning of Lin as Asian American rather than Taiwanese American obviates Lin's ethnic identity as Taiwanese American, aligning him with all Asians and thus all Chinese people. Such representations abstract Lin's particular story while supporting China's expressed position that China and Taiwan are "one China."[77]

Indeed, Lin's foundation website also abstracts his identity from his story by only once referring to him as "Asian American" and never referring to him as Chinese or Taiwanese. The only reference to his racial or ethnic identity states, "As one of the few Asian American professional basketball players, Lin has been passionate about speaking out about being AAPI and the importance of representation and empowerment in the APPI community."[78] Furthermore, in all of the interviews previously mentioned, several with ESPN, NBC, *Amanpour and Company*, and others, Lin's specific identity as Taiwanese American is barely mentioned, as he is always positioned as Asian American to appeal to a wider audience. While Lin may view his foundation as important to his advocacy work, and as he may use media interviews to tell his stories, Lin also participates in larger structures that modify his identity to conform to neoliberal logics and interests.

Lin also engages explicitly as an economic actor, maintaining a shoe deal with Xtep, a sport equipment manufacturing company in Hong Kong, and serving as LingoAce's brand ambassador. LingoAce's website, while offering Lin's biographical and professional background, never mentions Lin's ethnic identity as Taiwanese American, which is significant because LingoAce is a global technology company focused on Chinese and English language education. Instead, the website uses a quote from Lin in which he talks about growing up in California, but he does not reference his ethnic identity as Taiwanese when he says, "Growing up and playing basketball in California, I personally knew many kids that had to navigate through inequities in terms of access to education." The website then describes Lin as "growing up in the United States, with family living in Asia" in the following: "Jeremy knows firsthand

---

76. Fainaru-Wada and Fainaru, "NBA Owners."
77. Maizland, "Why China-Taiwan."
78. Jeremy Lin Foundation.

the struggles of having to learn a second language—growing up in the United States, with family living in Asia, Jeremy learned Mandarin Chinese as a child through traditional experiences."[79]

The obviation of Lin's Taiwanese American identity and the reference to Lin "growing up and playing basketball in California" and having "family living in Asia," rather than specifically stating he is Taiwanese American and has family in Taiwan, obviates his Taiwanese ethnicity. More specifically, Lin's younger brother, Joseph Lin, has played basketball professionally in Taiwan since 2015, where he currently plays for the New Taipei Kings. Arguably, collapsing Taiwan under "Asia" serves economic interests in appealing to a wider Asian market and, more specifically, avoids geopolitical tensions between Taiwan and mainland China.

Likewise, this rhetorical move elides Lin's politically progressive and social justice–oriented work and rhetorically constructs him as politically neutral. Butterworth argues that situating athletes as politically neutral reflects a broader tendency in the business of sports, as illusions of political neutrality stifle social justice activism; serve those in power, particularly white men in ownership and managerial positions; and thus maintain the centrality and normativity of whiteness and white power both within sport and society.[80] Such neutrality affirms neoliberal representations of the market as a value-free realm of economic exchange. Yet, this representation obscures the political stakes of this construction, as Asen and Kelly suggest in the introduction, and can only be achieved by obscuring, at least in this context, the very storytelling that functions centrally in Lin's efforts to articulate his standpoint. On these bases, the refashioning of Lin's identity exhibits the convergence of whiteness and neoliberalism. Addressing Lin's family heritage and current connections with Taiwan via his brother's career in Taiwan could have motivated audiences to seek understanding of the specific struggles and humanitarian issues in Taiwan, much of which are due to its relationship with China. Instead, imperatives of neoliberalism and whiteness required that this opportunity be avoided at all costs.

Altogether, these repositionings of Lin's identity to account for tensions between China and Taiwan and to extend his appeal as a brand ambassador for LingoAce suggest constraints on his agency—constraints that underscore the global power of geopolitics and economics guided by whiteness. Even as Lin seeks to rally varying members of the AAPI community (e.g., Chinese,

---

79. "LingoAce Appoints Jeremy Lin as Global Brand Ambassador," *Business Wire*, May 19, 2022, https://www.businesswire.com/news/home/20220519005155/en/LingoAce-Appoints-Jeremy-Lin-as-Global-Brand-Ambassador-percentC2percentA0.

80. Butterworth, "Sport and the Quest for Unity," 452.

Korean, Vietnamese, etc.) to work together, and even as he encourages AAPI people to engage in dialogue and try to understand and support other racially marginalized groups, he also is constrained by the global aspirations of the NBA and his own role as a brand ambassador with career and economic aspirations.

Conclusion

Examining basketball star Jeremy Lin's media representations and discourses allows for an opportunity to consider how athlete activists have the rhetorical power to invite audiences into social justice activism that may resist whiteness and racial violence. These discourses also reveal the need for scholars to consider how important calls for activism sometimes may highlight similarities across groups without accounting for important differences and relations of power. Although Lin did not engage in common expressions of athlete activism, like kneeling during the US National Anthem or wearing T-shirts with social justice messaging, his empathic sharing and listening through counterstories and his personal expression of his standpoint allow for intercultural education and coalition building grounded in a differential vision. Such rhetorical moves stand against strategies of division evident in discourses of whiteness that purport to illustrate a war of "identity politics" among marginalized communities. Instead, Lin's rhetoric centers AAPI voices and invites marginalized peoples, especially Black and AAPI people, to understand their colonized histories as related and interconnected, advancing a coalitional vision grounded in relationality.

While it is important to consider Lin's rhetoric in light of the BLM and Stop Asian Hate movements, understanding his rhetorical positioning within a capitalist and neoliberal global economy allows for a more nuanced understanding of the rhetorical economy of whiteness. Namely, Lin's positioning as Asian American rather than Taiwanese American allows for an illusion of political neutrality that favors NBA investments and Lin's brand associations with China. Such moves are not neutral, but rather, favor a rhetorical economy dependent upon white investors and Chinese consumers. In total, Lin's assertion of his agency in his activist role offers an opportunity for meaningful and effective leadership in the Stop Asian Hate movement. However, the global rhetorical economy of whiteness places constraints on his agency in how he and his image as a former NBA basketball player, Chinese pro basketball player, and influential athlete activist are represented within the context of China and Taiwan relations.

CHAPTER 7

Parasitic Movement in the Public Sphere

GEORGE (GUY) F. McHENDRY JR.
AND KYLE R. LARSON

In 2020 a relatively unknown activist named Chris Rufo began circulating through conservative media ecosystems in the United States. Ostensibly, he was sounding the alarm about a nefarious plot to institute racist curricula in public schools, government agencies, and private companies. He claimed such efforts—lumped under the moniker "critical race theory" (CRT)—institutionalized "anti-white racism."[1] *Critical Race Theory* is a specific discipline of legal scholarship established in the 1980s to better understand the creation, maintenance, and continued post–Second Reconstruction durability of white supremacy. Deeply dissatisfied with civil rights discourse's limitations in sufficiently dismantling white supremacy, these scholars worked to better "examine the relationship between that social structure [of white supremacy] and professed legal ideals."[2] Having little familiarity and engagement with this legal scholarship, activist rhetoric

---

1. Christopher F. Rufo (@realchrisrufo), "BREAKING: Parents in Virginia have filed a lawsuit against Albemarle County School Board for promoting race essentialism, collective guilt, and anti-white racism in public school," Twitter, December 23, 2021, https://twitter.com/realchrisrufo/status/1474088316614021142.

2. Kimberlé Crenshaw, Neil Gotanda, Gary Peller, and Kendall Thomas, "Introduction" in *Critical Race Theory: The Key Writings That Formed the Movement*, ed. Kimberlé Crenshaw, Neil Gotanda, Gary Peller, and Kendall Thomas (New York: New Press, 1995), xiii.

against CRT[3] fed off the power of a willing, well-networked media industry to circulate widely among publics invested in whiteness. Anti-CRT rhetoric effectively captured an enduring affective structure in rhetorical economies of whiteness. Its manufactured crisis had valence for and further incited those with fearful (mis)perceptions of group status and culture threats.[4] Claiming children especially as victims of CRT, conservative politicians exploited these accelerating fears as a permission structure for institutional political efforts. Rapidly, it resulted in the successful passing of anti-CRT state legislation against educational curricula discussing histories, perspectives, and concepts that do not actively present the United States as exceptional, democratic, and just. The federal government energized these legislative endeavors on September 22, 2020, via Executive Order 13950. With such momentum, politicians have been able to: limit educator speech; review, redesign, and reject curricula; take over local school boards; and ban books and scholarship.

The rapid ascent of anti-CRT rhetoric—from obscurity to enacted legislation—makes it a compelling case study for analyzing parasitic movement in the public sphere's affective economies of whiteness. Anti-CRT rhetoric emerges from a reactionary movement constitutive of and contributing to this post–civil rights period of "White Reconstruction."[5] Mobilized against steadily increasing efforts to address issues related to power, privilege, and oppression, this movement articulates anti-CRT rhetoric in a discursive assemblage with other appropriated and weaponized rhetorics like "political correctness," "identity politics," "cancel culture," and "woke." Its articulation with these rhetorics is yet another sublimation in the historically constituted discursive assemblages culpable for anti–affirmative action rhetoric and, earlier, anti-integration rhetoric. We examine this assemblage through our framework of parasitic publics. Doing so allows us to analyze the parasitic conditions available and processes undertaken when dominant publics invested in whiteness are threatened and/or challenged by the circulation, uptake, and ruptures of

---

3. We refer to *Critical Race Theory* as developed in scholarship by its full name, which we capitalize and italicize. We use the acronym "CRT" when discussing the concept deployed by anti-CRT rhetors. These different uses emerge from discrete discursive assemblages. We recognize that many scholars and activists use CRT as a nonpejorative acronym for this area of scholarship. Our distinction between the *Critical Race Theory* and CRT exists for the sake of clarity in this essay and not as a normative claim about how CRT ought to be used.

4. Maureen A. Craig, Julian M. Rucker, and Jennifer A. Richeson, "Racial and Political Dynamics of an Approaching 'Majority-Minority' United States," *The ANNALS of the American Academy of Political and Social Science* 677, no. 1 (2018): 204–14.

5. Dylan Rodríguez, *White Reconstruction: Domestic Warfare and the Logics of Genocide* (New York: Fordham University Press, 2021).

counterdiscourse.[6] It thus deepens understanding of a process by which publics invested in whiteness can uptake and mainstream the discourse of parasitic publics in order to buttress the assemblage of dominant discourses and maintain power arrangements beneficial to them. We first present a theoretical framework for this movement analysis with an overview of parasitic publics, affects, articulations, and assemblages. We then apply this framework to anti-CRT rhetoric, particularly focusing on the residual formations and affective processes of this frontlash's value production and exchange in the public sphere.

Parasitic Movement in Affective Economies—A Framework

In our 2019 *Rhetoric Society Quarterly* (*RSQ*) article, we argued that scholarship on (counter)publics would benefit from more critical attention to power differentials. If "counterpublic" can identify both Black feminist publics and white nationalist publics, then the conceptual framework lacks sufficient recognition of power. Publics circulate in and across asymmetrical structures of power, preconditioning the "social, discursive, affective process from which a public's rhetoric emerges."[7] Scholarship on (counter)publics must, as Robert Asen identifies, "account for the ways in which relations of power and symbolic and material resources influence production, circulation, and reception of discourse in the public sphere."[8] Attention to power differentials has also emerged in the third wave of whiteness studies. For instance, France Winddance Twine and Charles Gallagher argue the third wave emphasizes "an examination of how power and oppression are articulated, redefined, and reasserted through various political discourses and cultural practices."[9] Therefore, critical understanding of differently situated publics necessitates attending to the particular affective, discursive, and rhetorical specificities of their circulation.

With this in mind, we introduced and theorized "parasitic publics." Our conclusion offers the following definition based on analysis of a white nationalist public: "*Parasitic publics* are reactionary discursive spaces formed

---

6. Counterdiscourse refers to the circulation of rhetorics that challenge the status quo and disrupt centers of power within a society.

7. Kyle Larson and George F. (Guy) McHendry Jr., "Parasitic Publics," *Rhetoric Society Quarterly* 49, no. 5 (2019): 520.

8. Robert Asen, "Ideology, Materiality, and Counterpublicity: William E. Simon and the Rise of a Conservative Counterintelligentsia," *Quarterly Journal of Speech* 95, no. 3 (2009): 265.

9. Francis Winddance Twine and Charles Ghallagher, "Introduction: The Future of Whiteness: A Map of the Third Wave," *Ethnic and Racial Studies* 31, no. 1 (2008): 7.

residually and institutionalized affectively through the invention, circulation, and uptake of demagogic rhetorics."[10] By "formed residually," we emphasize the importance of parasitic publics as always fundamentally *historically situated* discursive spaces. By "institutionalized affectively," we emphasize the importance of affective circulation for parasitic processes of value production, rhetorical uptake, and discursive exchange in the public sphere when dominant publics experience strong counterdiscursive challenge and threat. Inattention to the transhistorical, transsituational assemblages in which and from which these publics circulate would fail to account for the affective economies that these publics rely upon to mainstream and/or bolster themselves in the public sphere and, in turn, close discursive space for others.

The discursive, rhetorical processes of parasitic publics are different from counterpublics and dominant publics. They do not experience the historical, contemporary power asymmetries against which counterpublics must circulate and intervene. While benefiting from the dominant power structure's privileging of particular constellations of identities and discourses, their circulation is also not hegemonic and ubiquitous enough in the public sphere to be a "dominant" public. To mainstream themselves within and thereby modify the dominant assemblage of publics, parasitic publics feed off of oppressive conditions in the public sphere. They take advantage of the dominance of a white habitus—which Eduardo Bonilla-Silva, Carla Goar, and David Embrick characterize as in the following way: "when everyday whites reproduce a racist habitus, they help legitimate social closure that discriminates by race."[11] Their demagogic rhetoric articulates with dominant discourses to exploit dominant publics' centripetal force, and it articulates against counterpublics to safeguard the (subsequently modified) assemblage of dominant publics against counterdiscursive challenge and threat.

For our analysis of anti-CRT rhetoric, we build upon this framework to deepen conceptual understanding of parasitic movement. We again draw upon the concepts of affect, articulation, and assemblage to elaborate on the affective economies of whiteness responsible for and contributing to the invention, circulation, and mainstreaming of parasitic discourses. Therefore, we now briefly present an overview of these concepts and their constitutive functions in affective economies before analyzing anti-CRT rhetoric.

Affect is pivotal to understanding parasitic movement, since its circulation acts as a central structuring factor to the contemporary precarious public

---

10. Larson and McHendry Jr., "Parasitic Publics," 535.
11. Eduardo Bonilla-Silva, Carla Goar, and David G. Embrick, "When Whites Flock Together: The Social Psychology of White Habitus," *Critical Sociology* 32, nos. 2–3 (2006): 248.

sphere.[12] "Affect" is also a notoriously slippery term. One can generally understand it as a bodily intensity or sensation.[13] One also can discuss it in terms like capacity, impression, energy, force, and potential. It can have the same connotation as "feeling" for this reason but demands critical inquiry into the circulation, encounter, and interpretation of its intensities in being felt or registered. Sara Ahmed artfully communicates this idea: "To be affected by something is to evaluate that thing. Evaluations are expressed in how bodies turn toward things."[14] It is often associated with "emotion," yet it is not equivalent to emotion because, like Ahmed suggests, the process of making sense of or understanding affect involves the emotional translation of affective intensities via discourse. In this way, affects are "profoundly conditioned by cultural forces or commonplaces."[15] As Deborah Gould states, "An emotion . . . squeezes a vague bodily intensity or sensation into the realm of cultural meanings and normativity."[16]

Social practices around race act as a locus of power for racist affects. Paula Ioanide examines the ways white publics become conditioned to racist affect. These ways of feeling race are not "individual matters; they are expressly cultural, socially shared, and political."[17] Affects are therefore embodied as habituations.[18] The residue of affective uptakes contributes to the formation, constitution, and expression of emotional dispositions: "Indeed, affect is what makes you *feel* an emotion."[19] Raymond Williams explains, for instance, that "structures of feeling" offer a contrast from "more formal concepts of 'worldview' or 'ideology.'"[20] They are "characteristic elements of impulse, restraint, and tone; specifically affective elements of consciousness and relationships: not feeling against thought, but thought as felt and feeling as thought."[21]

---

12. Lauren Berlant, *Cruel Optimism* (Durham, NC: Duke University Press, 2011).

13. Deborah Gould, "On Affect and Protest," in *Political Emotions: New Agendas in Communication*, ed. Janet Staiger, Ann Cvetkovich, and Ann Reynolds (New York: Routledge, 2010), 27.

14. Sara Ahmed, "Happy Objects," in *The Affect Theory Reader*, ed. Melissa Gregg and Gregory J. Seigworth (Durham, NC: Duke University Press, 2010), 23.

15. Jeff Pruchnic and Kim Lacey, "The Future of Forgetting: Rhetoric, Memory, Affect," *Rhetoric Society Quarterly* 41, no. 5 (2011): 484.

16. Gould, "On Affect and Protest," 27–28.

17. Paula Ioanide, *The Emotional Politics of Racism: How Feelings Trump Facts in an Era of Colorblindness* (Stanford, CA: Stanford University Press, 2015), 15.

18. Catherine Chaput, "Rhetorical Circulation in Late Capitalism: Neoliberalism and the Overdetermination of Affective Energy," *Philosophy and Rhetoric* 43, no. 1 (2010): 20.

19. Gould, "On Affect and Protest," 27–28.

20. Raymond Williams, "Structures of Feeling," in *Structures of Feeling: Affectivity and the Study of Culture*, ed. Devika Sharma and Frederik Tygstrup (Boston: De Gruyter, 2015), 23.

21. Williams, "Structures of Feeling," 23.

Williams defines these elements "as a 'structure': as a set, with specific internal relations, at once interlocking, and in tension."²² Structures of feeling or affective states represent the habituated animations of connections between elements reverberating within and from discourses.

Affect extends beyond, links, and attunes the elements in a discourse. Its circulation is *extra* in every sense. Affect does not causally evolve into emotion in the moment of its discursive interpretation, but remains ambiguous, incompletely understood, and ever-present. It manifests possibilities both to call upon residual and to generate emergent intensities, movements, rhetorics, and bodily encounters. Ahmed characterizes such circulation as an affective economy. It "suggests that emotions do not positively inhabit anybody or anything, meaning that 'the subject' is simply one nodal point in the economy, rather than its origin and destination."²³ Affect reverberates from historical conditions, animates social formations, and finds emotional expressions through resonance with and interpretation by discourses. Affective economies highlight the circulation, production, and interpretation of value in felt intensities between objects, bodies, cultural contexts, political norms, and flows of power. As an analytical concept, then, it draws critical attention to value production, circulation, and exchange in rhetorical economies. It therefore offers a way to trace parasitic value in blockages, flows, and movements of power through the material, the historical, the discursive, and the social.²⁴

Given the significance of discursive resonance and interpretation, understanding the specificity of a discourse is important to analyzing the affective circulation, uptake, and movement of a public. Discourses involve a wide array of social, cultural, and material elements (e.g., histories, ideologies, rhetorics, concepts, experiences, locations, bodies, objects). A discourse affectively and rhetorically links, networks, and interfaces seemingly different elements into the larger metastructure of an *assemblage*. Discourses can form and participate in even larger assemblages in their connections with other discourses and their elements. In fact, anti-CRT rhetoric exists within a larger assemblage of affective states, discursive elements, and rhetorical efforts concerning race, gender, and sexuality. For instance, anti-CRT legislation is joined by a similar assemblage of anti-transgender discourse. It has led to legislation banning transgender people from receiving basic recognition for their identity, having access to essential forms of gender-affirming health care, and participating in activities with children present. These assemblages (both specific and

---

22. Williams, "Structures of Feeling," 23.
23. Ahmed, "Happy Objects," 46.
24. Chris Mays, "From 'Flows' to 'Excess': On Stability, Stubbornness, and Blockage in Rhetorical Ecologies," *Enculturation* no. 19 (2015), https://enculturation.net/from-flows-to-excess.

collective) can be difficult to identify and recognize. After all, it is "an intensive network or rhizome displaying 'consistency' or emergent effects by tapping into the ability of the self-ordering forces of heterogeneous material to mesh together."[25] When aligned with dominant power structures, discursive assemblages can produce hegemonic assumptions, knowledges, and expectations that circulate and structure forceful expressions of inclusion-exclusion criteria in the public sphere. So, to understand the affective circulation cultivating a public and moving the public sphere, analyzing the discursive assemblages and power relations through which it constitutes itself is critical.

Discursive assemblages offer an affective sense of totality to elements, even as they may exhibit gaps and contradictions. The concept of rhetorical *articulation* is instrumental to this understanding. It helps explain how the nuances of and interactions between discursive elements find an affective unifying logic in an assemblage, enabling a variety of cultural expressions like those found in anti-CRT rhetoric. As a process of connection, articulation is a rhetorical means by which a discursive assemblage gains its appearance of totality. Ernesto Laclau and Chantal Mouffe explain articulation as "any practice establishing a relation among elements such that their identity is modified as a result of the articulatory practice."[26] It is the rhetorical act of assembling discursive elements in a process of contingent meaning-making. When elements articulate with one another, the relations between them produce something greater in the assemblage than the meaning of each discursive element separately. For Stuart Hall, articulation shows that "the so-called 'unity' of a discourse is really the articulation of different, distinct elements which can be re-articulated in different ways because they have no necessary 'belongingness.'"[27] Indeed, both are true: discourses are "resistant to internal criticism,"[28] and discursive assemblages are constituted by various elements—some of which are contradictory. While this might appear to be conceptually incoherent, attention to circulation in affective economies demonstrates that these contradictory elements are not *felt* or *experienced* as contradictions within the narrative into which they become arranged rhetorically and lived discursively. As Catherine Chaput acknowledges, "Beliefs . . . are affective

---

25. Mark Bonta and John Protevi, *Deleuze and Geophilosophy: A Guide and Glossary* (Edinburgh: Edinburgh University Press, 2004), 54.

26. Ernesto Laclau and Chantal Mouffe, *Hegemony and Social Strategy: Towards a Radical Democratic Politics* (New York: Verso, 1985), 105.

27. Stuart Hall, "On Postmodernism and Articulation: An Interview with Stuart Hall," ed. Lawrence Grossberg, *Journal of Communication Inquiry* 10, no. 2 (1986): 53.

28. James Paul Gee, *Social Linguistics and Literacies: Ideology in Discourses* (New York: Routledge, 1990), 179.

habituations rather than ideological errors."[29] Articulation explains the ways meaning for a public is always (re)made based on the affective habituations, material conditions, and power structures present in a discursive formation. Together then, the concepts of affect, assemblage, and articulation offer a framework with which to map, trace, and analyze the value production of anti-CRT rhetoric's circulation in the public sphere's economies of whiteness.

Parasitic Movement in the Frontlash of Anti-CRT Rhetoric

"Frontlash" best characterizes the anti-CRT movement. Vesla M. Weaver introduced the term to help explain the post–Jim Crow development of racist crime policies.[30] She defines frontlash as "the process by which losers in a conflict become the architects of a new program, manipulating the issue space and altering the dimension of conflict in an effort to regain their command of the agenda."[31] Those who experience the contemporary public sphere as reflecting a felt loss of position in past conflicts do not continue to organize from the same "defeated" position—or, as we will show, from a successfully challenged position no longer having valence in the public sphere. Instead, they sublimate this position into a new conflict. This sublimation attempts to not be perceived as violating the public sphere's established norms while also "rendering the results of the past conflict fundamentally unstable."[32] Weaver identifies three stages: issue (re)definition, manufacturing a new conflict (regularly via crisis); issue dominance, monopolizing accepted conflict interpretations and understandings; and issue capture, effectively making any continued opposition to this monopoly a political liability.[33] At the time of this writing, one can recognize anti-CRT rhetoric as in the second stage. With this in mind, our following analysis pinpoints recognizable exigencies for its frontlash in the public sphere, identifies residual formations of its sublimated position in rhetorical economies of whiteness, and describes rhetorical processes of its emotional pedagogy for affective institutionalization.

---

29. Chaput, "Rhetorical Circulation," 20.
30. Vesla M. Weaver, "Frontlash: Race and the Development of Punitive Crime Policy," *Studies in American Political Development* 21, no. 2 (2007): 230–65.
   31. Weaver, "Frontlash," 236.
   32. Weaver, "Frontlash," 236.
   33. Weaver, "Frontlash," 236.

Compounding Affective Ruptures as Networked Frontlash Exigencies

It is rare that a complex and relatively obscure academic theory (in terms of public familiarity) like *Critical Race Theory* becomes a flash point for conservative activism and sparks sustained national media attention. For this reason, identifying recognizable exigencies for this ascendency can help elucidate the specificities of its circulation within, across, and from economies of whiteness. Such identification, however, does not come without risks. It risks flattening the transhistorical, transsituational, and overdetermined complexities of circulation in the public sphere.[34] At the same time, attention to *compounding* intensities and ruptures can assist analysis of value production and exchange as long as it is understood as necessarily incomplete.[35] It therefore helps attune us to the dominant discursive development of valence for parasitic articulations and movements. In particular, anti-CRT rhetoric's intensity, urgency, and ascendancy is a frontlash response to a transhistorical, transsituational convergence of at least three contemporary exigencies.

Given the targets of anti-CRT state legislation and enforcement, one clear exigence is the steadily increasing efforts to address Diversity, Equity, and Inclusion (DEI) issues in schools, media, corporations, and governmental agencies. DEI has a significant discursive foundation in neoliberal multiculturalism. In practice, DEI initiatives often follow from the white racial frame with a procedural logic similar to corporate public relations. Many goals often implicitly, if not explicitly, are oriented toward capitalist consumption, essentialist representation, and token participation. These practices are rarely concerned with building and/or distributing participatory, liberatory power—they trade in perceived market demands. It, therefore, has increasingly become the deserved focus of counterdiscursive distrust and critique.

For instance, Angela Davis cogently communicates this critical position on DEI. She states, "If we stand up against racism, we want much more than inclusion. Inclusion is not enough. Diversity is not enough. And as a matter of fact, we do not wish to be included in a racist society."[36] Neoliberal multiculturalism, for this reason, tends to constantly shift and transform its rhetorical branding in response to emergent valence and critical publicity in the public sphere. Neoliberal multiculturalism manages "racial contradictions

---

34. Chaput, "Rhetorical Circulation," 12.
35. Chaput, "Rhetorical Circulation," 13.
36. Angela Davis, "Revolution Today," Centre de Cultura Contemporània de Barcelona, Barcelona, Spain, October 9, 2017, https://www.cccb.org/en/multimedia/videos/angela-davis/227656.

on a national and international scale for U.S.-led neoliberalism."[37] As such, it works to secure and maintain power through the rhetorical gentrification of counterdiscursive space. In appropriating emergent counterpublic rhetorics, dominant neoliberal publics siphon the critical valence of these rhetorics—a practice that Olúfẹ́mi O. Táíwò refers to as "elite capture."[38] These publics can then continue to frame the practices as "fulfilling" to wider publics. "Fulfilling" has two mutually reinforcing meanings here. Less importantly, it means the *rhetorical framing* of these practices as "effectual" in addressing contemporary contexts, conditions, and concerns. But more importantly, it means the *affective framing* of these practices as constituting their discursive position as "good people."

Neoliberalism is, after all, a fundamentally *reactionary* discursive assemblage. Its historical formation was a white liberal reactionary response against the newly gained publicness of marginalized populations who historically and contemporaneously experienced significant exclusions from public access, let alone public valence. Understood in its historical context, the emergence of neoliberalism's colonial logic of imperialist privatization has a clearly identifiable catalyst. Its material emergence is an affective expression of dominant discursive desire for the continued maintenance of existing asymmetrical power relations.[39] What do those invested in maintaining hegemonic, asymmetrical power do when people perceived to them as "undesirable," "illegitimate," or "second-class" gain access to the previously exclusive privilege of publicness and valence within the public sphere? They privatize . . . and construct privacy as the new privileged right.[40] White supremacy is an adaptable assemblage of conservative and liberal discourses in this way. Bartering for its continued existence, it becomes flexible, durable, and thereby enduring. But even neoliberal multiculturalism's paternalistic, tokenizing inclusion of "Others" is too much for the discursive assemblage from which anti-CRT rhetoric emerges.

A second recognizable exigence is the creation and circulation of *The 1619 Project*, a Pulitzer-winning series developed by Nikole Hannah-Jones in 2019. Its long-form journalism consists of essays that trace, as foundational to the

---

37. Jodi Melamed, "The Spirit of Neoliberalism: From Racial Liberalism to Neoliberal Multiculturalism," *Social Text* 24, no. 4 (2006): 13.

38. Olúfẹ́mi O. Táíwò, *Elite Capture: How the Powerful Took Over Identity Politics (and Everything Else)* (Chicago: Haymarket Books, 2022).

39. Wendy Brown, *In the Ruins of Neoliberalism: The Rise of Antidemocratic Politics in the West* (New York: Columbia University Press, 2019), 61.

40. Brown, *In the Ruins of Neoliberalism*, 104. See also Nancy Welch, *Living Room: Teaching Public Writing in a Privatized World* (Portsmouth, NH: Heinemann, 2008); and Gwendolyn D. Pough, *Check It While I Wreck It: Black Womanhood, Hip-Hop Culture, and the Public Sphere* (Boston: Northeastern University Press, 2004), 33.

United States, the enduring national impact of slavery from 1619 to present. It would be difficult to overstate the degree of white hostility directed toward this project for centralizing Black experiences in understanding the historical and contemporary reality of the United States. Dominant discourses invested in whiteness experienced it as a *felt* rupture in their affective economies. In renarrating the nation's founding and interrogating its mythic ideals through Black histories, experiences, and testimonies, *The 1619 Project* expressed a (counter)discourse of Black citizenship, even patriotism. This discursive assemblage fundamentally agitated affective economies of whiteness and disrupted mythic constructions of national identity and patriotism as always implicitly (or not so implicitly) racialized as white.

Whereas traditional DEI projects tend to serve the continued existence of institutional whiteness, *The 1619 Project* circulates Black critical memories and testimonies as a rhetoric of "insurrectionary genealogy." José Medina describes the power of such genealogies in the public sphere: "By opening up new ways to think about the past, genealogical investigations constitute critical interventions in the social imagination that can help us make our sense of a shared past more pluralistic and open to diversity."[41] These interventions then "can have a great impact on how we confront struggles in the present."[42] Such observations offer valuable insights into the affective intensity of dominant discourse's reactionary rhetorics against *The 1619 Project*. Critical memory, after all, is essential to the vibrance, sustainability, and revolutionary faculty of Black public spheres.[43] If national public memory is affectively felt or perceived as "white property" in rhetorical economies of whiteness,[44] then *The 1619 Project*'s circulation operates as a critical redistribution and democratization of public memory in the national public sphere. And with the release of curricular materials and supplementary resources for teachers to use when assigning its essays, the project also became easily articulated with DEI initiatives in the social imagination of dominant discourses. This articulation of compounding exigencies could then heighten the experienced intensities of

---

41. José Medina, *The Epistemology of Resistance: Gender and Racial Oppression, Epistemic Injustice, and Resistant Imaginations* (New York: Oxford University Press, 2013), 292.

42. Medina, *The Epistemology of Resistance*, 292.

43. Houston A. Baker Jr., "Critical Memory and the Black Public Sphere," in *The Black Public Sphere: A Public Culture Book*, ed. The Black Public Sphere Collective (Chicago: University of Chicago Press, 1995), 7. See also Carmen Kynard, *Vernacular Insurrections: Race, Black Protest, and the New Century in Composition-Literacies Studies* (Albany: State University of New York Press, 2013); and Ersula J. Ore, *Lynching: Violence, Rhetoric, and American Identity* (Jackson: University Press of Mississippi, 2019).

44. Catherine Prendergast, *Literacy and Racial Justice: The Politics of Learning after* Brown v. Board of Education (Carbondale: Southern Illinois University Press, 2003).

counterdiscursive circulation as a felt presence and therefore as an increasingly perceived threat.

A third recognizable exigency involves the Movement for Black Lives—from its emergence in 2013 to present. The movement has sustained counterdiscursive presence and pressure on dominant publics, institutions, and systems through their public-facing, direct action campaigns and kairotic protests. The movement has also built impressive community-facing organizations, networks, resources, and therefore local power. One can distinguish the responses to the racist murders of Ahmaud Arbery on February 23, 2020, of Breonna Taylor on March 13, 2020, and of George Floyd on May 25, 2020, as particularly notable moments here. The proximity of these murders compounded affective ruptures and (counter)public outrage, culminating in an especially massive international uprising. The *New York Times* suggested it might be the biggest movement in US history, reporting that four polls from the time "suggest that about 15 million to 26 million people in the United States have participated in recent demonstrations."[45] One must also credit the monumental scope and intensity of this uprising to the structure built and momentum generated by the Movement for Black Lives' internationalist political philosophy, decentralized leadership structure, and hybrid organizing praxis.

This particular moment especially appeared to pierce white consciousness and/or demand white responsiveness in a way and on a scale previously not experienced during earlier uprisings. Corporations released statements of support. Institutions announced plans to build anti-racist centers, programs, and curricula. White people purchased books on race and racism en masse. Even discussions on prison abolition circulated in mainstream public spheres. But as Derecka Purnell generally observed in reflection on this moment, "Those people [participating in demonstrations] weren't absorbed into organizations in such a way to build campaigns toward eliminating some of the kinds of violence that put them into the streets in the first place."[46] Much of the responsiveness did not extend beyond the performative or momentary: corporations did not translate statements into material actions; institutions walked back their promised plans; and many white people did not even read their

---

45. Larry Buchanan, Quoctrung Bui, and Jugal K. Patel, "Black Lives Matter May Be the Largest Movement in U.S. History," *New York Times*, July 3, 2020, https://www.nytimes.com/interactive/2020/07/03/us/george-floyd-protests-crowd-size.html.

46. Derecka Purnell, Olúfẹ́mi O. Táíwò, and Keeanga-Yamahtta Taylor, "After the Uprising, What Is to Be Done?: A Discussion of the Legacy of the 2020 Protests, the Growing Threat from the Right, and Building Movements," *Hammer & Hope* no. 1 (2023), https://hammerandhope.org/article/issue-1-article-5.

purchased books. Nevertheless, this moment was enough to be affectively disruptive for dominant publics. It would be especially experienced as inundating for those who perceive the superficial acknowledgement in these performative rhetorics as already alienating or threatening.

Residual Formations in the Sublimated Position of a Frontlash's Manufactured Crisis

Rather than representing a groundswell of grassroots concern and activism about *Critical Race Theory*, anti-CRT rhetoric instead operates as an astroturf movement. In other words, powerful organizations, networks, media, and people have manufactured CRT as a "grassroots" crisis requiring significant intervention in all levels of government. Chris Rufo, in particular, is widely credited as being responsible for the invention and ascendancy of anti-CRT rhetoric. A well-funded collective of conservative think tanks, organizations, media outlets, politicians, and activists assisted Rufo in rapidly manufacturing and mainstreaming a crisis around CRT. As Weaver states in theorizing frontlash, "Crises can provide opportunities to frame the introduction of a new problem," which enables a defeated group to circulate "'a new interpretation of events' and 'change the intensities of interest' in a problem."[47] This collective of establishment institutions, networks, and people is well-equipped for circulating rhetoric, directing attention, and building valence among the assemblage of dominant publics. The manufacturers of the CRT outrage also advanced legislative interventions against CRT. In this way, they have both created and positioned themselves as valued "saviors" to this "problem" perceived as threatening the well-being of *their* children and, by extension, the present and future well-being of *their* nation.

Reacting to the exigencies identified above, anti-CRT rhetoric articulates with and further exploits perceived culture and status threats in dominant discourses on citizenship. It draws upon a collection of attitudes, feelings, and beliefs (both old and new) to construct an assemblage for affectively redirecting and renarrating counterdiscursive movement in the public sphere. The assemblage from which anti-CRT rhetoric evolves particularly consists of reactionary rhetorical articulations against "political correctness," "identity politics," "cancel culture," and "woke." Shui-yin Sharon Yam notes that the repetition of recognizable rhetorical figures within affective networks allow them "to circulate and gain sufficient emotional valence and political

---

47. Weaver, "Frontlash," 236.

uptake."[48] Ahmed also observes, "How the object impresses (upon) us may depend on histories that remain alive insofar as they have already left their impressions."[49] Therefore, one can recognize this sublimating assemblage as assisting with the affective circulation, metonymic movement, and discursive uptake of anti-CRT rhetoric.

When Movement for Black Lives protests renewed public attention to systemic racism (especially for white people), affective economies of whiteness experienced this affective rupture as a crisis. Chaput explains, "Political and social crises emerge from an interruption in the rhetorical energies that sustain our structures of feeling, knowing, and experiencing the world."[50] Attention to affective responses, rhetorical articulations, and discursive movements is important in these moments of "discovery"—moments in which material myths and fantasies structuring and sustaining dominant discursive subjectivities are no longer tenable and therefore demand (re)explanations.[51] The compensatory frontlash movements of dominant publics invested in whiteness, for instance, can often seek to restabilize their rhetorical energies instead of radically transforming them.[52] In this stabilizing process of redefinition and reorganization, such a closed or stubborn "rhetoric system" can resist discursive uptakes outside of their assemblages and "reorganiz[e] itself entirely *within* itself in ways that maintain its continued integrity and stability."[53] By turning "within itself," a discursive assemblage can then also convert *"the residual" into "the present"* in the public sphere. In other words, it can accommodate parasitic articulations and advance parasitic movements.

During the Movement for Black Lives protests in the summer of 2020, for example, *Critical Race Theory* was not part of dominant discourse at the time. But the anti-CRT collective recognized the value of swiftly mobilizing to frame the existence of this academic discipline of legal scholarship (and not institutionalized racial oppression) as the real crisis deserving public attention, outrage, and intervention. Appropriating *Critical Race Theory* from its academic existence as legal scholarship, Rufo weaponized it into a popular strawperson threatening to dominant publics invested in whiteness. He invents versions of CRT that "preach freedom and equality, but are mere 'camouflages' for naked

---

48. Shui-yin Sharon Yam, "Affective Economies and Alienizing Discourse: Citizenship and Maternity Tourism in Hong Kong," *Rhetoric Society Quarterly* 46, no. 5 (2016): 417.
49. Sara Ahmed, *The Cultural Politics of Emotion* (New York: Routledge, 2015), 8.
50. Chaput, "Rhetorical Circulation."
51. Rishi Chebrolu, "The Racial Lens of Dylann Roof: Racial Anxiety and White Nationalist Rhetoric on New Media," *Review of Communication* 20, no. 1 (2020): 47–68.
52. Mays, "From 'Flows' to 'Excess.'"
53. Mays, "From 'Flows' to 'Excess.'"

racial domination."[54] This rhetorical appropriation is an articulation with white fear of racial power inversion. It is a structure of feeling in the rhetorical economies of whiteness dating back to enslavers' affective resistance to the humanization of enslaved Africans and the abolition of slavery.[55] Likewise, Rufo's "Briefing Book" instructs anti-CRT activists to "adopt language that is trenchant, persuasive, and resonates with the public."[56] Thus, he offers a series of redefinitions absent of context or fidelity to the scholarship, but with historically situated and/or residually present valence in the public sphere. Among his suggestions are "race-based Marxism," "state-sanctioned racism," "woke racism," and "racial engineering."[57] Echoed in the anti-CRT materials from both the Heritage Foundation and Citizens for Renewing America (CRA), Rufo's characterizations assemble a host of white anxieties, grievances, and entitlements into a rhetoric with a permission structure for those invested in whiteness to circulate (at least early on) with some level of deniability against charges of racism.[58]

Anti-CRT rhetoric is a residually present expression of citizenship and national identity discourses in the public sphere's affective economies of whiteness. Given the compounding exigencies and crises, anti-CRT rhetoric's intensity of affective circulation functions as a dominant discursive response to their perceived culture and status threat.[59] As Yam states, "In order to understand why the public subscribes to certain citizenship practices—particularly exclusionary ones motivated by collective fear and anxiety—so vigorously and passionately, rhetoric scholars must understand them not solely as deliberative acts but also as embodied, sticky, and permeating feelings that foreclose alternative articulations."[60] Anti-CRT rhetoric's foreclosure of alternative articulations here arguably does not consist of primarily confronting or responding to the emergent counterpublic rhetorics reverberating across the public sphere. While its intensity is an affective uptake and rhetorical acknowledgement of the epistemic friction resulting from a counterdiscursive movement, it instead maneuvers to specifically foreclose alternative articulations made possible via counterdiscursive uptake within the affective economies of whiteness for dominant and wider publics.

---

54. Christopher F. Rufo, "Critical Race Theory Briefing Book," June 6, 2021, https://cristopherrufo.com/crt-briefing-book/.

55. Patricia Roberts-Miller, *Fanatical Schemes: Proslavery Rhetoric and the Tragedy of Consensus* (Tuscaloosa: University of Alabama Press, 2009).

56. Rufo, "Briefing Book," 9.

57. Rufo, "Briefing Book," 9–10.

58. Yam, "Affective Economies," 423.

59. Craig, Rucker, and Richeson, "Racial and Political Dynamics."

60. Yam, "Affective Economies," 412.

These possible alternative articulations of national identity and citizenship arguably emerge from the convergence of previously mentioned affective crises, insurrectionary genealogies, and counterdiscursive movements. As we addressed in "Parasitic Publics," Jennifer Wingard builds from Ahmed's insights to offer a succinct framework for understanding the discursive construction of national identity and citizenship in the contemporary precarious public sphere. In particular, dominant publics define idealized national citizenry and community with "Others" and against "other Others."[61] "Others" are those that the nation uses as a means to *feel* benevolent through assimilationist or multicultural inclusion, and "other Others" are those that the nation *must* exclude or deport for the sake of defining community and national borders. This inclusion of the "Other," however, is premised upon participation in, articulation with, and/or assimilation into dominant discourses. Anti-CRT rhetoric expresses the position of assimilationist inclusion when describing color-consciousness as not "conducive" for developing children into "good citizens."[62] Based in the white racial frame, it reflects a dominant discursive postracial logic of "color-blindness."[63] Characterizing the "rhetorical labor of the postracial," Eric King Watts observes how "race is claimed as irrelevant, but blackness must be differentiated anyway; it must be reinvented and it must become an object of destructive force so that the entitlement of white male sovereignty can be re-authorized."[64] While asserting the irrelevance of race, the postracial relies upon the normalization of anti-Black violence for the discursive legitimation of white male authority. As Ersula Ore observes, "Color-blind rhetoric defends and perpetuates the contemporary racial order through interpretative frames that normalize racism."[65] Watts continues illustrating its resemblance to the cultural logic of "reverse racism": "From the perspective of the sovereign, prohibiting the reproduction of the black bio-threat body would itself undermine sovereignty, and *that* 'would be just plain racist.'"[66] Infringement upon this perceived "natural right" to anti-Black oppression

---

61. Jennifer Wingard, *Branded Bodies, Rhetoric, and the Neoliberal Nation-State* (Lanham, MD: Lexington, 2013), 5.

62. Citizens for Renewing America, "Combatting Critical Race Theory in Your Community: An A to Z Guide on How to Stop Critical Race Theory and Reclaim Your Local School Board," June 8, 2021, https://citizensrenewingamerica.com/issues/combatting-critical-race-theory-in-your-community/.

63. Joe R. Feagin, *The White Racial Frame: Centuries of Racial Framing and Counter-Framing* (New York: Routledge, 2013).

64. Eric King Watts, "Postracial Fantasies, Blackness, and Zombies," *Communication and Critical/Cultural Studies* 14, no. 4 (2017): 327.

65. Ore, *Lynching,* 124.

66. Watts, "Postracial Fantasies," 327.

then is *felt* as an impingement upon and even *experienced* as an existential threat to white male identity. "Post-race is really black disappearance" from recognition, consideration, and acknowledgement in the public sphere.[67] Publics invested in whiteness as a legitimating condition for citizenship therefore see the valence of maintaining the assimilationist inclusion-exclusion criteria and foreclosing alternative articulations of national identity.

In contrast to the assimilationist model, multicultural inclusion of the "Other" does not pretend race is irrelevant. But it is also often a paternalistic, tokenizing inclusion based on the fetishized representation of "Others." These "Others" are often only acceptable as insider-outsiders when perceived as "non-threatening" through the performance of whiteness and/or when necessary for the maintenance of inequitable systems.[68] Institutionalized DEI rhetorics and efforts are often indicative of this neoliberal "branding" of others—that is, indicative of a rhetorical, affective strategy for creating national identity without regard to difference or material circumstances.[69] Importantly, Rufo's (mis)characterization of *Critical Race Theory* conveniently widens the scope of anti-CRT rhetoric enough to encompass and implicate most contemporary DEI efforts. He notably began opposing diversity efforts as early as 2019 but had yet to label these efforts as examples of CRT.[70] He now advocates branding such diversity programs as "race reeducation programs."[71] This clear reference to communist reeducation camps articulates with anti-CRT rhetoric's rampant use of "Marxism" as a devil term with xenophobic underpinnings in its dominant discursive connotation of being "foreign" and "un-American." In doing so, anti-CRT rhetoric suggests a discursive-affective construction of citizenship at odds with even multicultural inclusion. While his "Briefing Book" does describe the goal as being "diversity without division,"[72] it would be more accurately expressed as "diversity only through assimilation and deference to whiteness."

bell hooks contributes additional insights here on the residual formations of anti-CRT rhetoric's frontlash construction of citizenship and its relationship to multicultural inclusion. In reference to Black domestic laborers living with the white families who employed them, she stated that "safety resided in the

---

67. Watts, "Postracial Fantasies," 327.

68. Larson and McHendry Jr., "Parasitic Publics," 528; and Alfonso Gonzales, *Reform Without Justice: Latino Migrant Politics and the Homeland Security State* (Oxford: Oxford University Press, 2014), 164.

69. Wingard, *Branded Bodies*, ix.

70. Christopher F. Rufo, "Cult Programming in Seattle," *City Journal*, July 8, 2020, https://www.city-journal.org/article/cult-programming-in-seattle.

71. Rufo, "Briefing Book."

72. Rufo, "Briefing Book."

pretense of invisibility."[73] This particular condition of safety refers to escaping direct violence by refraining from an embodied "assertion of subjectivity, equality" through direct eye contact.[74] Extending this to dominant discourses, white people "can live as though black people are invisible and can imagine that they are also invisible to blacks. Some white people may even imagine there is no representation of whiteness in the black imagination."[75] The exposure of these habituated beliefs as myths can indeed be a contemporary source of affective rupture and discursive intervention within rhetorical economies of whiteness. As hooks observes, "They think they are seen by black folks only as they want to appear."[76] It comes from the epistemic injustice of the white racial frame—the power to define, characterize, and control with consequence.[77] Such a fantasy evolving from the affective-material-discursive-rhetorical conditions of power in institutionalized white supremacy "makes whiteness synonymous with goodness."[78] Discovering whiteness not only to be seen outside of its own imperialist terms but also to learn its association with oppression, violence, and terror, those invested in whiteness can experience affective rupture and become discursively destabilized. This destabilization can produce affective states of anxiety, a structure of feeling related to the perceived and felt loss of the ability to control and define with consequence.

Parasitic publics can exploit this dominant affective state during the process of discovery. The construction of "good white people" is a central pillar in the public sphere's rhetorical economies of whiteness. To be clear, this affective-discursive construction is less about whiteness as actually *being* "good" in terms of social relationality, epistemic responsibility, and power distribution. Instead, it is much more about being *seen* as "good." For in its association with "goodness," whiteness denies its histories of violence. It ignores its discursive and rhetorical imperialism in the public sphere. It justifies its accumulation of wealth in racial capitalism. But as this association collapses, the white racial frame increasingly experiences the counterdiscursive pressure to contextualize, recognize, and atone.

And this, right here . . . is an opportune affective formation in the public sphere's assemblage of dominant publics for parasitic articulation and

---

73. bell hooks, "Representing Whiteness in the Black Imagination," in *Displacing Whiteness: Essays in Social and Cultural Criticism* (Durham, NC: Duke University Press, 1997), 340.
74. hooks, "Representing Whiteness," 340.
75. hooks, "Representing Whiteness," 340.
76. hooks, "Representing Whiteness," 340.
77. Herbert Blumer, "Race Prejudice as a Sense of Group Position," *Pacific Sociological Review* 1, no. 1 (1958): 5.
78. hooks, "Representing Whiteness," 340.

movement. While negotiating the experience of affective rupture and discursive destabilization from counterdiscursive movement, the manufactured crisis of anti-CRT rhetoric's frontlash further incites these affective uptakes so that the felt "anxiety and fear of losing control" can be parasitically "translated into an emotional discourse about threats."[79] Anti-CRT activists then offer these audiences ways to use institutional power structures to prevent the crisis they themselves invented. They implore readers to use open records laws to hunt for CRT, call members of Congress, run for positions on local school boards, seize control of curricula, take legal action, and use social institutions and media to grow anti-CRT advocacy networks. After all, dominant discourses of citizenship are not only about "branding and excluding the Other to reinforce the Self, nor . . . only about concretizing and asserting a cultural or national identity."[80] In affective economies of whiteness, dominant discourses of citizenship also have "significant affective functions that allow the existing citizenry to 'feel better' about themselves and their home during a time of crisis."[81] Anti-CRT rhetoric then is about affectively reestablishing the dominant discourses invested in whiteness as "happy," "good," and "morally superior."[82] In the same way that anti-CRT materials characterize color consciousness as not producing "good citizens," as we detail in the next section, apparently for anti-CRT rhetoric "upholding segregation once more became synonymous with practicing good citizenship."[83]

Affective Institutionalization via Frontlash's Emotional Pedagogy

Anti-CRT rhetoric's affective institutionalization relies upon emotional pedagogy for the attunement of citizenship discourse within the dominant assemblage of publics. One can understand emotional pedagogy as the rhetorical work of guiding people in "what and how to feel and for what to do in light of those feelings."[84] Yam explains the significance of emotional pedagogy for citizenship discourse: "Emotional pedagogy is a key instrument in the

---

79. Yam, "Affective Economies," 415.
80. Yam, "Affective Economies," 430.
81. Yam, "Affective Economies," 430.
82. Yam, "Affective Economies," 412.
83. Candace Epps-Robertson, *Resisting* Brown: *Race, Literacy, and Citizenship in the Heart of Virginia* (Pittsburgh: University of Pittsburgh Press, 2018), 25.
84. Gould, "On Affect and Protest," 33.

production, regulation, and (re)articulation of citizenry relationships."[85] She describes the technical process of affective uptake and discursive orientation flowing within and from the assemblage of dominant publics. She writes that "it translates permeating and dominant affects into a terministic screen that prescribes what emotional representations of the Others are acceptable, what kinds of feelings a 'proper' and 'loyal' citizen should have toward members and non-members, and how and to whom these feelings should be directed."[86] The emotional pedagogy of anti-CRT rhetoric offers deeper affective grounding within the public sphere's rhetorical economies of whiteness. It further affectively attunes and even latches dominant discursive attachments onto "a particular narrative and a set of values and practices that distinguish them from the Other."[87] With citizenship discourse articulated within and assembled through the contemporary precarious public sphere, the affective states of anxiety structuring dominant discourses on national identity provide these publics with "the moral and political justification for maintaining 'what is' (taken for granted or granted) in the name of future survival."[88] It provides a parasitic permission structure and mapped direction for dominant publics to renarrate the affective intensities and ruptures of counterdiscursive crises, memories, and movements into a demagogic discursive assemblage of anti-integration victimhood.[89] With this newly stabilized whiteness, these rhetors then appropriate the rhetorical style of counterdiscourse in order to position themselves, their children, and their country as existentially threatened victims of *Critical Race Theory*—all while also weaponizing their entrenched institutionalized power and the force of law to narrow and silence (counter) discursive space on systemic racism.

Anti-CRT rhetoric communicates the instructive imperative and procedure for those invested in whiteness to react defensively against threats to their identities. Nearly every document we analyzed attunes attention to the perceived threat of guilt as an affective state. Indeed, the experience of feeling guilty itself exists as evidence of harm in this affective economy of whiteness. The Heritage Foundation's model legislation, the CRA's model legislation, former president Donald Trump's Executive Order 13950, Tennessee's revised rules for the Department of Education, Texas Senate Bill 03, Florida Senate Bill 148, Oklahoma House Bill 1775, Iowa House File 802, and Georgia House Bill 1082 all ban any instruction that makes students experience guilt—with

---

85. Yam, "Affective Economies," 423.
86. Yam, "Affective Economies," 423–24.
87. Yam, "Affective Economies," 416.
88. Ahmed, *Cultural Politics*, 77.
89. Chebrolu, "Racial Lens of Dylann Roof," 60–61.

many providing an affective assemblage of related structures of feeling as well. For example, Executive Order 13950 bans federal funds from being used for programs where "any individual should feel discomfort, guilt, anguish, or any other form of psychological distress on account of his or her race or sex."[90] As an exemplar of this problem, it cites a "Smithsonian Institution museum graphic [which] stated that 'facing your whiteness is hard and can result in feelings of guilt, sadness, confusion, defensiveness, or fear.'"[91] Fear over the affective production of guilt is a central pillar of threat in anti-CRT rhetoric. In advocating for a curriculum premised upon the absence of guilt, this rhetoric introduces and generates four regulatory views on education for its emotional pedagogy. First, its positioning of guilt as a threat reorients discursive movement away from and against discomfort's affective capacity and educational role in intellectual growth.[92] Second, it reinforces the inclusion-exclusion criteria in the affective economy of whiteness, applying it to value assessments of student curriculum that neither applies to people of color expected to internalize whitewashed books and lessons, nor even acknowledges their presence as students. Third, it reveals exactly whom they see as in need of protection and whom they need to be seen in the public sphere as disregardable. Last, its use of seemingly neutral language relies upon and mobilizes the white racial frame to strengthen and protect the perceived "moral superiority" of whiteness in the public sphere with rhetorical deniability about the differential consequences and adverse impacts of the legislation.

Anti-CRT legislation is especially careful to outlaw feelings of guilt as a requirement, not guilt as a byproduct. This point receives special emphasis from the conservative Manhattan Institute's primer on "How to Regulate Critical Race Theory in Schools" in which James Copland explains that only material that suggests students *should* feel guilt are banned.[93] On the one hand, this distinction matters in terms of explicit instruction—a teacher cannot instruct that a student should feel guilty because they are white. At the same time, our analysis of this distinction in anti-CRT materials indicates it as a rhetoric designed for political uptake and mobilization, not principled education policy. In particular, it logically follows from the significant rhetorical attention in these propaganda action guides to the relationship between

---

90. Exec. Order No. 13950, 85 Fed. Reg. 60683 (Sept. 28, 2020).

91. Exec. Order No. 13950.

92. Charlene A. Carruthers, *Unapologetic: A Black, Queer, and Feminist Mandate for Radical Movements* (Boston: Beacon Press, 2018), 41.

93. James R. Copland, "How to Regulate Critical Race Theory in Schools: A Primer and Model Legislation," Manhattan Institute, August 2021, https://www.manhattan-institute.org/copland-critical-race-theory-model-legislation.

anti-CRT legislation and freedom of speech. Here is a representative sample of this attention: "This is not a free speech issue; it's a compelled speech issue ... Free speech was designed to protect the individual against the government, not to empower the government to force individuals to believe in fringe racial theories."[94] This rhetoric operates on the two interrelated levels of political uptake and mobilization. First, it anticipates criticism from other conservatives about unconstitutional violations of the First Amendment. Therefore, these distinctions assist in recruiting conservatives and others to circulate anti-CRT rhetoric under the political cover and public (mis)perception of being principled. Second, it positions CRT as compelled speech fully located in and coerced by "the government"—an ambiguous devil term without attention to the specific details about political party, representation, or power. After all, anti-CRT rhetoric circulates from a reactionary discursive space. Even when in dominant positions of institutional power, it must have a scapegoat to blame and concentrate power against. Framing CRT as institutionalized coercion allows them to organize these same institutional mechanisms against any perceived "enemies" (read: threats to hegemonic power).

Differentiating guilt as a requirement and guilt as a byproduct of legislation does not change the material outcomes for anti-CRT rhetoric. It is a technical distinction, not a material one. In the affective circulation of rhetorical economies of whiteness, the rhetorical slippage between "requirement" and "byproduct" in uptakes is not only possible but accommodated. The emotional pedagogy of anti-CRT rhetoric's affective circulation of outrage also actually conditions and incites such slippages. As such, guilt becomes a hallmark of CRT, despite the fact that *Critical Race Theory* views the production of white guilt as counterproductive. It is especially evident in Rufo's anti-CRT literature, suggesting activists frame anti-CRT legislation around the idea of coerced speech by the state: "The government does not have the right to force individuals to believe in race essentialism, collective guilt, or racial superiority theory." However, in defining where guilt emerges in CRT, the thread to compelled speech is lost:

> Critical race theory claims that individuals categorized as "White" are inherently responsible for injustice and oppression committed by white populations in the past. This concept is sometimes framed as "white guilt," "white shame," and "white complicity," which are psychological manifestations of collective guilt.[95]

---

94. Rufo, "Briefing Book," 11.
95. Rufo, "Briefing Book," 5.

None of these specific examples of terminology being associated with CRT involve coerced speech. Instead, they position guilt in terms of collective responsibility (rather than individual feeling). To misframe CRT as coerced speech then, he works to especially locate this world of individuals divorced from contexts. Thus, the mere possibility of guilt as an affective uptake becomes forced guilt.

While most of the Heritage Foundation's resources do not specifically mention guilt, they frequently link to Jonathan Butcher and Mike Gonzalez's Daily Signal article, "Feeling Guilty About Everything? Thank Critical Race Theory." Here, the idea of guilt becomes even more opaque, "We wrote our paper so that our policymakers and all Americans can better understand the genesis of the events that shook our own 'Summer of Hate' this year and are injecting the haunt of guilt—not opportunity—into every sector of our lives."[96] The rhetoric of guilt as "haunting" is particularly instructive given its possible association with an unresolved past tormenting the present. While we recognize legislative efforts to specify coerced feelings of guilt, it is essential to understand that various iterations of guilt (compelled, acknowledged, mentioned, and as a haunting) circulate within the same discursive assemblage, and "messages become rhetorically detached from their original meaning, thus primed for spreading misinformation and coordinating outrage."[97] After all, dominant discourses invested in whiteness experience any inconvenience produced by the proximity of "Others" and the need to recognize "Others" as "dramas of unfairness."[98] Guilt thus becomes a primary way anti-CRT advocates claim to be victims.

With reliance on articulations like exposure as coercive and guilt as harm, anti-CRT rhetoric enables the affective dimension of victimhood to surge through this collective assemblage. The discursive assemblage is shaped by the conceptual and stylistic excesses of white masculinity. Paul Elliott Johnson explains that "victimized, white men" are depicted "as the proper representatives of American identity. The idea of a fraught, imperiled, and perpetually marginalized white masculinity resonates broadly in America because white

---

96. Jonathan Butcher and Mike Gonzalez, "Feeling Guilty about Everything? Thank Critical Race Theory," Heritage Foundation, December 7, 2020, https://www.heritage.org/progressivism/commentary/feeling-guilty-about-everything-thank-critical-race-theory.

97. Brandi Lawless and Kristen L. Cole, "Troll Tracking: Examining Rhetorical Circulation of Anti-Intellectual Ideologies in Right-Wing Media Attacks," *Communication, Culture and Critique* 14, no. 1 (2021): 151.

98. Lauren Berlant, *On the Inconvenience of Other People* (Durham, NC: Duke University Press, 2022), 5.

masculinity's incoherence mirrors that of the U.S."[99] Indeed, white masculinity as a dominant discourse is increasingly experiencing counterdiscursive challenges to the presumed dominance of their identities and bodies. But even in this context, these dominant publics continue to operate in a public sphere affording them unearned power and privilege. The felt sense of collective victimhood here is about the public expression of an identity constructed as a "metaphor for power."[100] It is about publicness. It is a nostalgic desire for hegemonic control of publicness and valence in the public sphere. It is a longing for "not needing to know" transformed into an expression of "needing not to know."[101] These affective conditions are conductive for parasitic movement.

In particular, anti-CRT rhetoric's emotional pedagogy uses projective identification to reframe this guilt away from themselves and onto children as a means of not only moral justification in the public sphere but also of moral imperative to act against it. Children are a population constructed in affective structures, legal institutions, and social imaginaries as "in need of protecting" and "the future of the nation." We see slippage here, too, but one producing a "dominant positive affect" for them in the rhetorical economies of whiteness.[102] For in positioning themselves as "protectors" of those who "can't protect themselves," they also become protectors of the future of a nation-state *felt* as if it is "under siege" and "cannot protect itself." Therefore, their discursive reestablishing of themselves as "good people" is made possible through (white) masculine tropes of "protector" and "warrior" and "savior." Anti-CRT rhetorics weaponize the language of ownership ("your schools") in particularly instructive ways with this in mind. As the self-designated "protectors of children" and therefore "saviors of the nation's future," the weaponized language of possession further incites them to mobilize anger into collective outrage about the "loss" of what is perceived/assumed as "theirs." Thus, anti-CRT frontlash (re)attunes publics into the mobilization of emotional expressions with social valence in the rhetorical economies of white masculinity. In the public sphere, it works to continue fomenting distrust of public institutions and therefore in the continued devaluation of public education. In doing so, anti-CRT rhetoric represents an affective expression of this post–civil rights period of "White Reconstruction," ultimately organizing parasitic movement back toward a sublimated "segregation academies" model of privatized education.

---

99. Paul Elliott Johnson, "Walter White(ness) Lashes Out: *Breaking Bad* and Male Victimage," *Critical Studies in Media Communication* 34, no. 1 (2017): 15.
100. James Baldwin, *I Am Not Your Negro* (New York: Vintage International, 2017), 107.
101. Medina, *The Epistemology of Resistance*, 32.
102. Chaput, "Rhetorical Circulation."

Conclusion

Parasitic publics are reactionary discursive spaces formed residually and institutionalized affectively through the invention, circulation, and uptake of demagogic rhetorics. "Formed residually" emphasizes how parasitic discursive spaces are historically constituted. It draws attention to the historicity of circulation, articulation, and assemblage in affective economies. Parasitic publics involve residual formations of sublimated histories, positions, and attachments experienced as continuing felt intensities in circulatory encounters, uptakes, and repetitions of associated rhetorical objects. "Institutionalized affectively" emphasizes the importance of affective circulation for parasitic processes of value production, rhetorical uptake, and discursive exchange in the public sphere. As detailed in our analysis, compensatory movements of dominant publics invested in whiteness can often seek the comfort of restabilizing their rhetorical energies instead of radically transforming them in response to threatening counterdiscursive challenge. In this stabilizing process of redefinition and reorganization, dominant publics can draw upon and mobilize a collection of attitudes, feelings, and beliefs—both residual and present—to (re)construct a discursive assemblage for affectively redirecting and renarrating counterdiscursive movement. It offers an emotional pedagogy for dominant publics, redirecting key events and ideas into comforting narratives in which their sense of moral superiority and control is often reclaimed through affective states of victimhood and outrage. By turning "within itself" in this way, a discursive assemblage's conversion of "the residual" into "the present" can accommodate parasitic articulations and advance parasitic movements in the public sphere.

CHAPTER 8

Cisnormativity as Rhetorical Obstruction

The Silencing Effects of White and Cisgender Innocence

V. JO HSU

In February 2022, Texas Attorney General Ken Paxton issued an opinion declaring that gender-affirming health care for trans youth "can legally constitute child abuse."[1] Days later, Texas Governor Greg Abbott instructed the state's Child Protective Services (CPS) to investigate families of trans children. He also charged "all licensed professionals . . . including doctors, nurses, and teachers" to report instances of gender-affirming care, emphasizing that Texas law provides "criminal penalties for failure to report such abuse."[2] That same month, *Rhetoric Society Quarterly* published an article I had written about anti-trans rhetoric—specifically, about how right-wing activists and politicians mobilize anti-trans sentiment to enforce racist, ableist, and heteropatriarchal policies and attitudes. I believe strongly in the importance of rhetorical studies—for me, captured by Jay Dolmage as "the strategic study of the circulation of power through communication."[3] I find myself increasingly disheartened, however, by the gap between disciplinary spaces and the public conversations they *should* affect.

As a disabled trans person who moved to Texas at the peak of the 2020 COVID surge, I spent the past three years behind my computer screen, watching my world constrict. With each antivaccine conspiracy, with Texas's

---

1. Ken Paxton to Matt Krause, "Opinion No. KP-0401," February 18, 2022, 13.
2. Greg Abbott to Jamie Masters, February 22, 2022, https://gov.texas.gov/uploads/files/press/O-MastersJaime202202221358.pdf.
3. Jay Dolmage, *Disability Rhetoric: Critical Perspectives on Disability* (Syracuse, NY: Syracuse University Press, 2014), chap. Prosthesis.

prohibition on mask mandates, and with many politicians stoking transantagonism, the public spaces that I could occupy dwindled. I was writing with the hope of bell hooks's "theory as liberatory practice"[4]—naming, from experience, harms rendered illegible by dominant vernaculars. I was writing in the tradition of Johanna Hedva's Sick Woman Theory, which queries from the sickbed, "How do you throw a brick through the window of a bank if you can't get out of bed?"[5] How do you account for the uneven access of public spaces where political deliberations are waged? How do you craft resistance from the private and equally political sphere of coercive confinement? Writing had never felt more concretely like a lifeline—like the only tether that could hold me to a world drifting increasingly beyond my reach.

This chapter builds on hooks's and Hedva's liberatory theories, Cherríe Moraga's "theory in the flesh," Richard Delgado's "counterstory," and storytelling traditions from cultural rhetorics, which share in common the *deliberate use of story* to rupture dominant ways of knowing.[6] While marginal perspectives do not inherently bring incisive critique—and have too often been appropriated by academic disciplines[7]—Black feminists, Indigenous writers and artists, disabled activists, and other innovative creators have leveraged their stories to breach oppressive patterns and public complacency.[8] In cre-

---

4. bell hooks, "Theory as Liberatory Practice," *Yale Journal of Law & Feminism* 4, no. 1 (1991): 1–12.

5. Johanna Hedva, "Sick Woman Theory," *Mask Magazine*, 2016, 5, https://johannahedva.com/SickWomanTheory_Hedva_2020.pdf.

6. hooks, "Theory as Liberatory Practice"; Cherríe Moraga, "La Güera," in *This Bridge Called My Back*, ed. Cherríe Moraga and Gloria Anzaldúa, 4th edition (Albany: State University of New York Press, 2015), 22–29; Aja Y. Martinez, *Counterstory: The Rhetoric and Writing of Critical Race Theory*, CCC Studies in Writing & Rhetoric (Champaign: Conference on College Composition and Communication; National Council of Teachers of English, 2020); Malea Powell, Daisy Levy, Andrea Riley-Mukavetz, Marilee Brooks-Gillies, Maria Novotny, and Jennifer Fisch-Ferguson, "Our Story Begins Here: Constellating Cultural Rhetorics," *Enculturation*, no. 18 (October 25, 2014), http://enculturation.net/our-story-begins-here; Terese Guinsatao Monberg, "Like the Molave: Listening for Constellations of Community through 'Growing Up Brown' Stories," *Enculturation*, no. 21 (April 20, 2016), http://enculturation.net/like-the-molave; and V. Jo Hsu, *Constellating Home: Trans and Queer Asian American Rhetorics* (Columbus: The Ohio State University Press, 2022).

7. Jodi Melamed, *Represent and Destroy: Rationalizing Violence in the New Racial Capitalism* (Minneapolis: University of Minnesota Press, 2011); and Sujatha Fernandes, *Curated Stories: The Uses and Misuses of Storytelling* (New York: Oxford University Press, 2017).

8. Cherríe Moraga and Gloria Anzaldúa, eds., *This Bridge Called My Back: Writings by Radical Women of Color*, 4th edition (Albany: State University of New York Press, 2015); Patricia J. Williams, *The Alchemy of Race and Rights* (Cambridge, MA: Harvard University Press, 1991); Eli Clare, *Brilliant Imperfection: Grappling with Cure* (Durham, NC: Duke University Press, 2017); LeAnne Howe, "The Story of America: A Tribalography," in *Clearing a Path: Theorizing the Past in Native American Studies*, ed. Nancy Shoemaker (New York: Routledge, 2001), 29–48; and Thomas King, *The Truth about Stories: A Native Narrative* (Minneapolis: University of Minnesota Press, 2005).

ative nonfiction, the shape of this chapter might be described as a "braided essay," which interweaves multiple storylines. My experience entwines with more traditional analyses of anti-trans rhetorics to show how mainstream reportage and academic conventions center white, cisnormative perspectives. Portions of this essay will sidestep traditional argumentation. I do so strategically, querying what forms of writing dominate disciplinary and popular spaces, who benefits or profits from such writing, and what knowledge eludes these forms. I offer my experience not as a definitive account of any particular group or demographic, but to probe the conditions that universalize select perspectives as Truth.

Storytelling appears across numerous intellectual and cultural traditions, but my usage here participates specifically in trans-of-color critique. Drawing from Jules Gill-Peterson and Jian Neo Chen, I understand this approach as a mode of analysis that finds "solidarity and kinship" among those harmed by "radically different yet interrelated" systems of harm.[9] I focus on the imbrications of racism and transphobia, though the bodily and behavioral norms that govern racist and transphobic values traverse broader colonial, imperial, and ableist histories, as well as other areas of discrimination.[10] The terrains of racism and transphobia converge at the contrived boundaries of binary gender. As Black and decolonial feminists have long emphasized, conventional femininity and masculinity are premised on white middle-class norms and have often been used to dehumanize people of color. From the "effeminate" Asian man to the "angry Black woman," people of color have been stereotyped as too passive, too aggressive, hypersexual, and asexual—all in ways that violate acceptable gendered behavior.[11] The gender ideals encapsulated by "cisgender" are then only partially and conditionally accessible by people of color.[12] Transphobic policies often harm cisgender women and girls of color

---

9. Jian Neo Chen, *Trans Exploits: Trans of Color Cultures and Technologies in Movement* (Durham, NC: Duke University Press, 2019), chap. Introduction. See also Jules Gill-Peterson, "Trans of Color Critique before Transsexuality," *TSQ: Transgender Studies Quarterly* 5, no. 4 (2018): 606–20.

10. Chen, *Trans Exploits*; Clare, *Brilliant Imperfection*; and C. Riley Snorton, *Black on Both Sides: A Racial History of Trans Identity* (Minneapolis: University of Minnesota Press, 2017).

11. Patricia Hill Collins, *Black Feminist Thought: Knowledge, Consciousness, and the Politics of Empowerment*, 2nd edition (New York: Routledge, 2000); David L. Eng, *Racial Castration: Managing Masculinity in Asian America* (Durham, NC: Duke University Press, 2001); and Melissa V. Harris-Perry, *Sister Citizen: Shame, Stereotypes, and Black Women in America (For Colored Girls Who've Considered Politics When Being Strong Isn't Enough)* (New Haven, CT: Yale University Press, 2011).

12. Kai M. Green and Marquis Bey argue that Black cisgender women "have always already functioned in excess" of the universalized (implicitly white) "woman" as a category. Kai M. Green and Marquis Bey, "Where Black Feminist Thought and Trans* Feminism Meet: A Conversation," *Souls* 19, no. 4 (2017): 439.

(for example, gender policing in sports) and compound violence against trans people of color. Those who must survive this juncture of racism and cissexism are also better positioned to expose the codependences of racist and cissexist practices.

In 2022 racism and transphobia converged in conservatives' aggressive legislative agenda—one that sought to eliminate antiracist education, abortion access, and trans people in general. The proliferative bans on gender-affirming health care relied on the same racist logics that helped overturn *Roe v. Wade*. Trans people, queer people, and cisgender women's reproductive freedom are all viewed as threats to the continued proliferation—and socioeconomic influence—of white, middle-class US American families. By no coincidence, white supremacist groups have become an increasingly visible contingent of anti-choice movements.[13] The connections among transphobic legislation, antiabortion measures, and the censorship of US racial histories—the three major focal points of conservative platforms in 2022—should have been readily apparent. Yet, major media platforms continually missed this broader picture. The left's relative silence on trans topics enabled conservative politicians to disguise racist and heteropatriarchal agendas as necessary defenses against a "Transgender Leviathan"[14] or "Transgender Empire."[15] Paradoxically, to minimize their outspread harm, those same voices often insisted that such measures only affected the "tiny, tiny population" of US trans people.[16]

This chapter considers how whiteness, as an underlying logic, stifles rhetorical possibilities for people defending trans rights and reproductive freedom. One thread of this braided essay traces the unspoken cisnormativity that enables most anti-trans rhetorics. The other thread tracks the deliberate silencing that obstructs efforts toward exposing that cisnormativity. The two interweave to consider the discursive conventions that dictate how we, as rhetoricians and writers, make knowledge and where that knowledge can go. To

---

13. Renee Bracey Sherman and Lizz Winstead, "Patriot Front's Anti-Abortion Advocacy at March for Life Sends a Clear Message," NBC News, January 24, 2022, https://www.nbcnews.com/think/opinion/patriot-front-s-anti-abortion-advocacy-march-life-sends-clear-ncna1287952.

14. Pedro Gonzalez, "The Transgender Leviathan," American Principles Project, November 2022, https://americanprinciplesproject.org/wp-content/uploads/2022/11/2022_TransLeviathan_web.pdf.

15. Christopher F. Rufo [@realchrisrufo], "The Transgender Movement Has Conquered America Life. In a New Short Film, I Explain How the Movement Gained Power and Connect the Dots between Its Key Intellectuals, Billionaire Benefactor, and Large-Scale Medical Experiments in a Detroit Ghetto. This Is the Transgender Empire: Https://T.Co/UaQSGD5RL8," Twitter, July 12, 2023, https://twitter.com/realchrisrufo/status/1679143593238462464.

16. Emma Margolin, "Why the 'Tiny, Tiny' Transgender Population Should Matter to Donald Trump," MSNBC, May 13, 2016, https://www.msnbc.com/msnbc/why-the-tiny-tiny-transgender-population-should-matter-donald-trump-msna849046.

borrow again from Dolmage, I am studying the circulation of power through communication while querying *how power shapes where our communication can circulate.* If parts of this essay seem difficult or uncomfortable, they may be caused by my shortcomings in grappling with a novel form, but I hope, too, that readers will consider what *else*—what assumptions, what communicative practices, what prior understandings—may also inform such discomfort.

Cisnormativity, Whiteness, and Rhetorical Silence

In 1995 Thomas Nakayama and Robert Krizek called for an interrogation of whiteness as strategic rhetoric, attending to the perspectives that go unacknowledged through presumed universality.[17] Rhetoricians have since analyzed whiteness as "rhetorical silence."[18] Aimee Carrillo Rowe, for example, looks at how US feminism has reproduced racial exclusion by failing to name and address racial difference in gender-based oppression. Whiteness then exerts its power in part through a disappearing act. White perspectives, values, and conventions are so pervasive that they become the standard—even though many of us know and must live differently. Lopenzina calls such colonial erasure *unwitnessing,* an often "passive decision to maintain a particular narrative structure by keeping undesirable aspects of cultural memory repressed and inactive."[19] This strategic amnesia is also central to the machinations of neoliberalism, severing the present from the past to position each of us as isolated, independent actors.

Cisgender "innocence" is a confederate of whiteness's rhetorical silence. By "innocence," I mean the presumed and often *deliberate* disinterest of cisgender people when it comes to trans topics, experiences, and needs. Like whiteness, cisnormativity (itself a product of white supremacy) often operates as the unspoken standard against which all deviations are measured—a standard that needs continual reinforcing through measures such as anti-trans legislation. The pervasive framing of trans people as a "tiny segment of the

---

17. Thomas K. Nakayama and Robert L. Krizek, "Whiteness: A Strategic Rhetoric," *Quarterly Journal of Speech* 81, no. 3 (1995): 291–309.
18. Aimee Carrillo Rowe, "Locating Feminism's Subject: The Paradox of White Femininity and the Struggle to Forge Feminist Alliances," *Communication Theory* 10, no. 1 (2000): 64–80; and Carrie Crenshaw, "Resisting Whiteness' Rhetorical Silence," *Western Journal of Communication* 61, no. 3 (1997): 253–78.
19. Drew Lopenzina, *Red Ink: Native Americans Picking up the Pen in the Colonial Period* (Albany: State University of New York Press, 2012), 9.

population"[20] encourages cis people—even self-described "allies"—to distance themselves from the material conditions that endanger trans people. Through such chosen ignorance, many can declare that getting someone's pronouns right is "too hard" or that trans people have needlessly "complicated" matters of gender and sex,[21] while ignoring the intricate cultural constructions that determine normative pronoun and gender configurations.

Enabled by white rhetorical silence, cisnormativity functions as a set of behavioral and corporeal norms assumed to be desirable, "healthy," and "natural." As rhetorical *obstruction*, these presumed universal (mis)understandings render gender variance unintelligible through restrictive approaches to gender, race, and identity. In the section below, I map the rhetorical economies that establish and maintain cisnormativity. I then follow that cisnormativity through the pathologization of trans identity. I demonstrate how cisgender innocence occludes understandings of gender-expansive worlds and how it embeds assumptions that stigmatize gender difference and valorize white, middle-class values. My own experiences in writing about these values appear throughout as a sort of countertheory—an alternative set of conceptual tools that may help us "interrogate problems more deeply" and across differences.[22]

Cisnormativity as Rhetorical Economy

I began writing on the connection between transphobic legislation and reproductive control well before February 2022, but *Rhetoric Society Quarterly* published my article just weeks before Paxton's letter became public, when Texas again emerged as a frontier[23] of right-wing activism. Like many others who work on public rhetorics, I had already been thinking about the limitations of

---

20. Adam Serwer, "The Republican Party Finds a New Group to Demonize," *The Atlantic*, April 13, 2021, https://www.theatlantic.com/ideas/archive/2021/04/gops-war-trans-kids/618579/; see also Pamela Paul, "The Far Right and Far Left Agree on One Thing: Women Don't Count," *New York Times*, July 3, 2022, https://www.nytimes.com/2022/07/03/opinion/the-far-right-and-far-left-agree-on-one-thing-women-dont-count.html.

21. Kevin D. Williamson, "Of Course Haircuts Have Genders," *National Review*, June 9, 2022, https://www.nationalreview.com/2022/06/of-course-haircuts-have-genders/; TransgenderTrend [@Transgendertrd], "There Are Very Complicated Rules of Language Needed to Support the New Social Construction of 'Gender Identity' and It Doesn't Seem to Free Young People at All, but Tie Them into Analysing Every Aspect of Their Personalities in Terms of 'Gender.'" #genderID #conference #croydon," Twitter, June 23, 2018, https://twitter.com/Transgendertrd/status/1010581191676788736.

22. Christine Sleeter, "Building Counter-Theory about Disability," *Disability Studies Quarterly* 30, no. 2 (2010), http://dsq-sds.org/article/view/1244/1288.

23. And I mean this with all its colonizing implications.

our disciplinary genres.²⁴ What is the point of this knowledge if it stops at the boundaries of our fields? There is a particular helplessness in *theorizing* about anti-trans rhetoric—in screaming into paywalled journals—while watching that very rhetoric devastate your communities. This is how academia confines historically marginalized knowledges, commodifying them "as scholarly production" while positioning white perspectives as the arbiter of valid intellectual work.²⁵

I reached out to my university's Office of Public Affairs around the same time that one of the coordinators contacted me. They had come across my article, and we agreed that this seemed like a pressing topic to translate for a broader audience. We agreed that I would draft a public-facing argument that emphasized the interrelations among transphobia and other forms of structural harm. In brief:

1. Conservative fear mongering about a widespread "trans epidemic" focuses primarily on *"middle to upper middle class white girls."*²⁶
2. By describing gender-affirming care as "medical sterilization," anti-trans politicians and activists tap into anxieties about the reproductive futures of these white affluent children.
3. This focus on reproductive futures connects antiabortion politics directly to the surge in anti-trans hostility, both of which are inseparable from white nationalists' fear of declining white birthrates.

By white "girls," conservatives mean white transmasculine youth, whose reproductive futures are being curtailed for the same reasons that white supremacists enjoin white women to "sta[y] at home, submi[t] to male leadership,

---

24. Carmen Kynard and Bryan McCann, "Editor's Introduction," *Rhetoric, Politics & Culture* 1, no. 1 (Summer 2021): v–xiii.

25. Mitsuye Yamada, "Invisibility Is an Unnatural Disaster: Reflections of an Asian American Woman," in *This Bridge Called My Back,* ed. Cherríe Moraga and Gloria Anzaldúa, 4th edition (Albany: State University of New York Press, 2015), 30–35; Maria Cotera, "'Invisibility Is an Unnatural Disaster': Feminist Archival Praxis after the Digital Turn," *South Atlantic Quarterly* 114, no. 4 (2015): 781–801; and Dan Berger, "Subjugated Knowledges: Activism, Scholarship, and Ethnic Studies Ways of Knowing," in *Critical Ethnic Studies,* ed. Nada Elia, David M. Hernández, Jodi Kim, Shana L. Redmond, Dylan Rodríguez, and Sarita Echavez See. (Durham, NC: Duke University Press, 2020), 215–28.

26. Megyn Kelly, "Abigail Shrier on the Teen Trans Trend, Feminism and Technology," *Megyn Kelly Show,* October 19, 2020, Episode 12, 38:56–39:00, https://podcasts.apple.com/us/podcast/abigail-shrier-on-teen-trans-trend-feminism-technology/id1532976305?i=1000495240932, emphasis added. As in all her rhetoric, Shrier refers to trans children by their gender assigned at birth.

[and] bea[r] lots of children."²⁷ Queerness, white women's reproductive freedom, and people of color in general all jeopardize the primacy of the white nuclear family. In fact, conservatives consistently describe trans people—and our supposed "gender ideology"—as "destroying American families."²⁸ Mirroring that language, Trump presidential advisor Stephen Miller cites abortion as a strategy to "destroy the nuclear family."²⁹ The whiteness of this family is, of course, often silently asserted—as it is when conservatives describe "critical race theory" as a denial of "parental rights."³⁰

The recent surge of such rhetoric responds to a perceived destabilization of white elites' power. As Abigail Shrier explains to the Independent Women's Forum, "A lot of these [trans youth] . . . are middle to upper middle class white girls, and they know that that's not such a great identity to have today but they can't choose a different race, right?"³¹ This theory, amplified

---

27. Annie Kelly, "The Housewives of White Supremacy," *New York Times*, June 1, 2018, https://www.nytimes.com/2018/06/01/opinion/sunday/tradwives-women-alt-right.html; see also Nancy S. Love, "Shield Maidens, Fashy Femmes, and TradWives: Feminism, Patriarchy, and Right-Wing Populism," *Frontiers in Sociology* 5 (2020), https://doi.org/10.3389/fsoc.2020.619572.

28. Doug Mainwaring, "Dr. Ben Carson Says COVID Mandates, Mask Wearing, Gender Ideology Are Child Abuse," LifeSite, February 25, 2022, https://www.lifesitenews.com/news/dr-ben-carson-slams-covid-mandates-mask-wearing-gender-ideology-as-child-abuse/.

29. Stephen [@StephenM] Miller, "Destroy Nuclear Family, Discourage Childbirth, Promote Abortion as 'Family Planning'—Replace Religion with Regime Ideology—Put Gov't between Parents & Children—Use Schools & Corps to Instill Woke Propaganda, Sow Gender Confusion, Teach Hatred of Self/Family/Faith/Nation (2/3)," Twitter, July 1, 2022, https://twitter.com/StephenM/status/1542891404799709188.

30. Melissa Moschella, "Critical Race Theory, Public Schools, and Parental Rights," Heritage Foundation, March 24, 2022, https://www.heritage.org/education/commentary/critical-race-theory-public-schools-and-parental-rights.

31. Beverly Hallberg, "Abigail Shrier on Her New Book: Irreversible Damage: The Transgender Craze Seducing Our Daughters," She Thinks, 6:51–7:02, https://www.iwf.org/2020/09/04/abigail-shrier-on-her-new-book-irreversible-damage-the-transgender-craze-seducing-our-daughters/ (accessed June 10, 2022).

throughout anti-trans media,[32] asserts that "woke culture"[33] has put such pressure on white middle-class people that children are "tak[ing] cover in victim groups."[34] Conspiracy theories perpetuated by Christopher Rufo, James Lindsay, and the journalists who amplify them position "gender theory" as one of the "suite of fields, alongside CRT [critical race theory]" terrorizing white students and separating them from "family, religion, and culture."[35] Prohibiting lessons about racial histories and LGBTQ identities only shelters select kids while endangering others. Conservatives' rhetoric about defending children and families then draws a dividing line between those *for* whom these policies offer protection and those *from* whom such policies protect. While the anti-CRT panic positions itself as a defense against "radical" classroom changes, it is also about preserving the history and status quo of many US educational systems—securing "whiteness as a national inheritance" and passing socioeconomic capital from one generation of white elites to the next.[36]

The Office of Public Affairs connected me with an editor for a national publication, who commissioned an eight-hundred-word article from me. No matter how I arranged my words, however, I could not shape my argument to her satisfaction. In her limited feedback, she repeated that my claims were

---

32. Upon its release, Shrier's book topped Amazon sales lists for LGBTQ Studies and Transgender Studies. Republicans selected her to testify against the Equality Act, whereupon she focused entirely on the fabricated threat of transgender predators. She's also been in conversation with right-wing figures such as Arkansas Senator Tom Cotton, podcaster Joe Rogan, conservative journalist Ben Shapiro, and Fox's Tucker Carlson, and many others. Abigail [@AbigailShrier] Shrier, "Always a Pleasure to Be Invited into @TuckerCarlson. Here's the Clip (in Two Parts) for Those Who Missed It," Twitter, May 29, 2021, https://twitter.com/AbigailShrier/status/1398443037202788352; Abigail [@AbigailShrier] Shrier, "Thanks @benshapiro for Having Me on the Sunday Special to Discuss Book Banning, the Illiberal Left, and What's Going on with These Teenage Girls: Https://Youtu.Be/9uSlmfp7euo via @YouTube," Twitter, November 22, 2020, https://twitter.com/AbigailShrier/status/1330553881906933760; Joe Rogan, "Abigail Shrier," *The Joe Rogan Experience*, n.d., https://open.spotify.com/episode/4SIh4Pt39AtGQYzMJMNkv1?si=5176700cdcb34c87; and Tom Cotton, "Could the GOP Become the Party of Women? Sen. Tom Cotton Says It Already Has," interview by Abigail Shrier, November 4, 2021, https://abigailshrier.substack.com/p/could-the-gop-become-the-party-of.

33. Dave Aucoin, "Parents: Wake Up to WOKE Culture," Family Policy Alliance, August 27, 2020, https://familypolicyalliance.com/issues/2020/08/27/parents-wake-up-to-woke-culture/.

34. Abigail Shrier, *Irreversible Damage: The Transgender Craze Seducing Our Daughters* (Washington, DC: Regnery Publishing, 2020), xxiii.

35. Kathryn Joyce, "Meet James Lindsay, the Far Right's 'World-Level Expert' on CRT and 'Race Marxism,'" *Salon*, February 17, 2022, https://www.salon.com/2022/02/17/meet-james-lindsay-the-far-rights-world-level-expert-on-crt-and-race-marxism/; James Lindsay, *Race Marxism* (Orlando, FL: New Discourses, LLC, 2022); and Helen Pluckrose and James Lindsay, *Cynical Theories: How Activist Scholarship Made Everything about Race, Gender, and Identity-and Why This Harms Everybody* (Durham, NC: Pitchstone Publishing, 2020).

36. Donald Yacovone, *Teaching White Supremacy: America's Democratic Ordeal and the Forging of Our National Identity* (New York: Pantheon Books, 2022), xiv.

"too complicated" for lay audiences. As I tried to respond to each individual point, I began to see that what she called "complicated" were layers of meaning obscured by the universalization of white, cisgender perspectives. For example, she refuted my claim that CPS has been used to police Black mothers, responding that "actions are criminalized, not people." As Dorothy Roberts explains, however, every state institution—including public assistance, education, health care, child welfare, and prisons—participates in the "policing of Black motherhood," resulting in the treatment of particular *people* as criminally suspect.[37]

Due to racial stereotypes, ongoing disenfranchisement, and criminal punishments for outcomes of poverty, Black children are far more likely than their white counterparts to be removed from their parents. The foster care system then establishes a "foster-care-to-prison pipeline"[38] where the vulnerabilities inherent to foster care leave these children far more likely to end up in juvenile detention centers and/or adult prisons. Children who run away from foster care might be forced into sex work or other underground economies, where they are more likely to be arrested. In this way, CPS and the carceral system, in Roberts's words, "*criminalize children.*"[39] When Governor Abbott instructed CPS to investigate gender-affirming families, he then further empowered an institution used to separate and persecute Black families.

The editor, however, responded from a perspective where criminality is a result of one's actions rather than a label assigned to how one is perceived. Like most editors in the United States, she is cisgender, heterosexual, and white.[40] Regardless of intent, her feedback reinforces the presumed universality of white perspectives. Even the *Oxford English Dictionary* provides, as its first definition for "criminalize (v)": "To turn (a person) into a criminal, esp.

---

37. Dorothy Roberts, "How the Child Welfare System Polices Black Mothers," *S&F Online* 15, no. 3 (2019), https://sfonline.barnard.edu/how-the-child-welfare-system-polices-black-mothers/. See also Dorothy E. Roberts, *Torn Apart: How the Child Welfare System Destroys Black Families—and How Abolition Can Build a Safer World* (New York: Basic Books, 2022).

38. Roberts, "How the Child Welfare System Polices Black Mothers."

39. Dorothy [@DorothyERoberts] Roberts, "To Make Matters Worse, Children Who Run Away from Foster Care and Are Forced by Adults or Hunger into Sex Work, Are Often Arrested and Detained. One of the Ways CPS & the PIC Collaborate to Criminalize Children—and Reasons Why We Should Abolish Them," Twitter, February 10, 2022, https://twitter.com/DorothyERoberts/status/1491786283118575632, emphasis added. It is beyond the scope of this chapter, but whiteness also mobilizes immigration policies and enforcement to isolate and "adultify" migrant children. See Laila Hlass, "Adultification of Immigrant Children," *Georgetown Immigration Law Journal* 34, no. 2 (2020): 199–262.

40. Gabriel Arana, "Decades of Failure," *Columbia Journalism Review*, Fall 2018, https://www.cjr.org/special_report/race-ethnicity-newsrooms-data.php/.

by making his or her activities illegal."⁴¹ Her objection then does not emerge from some archaic set of language rules but from an assumption that the US penal system targets behaviors and not people. Dismissing the systemic drivers of criminalization further occludes the ways state institutions serve white wealth and power.

When Ky Peterson, a Black trans man, was arrested for shooting a man *who was in the process of raping him,* the police and the prosecutor claimed Ky did not look like a victim—despite a rape kit that corroborated his story. Ky was sentenced to twenty years in prison and was incarcerated for fifteen years with five years of probation. George Zimmerman, meanwhile, was acquitted for murdering Trayvon Martin while the seventeen-year-old Black boy was walking home. Both cases took place in states with Stand Your Ground (SYG) laws, but only one person appeared entitled to that ground. In criminalizing Peterson and defending Zimmerman's murder of Trayvon Martin, SYG laws codify Black criminality and subordinate Black lives to white (and white-adjacent) property rights.⁴²

Of course, I could not provide a deep history of US law in eight hundred words—let alone do so with enough room for an argument addressing the novel threats of 2022. My revision provided a condensed summation of how systemic racism assigns criminality to people regardless of their actions—how no amount of law-abiding behavior or respectability politics can protect many Black, Indigenous, trans, queer, disabled, and/or poor folks from legal persecution. This was, however, only one of many things I had to explain. The editor also asked that I do the following:

> Define terms such as "cisgender" and "gender dysphoria."
> Explain why trans communities and Black communities are not separate, discrete communities (i.e., explain that Black trans people exist).
> Provide defenses of the single study that describes trans identity as social contagion, which has been widely discredited by experts in the field.
> Explain why white nationalists would want to outnumber people of color.

I hollowed out at least four hundred words from the essay to make room for fundamental definitions. I explained that plenty of people identify as both Black and trans—and that the perspectives of those with multiple marginalized identities can provide (though do not guarantee) more comprehensive

---

41. Oxford English Dictionary, "criminalize, v.," 3rd edition, March 2022, https://www.oed.com/view/Entry/271579?redirectedFrom=criminalize.

42. Caroline E. Light, *Stand Your Ground: A History of America's Love Affair with Lethal Self-Defense* (Boston: Beacon Press, 2017).

views of structural transformation and justice. I provided Lisa Littman's inconsequential defense of her 2018 study. To demonstrate how population control factors into white supremacy, I quoted Tucker Carlson. The Fox News host had helped mainstream the Great Replacement Theory, accusing Democrats of plotting to "import an entirely new electorate from the Third World and change the demographics of the U.S."[43] Even the language of "importation" regards migrant people as commodities—ones that might add to or detract from white capital.

Perhaps I had been assuming too much baseline knowledge on the part of readers. However, other authors that the editor had published used "traditional families" (meaning heteronuclear families) and "liturgy" and "sacrament" (meaning Christian rites) without definition. These words and phrases require knowledge particular to Western Christian contexts—without which they would have different meanings. Writers also frequently invoke Constitutional amendments with little to no explanation, assuming that readers are largely situated in the United States and are conversant in Constitutional law. The "general public" that the publication describes as its audience is delimited by the premises editors and writers leave unstated, which readers must supply. If generalist publications conform to presumed "common knowledge," then the preemptive assumption that trans topics are too marginal for public attention will ensure that majoritarian audiences never have to confront gender diversity. When editors and writers anticipate and tailor to the limitations of cisnormative lenses, then generalist publications can never move beyond rudimentary discussions of gender.

The Premises of Cisnormativity

With the absence of trans-affirming voices in public circulation, public naivete often fills in cisnormative premises to support transphobic conclusions. The term in classical rhetoric is *enthymeme*: a line of reasoning that leaves a premise—usually a shared assumption—unstated. Matthew Jackson unpacked the enthymemes of white supremacy, offering as example:

> Premise (missing): White men are credible witnesses.

---

43. Tucker Carlson quoted in Kaleigh Rogers, "The Twisted Logic behind the Right's 'Great Replacement' Arguments," FiveThirtyEight, May 26, 2022, https://fivethirtyeight.com/features/the-twisted-logic-behind-the-rights-great-replacement-arguments/.

Premise (provided): The officer is a white policeman.
Conclusion: The officer is a credible witness.[44]

The complementary reasoning then follows:

Premise (missing): Nonwhite people are not credible witnesses.
Premise (provided): The victim and their family are not white.
Conclusion: The victim and their family members are not credible witnesses.

A wealth of scholarship has since examined the prominence of enthymemes in white supremacist rhetoric.[45] In disability studies, James Cherney has also considered ableism as enthymematic. Ableist assumptions supply unspoken premises that disability is inherently undesirable, unnatural, or otherwise inferior.[46] Likewise, cisnormativity provides implicit values that render trans people as deviant and/or disposable.

Rhetorics opposing gender-affirming health care, for instance, rely on cisnormative views of gender variance as inherently "unhealthy." The American College of Pediatricians,[47] which has been designated a hate group by the Southern Poverty Law Center, emphasizes that masculinizing hormone replacement therapy (HRT) "rais[es testosterone] levels 10–40 times above the female reference range."[48] They use this point as evidence that "transgender intervention harms children" even though the 10–40 times increase in testosterone is the *purpose* of the intervention and is within the expected range for cisgender men. Likewise, Paxton's legal opinion describes HRT as providing "suprophysiologic doses of testosterone to females" and "suprophysiologic

---

44. Matthew Jackson, "The Enthymematic Hegemony of Whiteness: The Enthymeme as Antiracist Rhetorical Strategy," *JAC* 26, no. 3/4 (2006): 605.

45. Krista Ratcliffe, "In Search of the Unstated: The Enthymeme of/and Whiteness," *JAC* 27, no. 1–2 (2007): 275–89; Martin Camper and Zach Fechter, "Enthymematic Free Space: The Efficacy of Anti-Stop-and-Frisk Arguments in the Face of Racial Prejudice," *Argumentation and Advocacy* 55, no. 4 (2019): 259–81; and Danny Rodriguez, "Countering Racial Enthymemes: What We Can Learn about Race from Donald J. Trump," *Constellations: A Cultural Rhetorics Publishing Space* no. 3 (November 23, 2020), https://constell8cr.com/issue-3/countering-racial-enthymemes-what-we-can-learn-about-race-from-donald-j-trump/.

46. James L. Cherney, "The Rhetoric of Ableism," *Disability Studies Quarterly* 31, no. 3 (2011), https://dsq-sds.org/index.php/dsq/article/view/1665/1606.

47. Not to be confused with the American Academy of Pediatrics, which is the professional association of pediatricians, and endorses gender-affirming care.

48. "Transgender Interventions Harm Children," American College of Pediatricians, https://acpeds.org/transgender-interventions-harm-children (accessed June 11, 2022).

doses of estrogen to males."⁴⁹ The unspoken premise is that these trans people are still inherently cisgender and therefore their hormone treatments should be undesirable. Like most anti-trans politicians, Paxton refuses to recognize trans identity, and he measures trans embodiment by prejudicial standards created to regulate so-called deviant bodies. These are the same metrics that pathologize gender-nonconforming cisgender people like Caster Semenya, whose endogenous hormones exceed the "normal" bounds dictated by Western medicine.

Cisnormative logic appears even more clearly in discourse around "detransitioners"—a term anti-trans activists use for people who once identified as trans but then transitioned back to their sex assigned at birth. The very word "detransition" assumes a linear, binary view of trans experience and maintains cisgender identity as the ideal. So-called "detransitions" are then framed by conservatives as failures—both of the individual and of the medical system. Stories about detransition frequently emphasize the effects of HRT or surgery, focusing on traits that make it difficult for a person to "pass" as cisgender. To support Arkansas's "SAFE" Act, the first law in the United States to prohibit gender-affirming care for minors, Republicans brought in Billy Burleigh. A self-described detransitioner, Burleigh detailed for legislators the process of his genital surgery and its complications⁵⁰—even though no doctors in Arkansas had performed *any* gender-affirming surgeries on minors.⁵¹ Capitalizing on this fear of "irreversible" gender-bending, a "Parent Resource Guide" compiled by major anti-trans organizations emphasizes that cross-sex hormones can cause "the growth of breast tissue in males and a lowered voice in females."⁵² Like Paxton's usage of "supraphysiologic," these claims refer to trans people by their birth-assigned sex and rely on ciscentric bodily norms to suggest that the outcomes of trans medical care are inherently harmful.

These misleading and often overtly false claims about trans people and health care enlist cisgender innocence to complete their reasoning. "A lowered voice in females" is not inherently undesirable, harmful, or negative in any

---

49. Paxton to Krause, "Opinion No. KP-0401," February 18, 2022, 1.

50. House Public Health, Welfare, and Labor Committee, "HB 1570: The Save Adolescents from Experimentation (SAFE) Act," 93rd General Assembly, March 9, 2021, https://senate.arkansas.gov/todays-live-stream-meetings/archived-meetings/.

51. Sabrina Imbler, "In Arkansas, Trans Teens Await an Uncertain Future," *New York Times*, January 18, 2022, https://www.nytimes.com/2022/01/18/health/transgender-adolescents-arkansas.html.

52. Minnesota Family Council, "Responding to the Transgender Issue: Parent Resource Guide" (Family Policy Alliance, The Heritage Foundation, The Kelsey Coalition, Parents of ROGD Kids, and Women's Liberation Front, 2019), 24.

way. Rather, readers are supposed to fill in the assumption that lower voices are unfeminine and therefore misplaced in feminine bodies:

> Premise (missing): Failure to conform to feminine expectations is inherently harmful or undesirable.
> Premise (missing): Lower voices are unfeminine.
> Premise (missing): These transmasculine youth are really cis girls.
> Premise (provided): Testosterone will cause a lower voice in "girls."
> **Conclusion: Testosterone is harmful to "girls."**

Likewise, transitioning more than once is not bad in itself, but cisnormative views presume that gender should be a permanent destination. A genuinely (trans)formative view of gender would allow for infinite plasticity and dynamism throughout one's life. Cisnormativity adds the premise that every change in gender identity is unwelcome—a fact exacerbated by a world that punishes gender variance. Enthymemes are especially powerful in burying hegemonic values so that they become common sense—so that the word "detransitioner" can sound like a tragedy all on its own.

The editor never responded to my revisions. Instead, she contacted an administrator in my university's Office of Public Affairs. Without notifying me, she shared my draft with him. I knew very little about the administrator except that he had published in a major platform for anti-trans journalists and that he had written extensive praise of an author currently proliferating anti-trans misinformation. When he finally reached out to me, it was May. Justice Alito's draft opinion on *Roe v. Wade* had just been leaked. The conservative majority of the US Supreme Court planned to overturn a fifty-year-old decision supporting abortion access. Meanwhile, Alabama declared it a felony to provide gender-affirming care for people younger than nineteen.[53] Meanwhile, Florida's Department of Health issued "guidance" condemning any form of social or medical transition.[54] Meanwhile, South Dakota banned "Critical Race Theory" in K–12 education, and the Florida Department of Education rejected fifty-four math textbooks because they "included references to Critical Race

---

53. Rick Rojas and Tariro Mzezewa, "Alabama Lawmakers Approve Ban on Medical Care for Transgender Youth," *New York Times*, April 7, 2022, https://www.nytimes.com/2022/04/07/us/alabama-transgender-youth-bill.html.

54. "Treatment of Gender Dysphoria for Children and Adolescents," Florida Department of Health, April 20, 2022, https://content.govdelivery.com/accounts/FLDOH/bulletins/3143d4c.

Theory (CRT)" and/or "the unsolicited addition of Social Emotional Learning (SEL)."[55]

I read about the Supreme Court opinion after my plane landed in Florida, where I was being treated at Nova Southeastern University's Institute for Neuro-immune Medicine (INIM). The first research/care facility of its kind in the United States, the INIM specializes in postviral conditions, which medicine has known of since at least the 1960s. In 1969 the World Health Organization named myalgic encephalomyelitis (ME, or sometimes ME/CFS) a neurological disease in the ICD-8. Still poorly understood, ME is a chronic, inflammatory, neuroimmune condition often triggered by a viral infection, more commonly found in people assigned female at birth. By the '80s and '90s it was stereotyped as the "yuppie flu," with some psychiatrists arguing that (cis) women in particular were suffering the consequences of a feminist world. Journalist Hillary Johnson explains the pervasive assumption "that women who get this disease, they almost deserve it, because they stepped out of bounds, they got educations, they got graduate degrees, they were working in professions that men typically work in."[56] This misogynistic premise then encouraged the blatant neglect of ME for many decades.

Even though researchers found ample proof of ME's physiological origins, including immune irregularities, mitochondrial dysfunction, and autopsies that revealed extreme spinal inflammation,[57] the CDC continued to ignore its urgency until 2020. Long COVID emerged as the most recent iteration

---

55. FDOE Press Office, "Florida Rejects Publishers' Attempts to Indoctrinate Students," Florida Department of Education, April 15, 2022, https://www.fldoe.org/newsroom/latest-news/florida-rejects-publishers-attempts-to-indoctrinate-students.stml.

56. Maya Dusenbery, *Doing Harm: The Truth about How Bad Medicine and Lazy Science Leave Women Dismissed, Misdiagnosed, and Sick* (New York: HarperOne, 2017), 261.

57. Mark Vink, "The Aerobic Energy Production and the Lactic Acid Excretion Are Both Impeded in Myalgic Encephalomyelitis/Chronic Fatigue Syndrome," *Journal of Neurology and Neurobiology* 1, no. 4 (2015): 6; Bruce M. Carruthers, Anil Kumar Jain, Kenny L. De Meirleir, Daniel L. Peterson, Nancy G. Klimas, A. Martin Lerner, Alison C. Bested, Pierre Flor-Henry, Pradip Joshi, A. C. Peter Powles, Jeffrey A. Sherkey, and Marjorie I. van de Sande, "Myalgic Encephalomyelitis/Chronic Fatigue Syndrome: Clinical Working Case Definition, Diagnostic and Treatment Protocols," *Journal of Chronic Fatigue Syndrome* 11, no. 1 (2003): 7–115; Sarah Myhill, Norman E. Booth, and John McLaren-Howard, "Targeting Mitochondrial Dysfunction in the Treatment of Myalgic Encephalomyelitis/Chronic Fatigue Syndrome (ME/CFS)—a Clinical Audit," *International Journal of Clinical and Experimental Medicine* 6, no. 1 (2012): 1–15; and Yasuhito Nakatomi, Kei Mizuno, Akira Ishii, Yasuhiro Wada, Masaaki Tanaka, Shusaku Tazawa, Kayo Onoe, Sanae Fukuda, Joji Kawabe, Kazuhiro Takahashi, Yosky Kataoka, Susumu Shiomi, Kouzi Yamaguti, Masaaki Inaba, Hirohiko Kuratsune, Yasuyoshi Watanabe, "Neuroinflammation in Patients with Chronic Fatigue Syndrome/Myalgic Encephalomyelitis: An ^{11}C-(R)-PK11195 PET Study," *Journal of Nuclear Medicine* 55, no. 6 (2014): 945–50.

of postviral illness, and researchers and CDC authorities began comparing long COVID symptoms with those of ME.[58] By 2021, researchers were asking whether long COVID and ME/CFS were really "one and the same."[59] Half a century after ME was identified and named, the US government devoted resources to researching and addressing postviral conditions, but efforts remain slow and opaque.[60]

There have been patient deaths attributed to ME, but one of the condition's most insidious features is that it can bleed so much life without killing you. Like many other patients with chronic illness—and, for that matter, trans people—ME patients are at significantly higher risk for suicide. As with trans people, the elevated suicidality (estimated approximately ten times higher for people with moderate/severe ME than for the general population)[61] is not an innate characteristic, but a product of environments that ignore or even amplify our pain. Studies on both trans people and ME patients are limited by scarce financial investment—a reflection of our perceived value, or lack thereof, for the nation's (re)production. What limited knowledge exists has linked suicidality in ME patients to a lack of resources and understanding, to the loss of employment and relationships, and to chronic and untreated pain.[62] Even if the root cause is still unknown, much of the stigma, the medical maltreatment, and the social ostracization are very much changeable.

---

58. Moises Velasquez-Manoff, "What If You Never Get Better from Covid-19?," *New York Times*, January 21, 2021, https://www.nytimes.com/2021/01/21/magazine/covid-aftereffects.html; and Timothy L. Wong and Danielle J. Weitzer, "Long COVID and Myalgic Encephalomyelitis/Chronic Fatigue Syndrome (ME/CFS)—A Systemic Review and Comparison of Clinical Presentation and Symptomatology," *Medicina* 57, no. 5 (2021): 418.

59. Columbia Public Health, "Is Long COVID Really Chronic Fatigue Syndrome by Another Name?," Columbia Mailman School of Public Health, August 6, 2021, https://www.publichealth.columbia.edu/public-health-now/news/long-covid-really-chronic-fatigue-syndrome-another-name.

60. Rachel Cohrs Zhang, "'A Slow-Moving Glacier': NIH's Sluggish and Often Opaque Efforts to Study Long Covid Draw Patient, Expert Ire," STAT (blog), March 29, 2022, https://www.statnews.com/2022/03/29/nih-long-covid-sluggish-study/.

61. Lily Chu, Meghan Elliott, Eleanor Stein, and Leonard A Jason, "Identifying and Managing Suicidality in Myalgic Encephalomyelitis/Chronic Fatigue Syndrome," *Healthcare* 9, no. 6 (2021): 629.

62. Andrew R. Devendorf, Stephanie L. McManimen, and Leonard A. Jason, "Suicidal Ideation in Non-Depressed Individuals: The Effects of a Chronic, Misunderstood Illness," *Journal of Health Psychology* 25, no. 13–14 (2020): 2106–17; and Stephanie L. McManimen, Damani McClellan, Jamie Stoothoff, Leonard A. Jason, "Effects of Unsupportive Social Interactions, Stigma, and Symptoms on Patients with Myalgic Encephalomyelitis and Chronic Fatigue Syndrome," *Journal of Community Psychology* 46, no. 8 (2018): 959–71.

Gender Illegibility: Missing Premises as Uncommon Knowledge

The administrator's suggestions were rather different from those of the editor. Trusting his promise to help me place this article, I gutted the essay again and filled it with his provisions. While he and I nuanced sentences, the *New York Times* published a misleading overview of medical literature about "detransition." Reporter Azeen Ghorayshi writes: "Research from the 1990s and 2000s had suggested that many children diagnosed with gender identity disorder (a psychological diagnosis that no longer exists) would resolve their gender difficulties after puberty, typically by ages 10 to 13."[63] The article shuffles through predictable both-sidesism, sharing some clinicians' speculations about "peer influence on social media platforms." Claims about "detransition" rely on studies spanning five decades of medical transphobia. Many of these studies were performed on children who did not identify as trans, and some aimed explicitly to *prevent* trans identity.[64] By entertaining speculations about whether adolescents' "gender difficulties" would "resolve," Ghorayshi implicitly endorses cisgender identity as the ideal outcome for trans youth. Ghorayshi also neglects to consult actual trans patients for the article, relying on cisgender researchers' and clinicians' opinions. In doing so, Ghorayshi echoes much of mainstream reporting *and* medical literature, which treat trans people as objects of study rather than as authorities of their own experiences.

When the administrator was satisfied with my revisions, he sent them to the director of his unit, who determined that the essay was not fit for an audience. The brief note that came back to me was a demand that I revise my op-ed to address the "other side." Days after I received this feedback, the news cycle ruptured again. A white supremacist carried an AR-15 into a grocery store in Buffalo, New York, where he murdered ten Black people. The "Great Replacement Theory" that fed this hatred became the focus of public conversation. What the editor had regarded as a "fringe" idea months ago was *now*, too late, of mainstream interest. Within a week of the Buffalo shooting, the editor published an explainer on the Great Replacement Theory. It was authored by two white men, despite the many academics of color who are experts on such

---

63. Azeen Ghorayshi, "Doctors Debate Whether Trans Teens Need Therapy Before Hormones," *New York Times*, January 13, 2022, https://www.nytimes.com/2022/01/13/health/transgender-teens-hormones.html.

64. Julia Temple Newhook, Jake Pyne, Kelley Winters, Stephen Feder, Cindy Holmes, Jemma Tosh, Mari-Lynne Sinnott, Ally Jamieson, and Sarah Pickett, "A Critical Commentary on Follow-up Studies and 'Desistance' Theories about Transgender and Gender-Nonconforming Children," *International Journal of Transgenderism* 19, no. 2 (2018): 212–24.

white supremacist fictions.⁶⁵ A month later, the US Supreme Court formally overturned *Roe v. Wade* and legal scrambles to protect or eliminate abortion ignited across the country.

Days bled together with unrelenting catastrophe. A ten-year-old girl from Ohio was denied an abortion and traveled to Indiana, where the doctor who performed that abortion was placed under investigation. People with autoimmune conditions lost access to medications that could, hypothetically, be used to induce miscarriage.⁶⁶ Brazil Johnson was murdered in Milwaukee, Martasia Richmond in Chicago, and Keshia Chanel Geter in Augusta—all Black trans women between the ages of twenty-six and thirty. The COVID-19 pandemic screamed into its third year, claiming over one million lives in the United States—disproportionately Native American, Pacific Islander, Black, and disabled lives. All this time, mass shootings punctuated the news like a gruesome backbeat: a Taiwanese church in Laguna Woods; an elementary school in Uvalde; a hospital in Tulsa; Chicago, Philadelphia, Chattanooga, Allen, Highland Park, Greenwood, and Maquoteka. By the time (/if) this chapter makes it to print, we will have lost so many more people to preventable illness, to racial violence, to a virulent hatred of trans people, and to the mass death required to sustain white supremacy.

Still, trans people remain the scapegoat for a nation on fire. In Uvalde, Texas, Salvador Ramos massacred nineteen elementary school students and two teachers while 376 police officers stood outside. Users on 4chan circulated a photo of a completely unrelated trans woman from Georgia, claiming she was the shooter.⁶⁷ The theory lit across conservative media, repeated by Arizona Congressman Paul Gosar and the *Daily Wire*'s Candace Owens.⁶⁸ All too predictably, a trans teen in Texas was attacked by four cis men who blamed trans people for the shooting. When the Rainbow Youth Project tried reporting the assault, the El Paso Police Department refused to respond.⁶⁹

---

65. Jodi A. Byrd, *The Transit of Empire: Indigenous Critiques of Colonialism* (Minneapolis: University of Minnesota Press, 2011); Leo R. Chavez, *The Latino Threat: Constructing Immigrants, Citizens, and the Nation*, 2nd edition (Stanford, CA: Stanford University Press, 2013); and Iyko Day, *Alien Capital: Asian Racialization and the Logic of Settler Colonial Capitalism* (Durham, NC: Duke University Press, 2016).

66. Sonja Sharp, "Post-Roe, Autoimmune Patients Lose Access to a Crucial Drug," *Los Angeles Times*, July 11, 2022, https://www.latimes.com/california/story/2022-07-11/post-roe-many-autoimmune-patients-lose-access-to-gold-standard-drug.

67. Jo Yurcaba, Ben Goggin, and Ben Collins, "Trans Woman's Photo Used to Spread Baseless Online Theory about Texas Shooter," NBC News, May 25, 2022, https://www.nbcnews.com/nbc-out/out-news/trans-womans-photo-used-spread-baseless-online-theory-texas-shooter-rcna30511.

68. Yurcaba, Goggin, and Collins, "Trans Woman's Photo."

69. Donald Padgett, "Texas Trans Girl Attacked after False Uvalde Claims Spread Online," *The Advocate*, May 27, 2022, https://www.advocate.com/news/2022/5/27/texas-trans-girl-attacked-after-false-uvalde-claims-spread-online-el-paso.

This transantagonism was not unique to conservative media. When *Roe v. Wade* was overturned, a baffling number of journalists pitted trans inclusion against the rights of cisgender women. In *The Atlantic*, Helen Lewis opined that "the left has declared a war on saying 'women.'"[70] The *New York Times*' Michael Powell claimed that "women" is a "vanishing word" in the "abortion debate,"[71] and Pamela Paul lamented, "In a world of chosen gender identities, women as a biological category don't exist."[72] These authors, echoing the broader anti-trans narrative, often referred to trans men and women interchangeably. Paul's complaint, for example, was that using the phrase "pregnant people" to include trans men and nonbinary people was "erasing women." As evidence, though, she argued that cis women had been so "accommodating" by allowing trans women into "[implicitly cis] women's" spaces. Paul's writing ignores the many transmasculine and nonbinary people who need abortion access, and the many barriers we already face in attaining such care. By insisting on "women" as the most accurate label for those who need abortion access, and accusing transmasculine folks of erasing "women," she ironically erases trans women. Reflecting most conversations around reproductive choice, Paul's article regards abortion-related activism—and other "women's" spaces—as the rightful territory of cisgender women, establishing grounds on which all trans people become intruders. Moreover, this argument about femininity being assailed by gender variance draws from a long history of white femininity—and white women's victimhood—justifying the murder, incarceration, and expulsion of people of color.[73]

Paul's messy conflation of trans people, like the unabashed misrepresentation of gender-affirming care, depends on audience illiteracy in gender dynamism—a strategic forgetting of how colonialism continues to contrive and regulate gender norms. When binary gender is the unchallenged standard, many expressions of gender difference appear "too complicated" to parse. "Complicated," in this case, means that the premises that would provide clarity are *not* common knowledge and are not given public space to *become* common knowledge:

---

70. Helen Lewis, "The Abortion Debate Is Suddenly About 'People,' Not 'Women,'" *The Atlantic*, May 14, 2022, https://www.theatlantic.com/ideas/archive/2022/05/abortion-rights-debate-women-gender-neutral-language/629863/.

71. Michael Powell, "A Vanishing Word in Abortion Debate: 'Women,'" *New York Times*, June 8, 2022, https://www.nytimes.com/2022/06/08/us/women-gender-aclu-abortion.html.

72. Paul, "The Far Right and Far Left Agree on One Thing."

73. For more on the role of white femininity—and victimhood—in enforcing colonial structures of race and gender, see Hannah Noel, *Deflective Whiteness: Co-Opting Black and Latinx Identity Politics* (Columbus: The Ohio State University Press, 2022).

Premise (stated): Some people are advocating for trans-inclusive language in struggles for abortion access.

Premise (missing): Strict gender roles are integral to white supremacist movements.

Premise (missing): Enforcing strict gender roles involves both the control of cis women's bodies and reproductive options *and* the erasure/elimination of transgender people.

Conclusion (missing): Anti-abortion and anti-trans politics serve the *same* right-wing agenda.

With the undercurrent of whiteness buried in historical silence, conservatives stoke transantagonism as political diversion. As white gender norms condition the very limited public vocabulary for gender variance, anti-trans movements are free to equate trans identity with prosecutable sexual behaviors, further stigmatizing and—yes—criminalizing gender-nonconforming people.

This blanket persecution of gender variance can be seen in a viral tweet by conservative journalist Andy Ngo. Ngo shared a video of "drag story time" from DC Pride, which should have been mundane footage if it weren't for extant assumptions about gender diversity. The video shows a person in a red dress seated before a young audience, reading from a picture book. Ngo's caption reads: "There was a drag queen story time event for young children at the Capitol Pride Parade event in Washington, DC."[74] Ngo's straightforward statement leaves the central premise unsaid: that there is something inherently perverse about drag queens sharing time with children. His audience leaps to that conclusion with him, with replies such as "Parents of these kids should be sent to jail" and "Child services where are you?"[75] The outrage Ngo provokes depends on white, cisgender norms as the unmarked standard by which all other experiences are assessed. Because cisnormativity assigns deviance to any divergence from gender norms, and because cisgender people are often sheltered from worlds beyond gender normativity, conservatives use innocuous images and videos of drag queens as spectacles. Had the drag queen been a cisgender woman in the same dress reading the same book in the same setting, it would be unimaginable for conservatives to espouse the same anger—let alone for Ngo's scant description to elicit calls for imprisonment or CPS

---

74. Andy [@MrAndyNgo] Ngô, "There Was a Drag Queen Story Time Event for Young Children at the Capitol Pride Parade Event in Washington, DC. Video by @MiaCathell," Twitter, June 12, 2022, https://twitter.com/MrAndyNgo/status/1535849526514286593.

75. SFA—квино [@Kwinoh_], "Child Services Where Are You??," Twitter, June 12, 2022, https://twitter.com/Kwinoh_/status/1535853262473142273.

investigations. The recent moral panic around drag queens[76] then relies on audiences to hold and enforce normative conceptions of gender—and of what sorts of identities are criminal.

Many journalists, health care providers, and politicians have accurately described attacks on trans youth as "solving a problem that doesn't exist."[77] More than that, though, they are marking trans people *as* the problem while *creating* crises that trans communities must address. Trans people are already particularly vulnerable to discrimination across professional, educational, and social contexts. The legislative climate has diverted attention from the monumental work of combating extant transphobia—and its accompanying racism, ableism, and misogyny. The hundreds of bills assailing trans youths' access to health care, to sports participation, to inclusive classrooms, or to quite frankly take up public space has consumed the already-scarce resources available to trans communities. Meanwhile, Republicans' transantagonistic maneuvering has placed gender-affirming families under investigation, forced trans people out of their home states, denied trans youth desperately needed care that has harmed their well-being, and excluded them from school curricula and athletic participation.

These new crises are important and demand attention. They are also, however, largely experienced by better-resourced, middle- and upper-class trans people. In the United States, even basic health care remains largely inaccessible to many transgender people.[78] As difficult and unjust as it is to be forced out of one's home state due to discriminatory policies, many families do not have the resources or freedom to relocate. As important as athletics are—for all the reasons that Republicans recite in their attacks on trans women—sports participation alone will not address the pervasive bullying faced by trans and gender-nonconforming children, the discrimination they'll encounter in classrooms and workplaces, or their vulnerability to family rejection and housing instability. When conservatives channel their resources and attention into manufactured problems, they also direct *our* resources and attention away from conditions that *already* endanger vulnerable trans people.

---

76. Melissa Gira Grant, "The Right-Wing War on Trans Youth Was Hiding in Plain Sight," *New Republic*, May 4, 2021, https://newrepublic.com/article/162289/republican-war-trans-youth-drag-queen-story-hour.

77. Stephen Gruber-Miller, "Transgender Girls Would Be Barred from Playing Girls' Sports under Iowa Republican Bill," *Des Moines Register*, February 9, 2022, https://www.desmoinesregister.com/story/news/politics/2022/02/09/iowa-house-republicans-propose-bill-restricting-transgender-athletes-girls-sports/6726829001/.

78. Ayden I. Scheim, Kellan E. Baker, Arjee J. Restar, and Randall L. Sell, "Health and Health Care among Transgender Adults in the United States," *Annual Review of Public Health* 43, no. 1 (2022): 503–23.

Whiteness then operates as rhetorical obstruction on multiple levels in anti-trans politics. In motivating the aggressive dismantling of transgender health care, it creates additional challenges for communities that often already struggle to find safety and security. By embedding and excusing ignorance about gender diversity in our everyday communication, whiteness-as-cisnormativity constrains the arguments that can be made effectively and concisely in public arenas. Finally, when editors and other gatekeepers *anticipate* and then cater to that ignorance, they further limit the rhetorical possibilities around trans politics and liberation. If messaging about trans health care needs to reiterate medical "best practices" all the time just to counter unabashed disinformation, then it will be all the more difficult to critique the very limiting logics behind those medical practices.[79] And, it will be exceptionally hard to make legible a world where *all* trans people—not just those who want to and can conform to cis-adjacent embodiment—can be safe and free.

Notably, these patterns are not particular to transgender politics. Rhetoric that bends to majoritarian views will perpetuate majoritarian values. What results are often "top down" approaches to "justice" that focus on the needs of those with better access to public platforms and whose stories are more legible—and sympathetic—to mainstream audiences. As a technology of attention, rhetoric can also redirect our focus. It can tell the stories of those most affected and trace their experiences to the institutions that perpetuate far-reaching harm. That is, I'm telling you this story not because I need you to relate to it, or to even arrive at my same conclusions, but because I hope it might help map the sprawling reach of white supremacy and a shared need to dismantle its machinations.

Coda: On Courage and Complexity

In my first year of my first faculty position, a colleague asked me for input on his syllabus. He was teaching a new course exploring literary and philosophical works on "justice." He shared with me a semester's worth of readings by canonical white men and requested that I help fill the one week he'd designated for "women, people of color, and LGBTQ" authors and theorists. I wrote back emphasizing that women, people of color, queer folks, and all those at

---

79. Jules Gill-Peterson, *Histories of the Transgender Child* (Minneapolis: University of Minnesota Press, 2018); Stef M. Shuster, *Trans Medicine: The Emergence and Practice of Treating Gender* (New York: New York University Press, 2021); and Hil Malatino, *Queer Embodiment: Monstrosity, Medical Violence, and Intersex Experience* (Lincoln: University of Nebraska Press, 2019).

the intersections of those identities had done groundbreaking work on the ideas he was exploring. I appended a long list of readings that aligned with the themes of his course, pointing to ways they might complement his curriculum beyond the single week. He responded by thanking me for the suggestion but added that concepts like intersectionality were "too complicated" for his students.

We taught the same students. Across the universities where I have worked, students have deftly applied challenging concepts that dis/articulate mechanisms of power, working from a vast range of positionalities and backgrounds. I have witnessed the ways these vocabularies augment students' approaches to their own histories, to their communities, and to the ways they engage others. I have *been* that student—simultaneously awed and furious at how long it took me to find words for the coercions and complicities that have shaped my life. I continue to be that student, my worldview expanding with the classes I teach, with the colleagues who engage me, and with every generous conversation that stretches across difference.

Surrounded by so much hostility, I sometimes wonder how far words can really take us. I also remember the feats small and large that words have enacted for me—how *queer* splayed open a world of breathtaking possibility; how *ableism* lifted me from isolation and self-blame; how *postviral illness* connected millions of ME/CFS patients with the millions more experiencing long COVID. I remember the gift it was to watch a student grasp how *compulsory heterosexuality* exposes normative life paths and how *disability justice* envisions a world where humans are valued regardless of their capacity for labor and production. I don't think the colleague and I differ in teaching ability. Rather, I trusted my students to grapple with "complex" concepts, and they trusted I would direct them toward knowledge that was worth the struggle.

No single perspective can hold the complexity of a world wrought of animus and domination. We could each spend a lifetime prying our hearts open to the wounds and fears of others and never come close to grasping the expanse of human experience—all the myriad ways we can hurt and soothe one another. But I do think that it's worth trying; there are too many lives at stake. As we careen into a third year of a global pandemic—quite possibly a fourth by the time this chapter goes to print—I am thinking about the 7 percent of all US adults who are currently experiencing long COVID, who are disproportionately trans, disproportionately Latinx or multiracial, and who must survive this world that refuses to heed their suffering.[80] The causes of

---

80. Center for Disease Control and Prevention, "Long COVID—Household Pulse Survey," July 19, 2022, https://www.cdc.gov/nchs/covid19/pulse/long-covid.htm.

these health disparities are, well, intersectional. I am writing with the hope that words can still be liberatory practice, with the faith that someone is willing to meet the challenges of connection. So tell me, reader, what is the shortest distance between where you and I each begin? What stories will carry us across?

AFTERWORD

The Endgame of Whiteness

THOMAS K. NAKAYAMA

This collection of essays on whiteness highlights the contemporary rhetorics of whiteness through fascinating case studies. Whiteness, of course, is not monolithic, and there is no singular rhetoric of whiteness that defines it. However, it should be noted that it functions and reproduces itself from a position of power and privilege that sets it apart from other racial rhetorics in the United States.

I've long thought about the issues facing whiteness and how whiteness functions to resecure its social position of power in a range of contexts. Over the past forty years, I've watched whiteness morph in various ways, highlighting its dynamic nature. And I've also watched it retain some of its same rhetorical strategies that point to its enduring static nature. In 1995, I argued that whiteness was a strategic rhetoric as it resecured its unique and privileged position through rhetorical strategies that come from a position of power.[1]

When the COVID-19 pandemic settled over the United States, health researchers noted the differential impact that it was having on Brown and Black people. Three years later, racial differentials concerning COVID-19 have shifted as white people are now dying at a higher rate than any other racial/

---

1. Thomas K. Nakayama and Robert L. Krizek, "Whiteness: A Strategic Rhetoric," *Quarterly Journal of Speech* 81, no. 3 (1995): 291–309.

ethnic group.² In the intervening three years, from 2020 to 2023, we have witnessed a range of discourses that have shaped people's responses to the virus. It has been racialized, for example, as the "China virus" or "Kung flu." Resistance to the vaccines and mask mandates had been organized as a move toward "freedom." Various solutions were offered that were not medically supported, such as taking Ivermectin.

This change in the impact of COVID-19 on white people has led me to wonder if we are beginning to see the endgame of whiteness as it confronts a rapidly changing, racially diverse society in the context of globalization. This decline in the white population, due to a variety of factors, is challenging whiteness. At first glance, the rhetorical discourses that argue against vaccination and against wearing masks appear anything but strategic.

In August 2017, the "Unite the Right" rally was held at the University of Virginia and the city of Charlottesville, Virginia. At this rally, white nationalists chanted, "Jews will not replace us," among other slogans.³ For many Americans, this event brought the Great Replacement Theory to the front and center of racial rhetorics. This theory posits that nonwhites will replace whites and that this phenomenon is something to fear. In contemporary writing, increased references to this theory have been "attributed to Renaud Camus, a French writer who wrote 'Le Grand Remplacement' (which translates to 'The Great Replacement') in 2011."⁴ Interestingly, "although 'The Great Replacement' has never been published in English, it has been translated on far-right websites and endorsed by white supremacist Richard Spencer and disgraced former Iowa congressman Steve King."⁵ Camus is more concerned about the replacement of white people with Muslim immigrants in France, but his ideas are also used to fit the situation in the United States. In France, the national census does not classify people into racial categories. In contrast, the US Census identifies Middle Eastern/North Africans as "white," although attempts

---

2. Akilah Johnson and Dan Keating, "Whites Now More Likely to Die from Covid than Blacks: Why the Pandemic Shifted," *Washington Post*, October 19, 2022, https://www.washingtonpost.com/health/2022/10/19/covid-deaths-us-race/.

3. Hawes Spencer and Sheryl Gay Stolberg, "White Nationalists March on the University of Virginia," *New York Times*, August 11, 2017, https://www.nytimes.com/2017/08/11/us/white-nationalists-rally-charlottesville-virginia.html.

4. Dustin Jones, "What Is the 'Great Replacement' and How Is It Tied to the Buffalo Shooting Suspect?," NPR, May 16, 2022, https://www.npr.org/2022/05/16/1099034094/what-is-the-great-replacement-theory.

5. Gillian Brockell, "The Father of 'Great Replacement': An Ex-Socialist French Writer," *Washington Post*, May 17, 2022, https://www.washingtonpost.com/history/2022/05/17/renaud-camus-great-replacement-history/.

were made to create a different category for them in the 2020 Census. They are not simply "white" or "other" in the United States.[6]

While some think that "the 'great replacement' theory has roots in French nationalism books dating back to the early 1900s,"[7] others note that "these theories were popularised by the 1916 book *The Passing of the Great Race*, written by Madison Grant, a lawyer, eugenicist and conservationist from New York."[8] I am less interested in identifying the "origin" of this replacement theory, whether from French intellectual history or American intellectual history or somewhere else, but I suspect that it has much deeper roots than either of these two traditions. The nineteenth-century Chinese Exclusion Act points to an earlier concern about race and immigration.

In his book, *Dying of Whiteness: How the Politics of Racial Resentment Is Killing America's Heartland,* Jonathan Metzl uses the metaphor of the castle, which represents the self-destructive and obfuscating promise of fortifying white supremacy against external challenges, to describe the ways that whiteness has embedded its own inability to respond to health crises.[9] In his case, Metzl focused on the Affordable Care Act (ACA) and the ways that larger institutions responded to it. For example, a number of states refused to expand Medicaid for their residents, even though its expansion would have helped millions of people. Although he focused on the ACA, Metzl's analysis is relevant to the nation's response to COVID-19.

COVID-19, of course, is not limited to any racial or ethnic group. An effective response to the virus would involve collaborating and working with others across racial and ethnic groups. Instead, calls to get vaccinated were met with resistance among some Americans who did not trust the medical experts. Mask mandates were also seen as another example of government overreach that compromised our "freedom." Flight attendants were one of the groups that received a lot of push back when enforcing the mask mandate. By the end of April 2022, when the mask mandate was dropped by a federal

---

6. Marie-Odile Hobeika and Thomas K. Nakayama, "Check-mate: The MENA/Arab Double Bind," in *Negotiating Identity and Transnationalism: Middle Eastern and North African Communication and Critical Cultural Studies,* ed. Haneen Ghabra, Fatima Zahrae Chrifi Alaoui, Shadee Abdi, and Bernadette Marie Calafell (New York: Peter Lang, 2020), 14–31.

7. Jones, "What Is the 'Great Replacement.'"

8. Steve Rose, "A Deadly Ideology: How the 'Great Replacement Theory' Went Mainstream," *The Guardian,* June 8, 2022, https://www.theguardian.com/world/2022/jun/08/a-deadly-ideology-how-the-great-replacement-theory-went-mainstream.

9. Jonathan M. Metzl, *Dying of Whiteness: How the Politics of Racial Resentment Is Killing America's Heartland* (New York: Basic Books, 2019).

judge's ruling, there had already been 807 unruly passenger events according to the Federal Aviation Administration.[10]

Metzl's castle highlights the ways that the threat to whiteness comes from outside the castle. These threats to whiteness are reinforced by rhetorical moves such as former president Trump naming the virus the "China virus." Immediately afterward, the hashtag #chinavirus began trending on Twitter and was associated with racist content when compared to tweets that used the hashtag #covid19.[11]

Although it is probably not necessary to point out that white Americans are not the indigenous people of the United States, fears about replacement recognize the tenuous nature of claims about who belongs and what our society looks like. For example, when white people tell Others to go back to wherever they came from, they assert a claim on indigenousness that only whiteness can make.[12] Sometimes called nativism, this rhetoric positions white people as the true natives to the United States.

It may seem ironic that the white Europeans who engaged in a great replacement themselves are now concerned about being replaced. This means that "counterarguments to the great replacement theory would point out that, if anyone has grounds for complaint, it is the Indigenous people of North and South America, Australia and New Zealand, Africa and many other parts of the world, who have been 'replaced' by colonial settlers."[13] Yet the rhetoric of whiteness has tried to position white people as victims of a global world in which they—the "indigenous" people of the United States—are being replaced.

Rather than viewing this claim to victimage as ironic, I want to suggest that whiteness knows that whiteness is fragile as it rests on a rhetorical notion of indigeneity and belongingness that does not exist. Based on its history, whiteness knows that it has replaced Indigenous people. The status of whiteness can be challenged, and others may replace this claim. The fear is that Others may follow a similar path and claim indigeneity and belongingness that displaces the current ideological holders of the title "Americans."

This pattern of whiteness is repeated worldwide. When we think of "Australians," we tend to imagine the people who descended from European

---

10. Nathan Diller, "Mask Police No More: Flight Attendants Relieved to See Mandate Dropped," *Washington Post*, April 27, 2022, https://www.washingtonpost.com/travel/2022/04/27/flight-attendants-mask-mandate-drops/.

11. Yulin Hswen, Xiang Xu, Anna Hing, Jared B. Hawkins, John S. Brownstein, and Gilbert C. Lee, "Association of '#covid19' Versus '#chinesevirus' with Anti-Asian Sentiments on Twitter: March 9–23, 2020," *American Journal of Public Health* 111, no. 5 (2021): 956–64.

12. At particular points in this essay, I capitalize Other(s) to refer to those who fall outside of an imagined community of indigenous white people worldwide.

13. Rose, "Deadly Ideology."

immigrants and not the Indigenous people. This pattern repeats with "Canadians" and, of course, "Americans." Within the framework of whiteness, it makes sense to tell Others to "go back to where you came from." This phrase is so well-established in contemporary rhetoric that it serves as the title of a book by a Pakistani American author who reflects on his own experiences with prejudice, whiteness, and American culture.[14] The demand that one should "go back" functions as a strategic rhetoric that defends whiteness from outsiders.

Here we can see the self-destructive nature of Metzl's castle. The threat is constructed as outside of whiteness. Whatever is not white is the threat, despite the notion that whiteness itself is a rhetorical construction. Yet this notion does not relieve the tensions that fuel replacement theory and the changing social landscape. The data note: "In the US, the white population fell for the first time in history in the 2020 census. Proportionally, white Americans are at all-time low, making up 61.6% of the population, compared with 72.4% in 2010 and almost 90% in 1940."[15] These changes can be viewed as replacement. Whiteness is not positioned to work with Others to take on contemporary challenges such as COVID-19. It cannot see beyond whiteness, as whiteness is an overarching worldview.

In response to these changing demographics, the rise of Trumpism can be seen as a response. "Making America Great Again" reflects a nostalgia for a past in which whiteness was normative and not challenged. The castle is embracing a view of whiteness in which there is an urgent need to regain the assumed connection between whiteness, power, and Americanness. Yet this has resulted in a rise in fascist tendencies. Despite fascism being "riddled with internal contradictions, but no less of a threat to democracy. Donald Trump is an aspiring autocrat out solely for his own power and material gain. By giving this movement a classically authoritarian leader, Trump shaped and exacerbated it, and his time in politics has normalized it."[16]

Here I wonder if the endgame of whiteness is not to accept being a minority among many other racial minorities in the United States but instead to embrace a nondemocratic fascism that keeps whiteness in power, or to bring down the nation if whiteness cannot be the powerful force that calls all the shots? Is it not worth living in a nation where whiteness is no longer the powerful force that it once was? These are all questions that need to be addressed, as we see what happens in the coming years. Will white Americans continue

---

14. Wajahat Ali, *Go Back to Where You Came from and Other Helpful Recommendations on How to Become American* (New York: W. W. Norton, 2022).

15. Rose, "Deadly Ideology."

16. Jason Stanley, "America Is Now in Fascism's Legal Phase," *The Guardian*, December 22, 2021, https://www.theguardian.com/world/2021/dec/22/america-fascism-legal-phase.

to be the primary group dying from COVID-19? As their numbers continue to decline, will there be more desperation to grasp on to a past that is no longer attainable? There is a lot at stake here, and I urge everyone to pay attention and think about what is happening. If the endgame of whiteness is to destroy the castle, rather than living in a castle where whiteness is not dominant, then the strategies to maintain white domination in the castle will become even more extreme. We have time to choose an alternative path in building a different castle, but whiteness is strategic. It comes with power. Therefore, the threat to the castle may be within the castle of whiteness. My point runs counter to the way that whiteness views the threat to the castle: the threat to Metzl's castle is not always outside the castle.

CONTRIBUTORS

GODFRIED ASANTE (he/him) is an associate professor of communication at San Diego State University. He has a PhD in intercultural communication from the University of New Mexico. Asante's primary areas of research include human rights, critical dialogue, and intercultural communication. The goal of his research is to identify ways to build individual and organizational capacity of LGBTQI-focused human rights NGOs and activists and to develop culturally relevant ways to do human rights advocacy work in international settings. He has published essays in journals including *Howard Journal of Communications*, *Communication Theory*, and *Quarterly Journal of Speech*.

ROBERT ASEN (he/him) is the Stephen E. Lucas Professor of Rhetoric, Politics, and Culture in the Communication Arts Department at the University of Wisconsin–Madison. Engaging relationships among rhetoric, critical theory, and the public sphere, Asen explores ideas and practices that may promote just, equal, and free democracies as well as contemporary threats to democracy like neoliberalism, white nationalism, and authoritarianism. Asen is the author of numerous books, including, most recently, *School Choice and the Betrayal of Democracy: How Market-Based Education Reform Fails Our Communities* (2021), and he has coedited multiple volumes, including *Text + Field: Innovations in Rhetorical Method* (2016).

CHARLES ATHANASOPOULOS (he/him) is an assistant professor of African American and African Studies and English at The Ohio State University. His research interests lie at the intersection of Black rhetorical studies, cultural studies, and media studies. His forthcoming book project, *Black Iconoclasm: Public Symbols, Racial Progress, and*

Post/Ferguson America, offers an alternative approach to thinking about Blackness and iconoclasm aimed toward uprooting the rigid social codes of Western man.

PAULAMI BANERJEE (she/her/hers) is a postdoctoral researcher at the State University of New York, College of Environmental Science and Forestry. She completed her doctoral degree in environmental science and engineering from the University of Texas at El Paso, along with a visiting assistant professorship at Boise State University and a postdoctoral research fellowship and lectureship at the University of Texas at Austin. She has published journal articles and book chapters related to her scholarship on global environmental conservation and politics, such as her extensive multisited ethnographic fieldwork in East Sikkim, India, on adaptive natural resource management and public participation.

ANNE BONDS (she/her) is a professor of geography and urban studies at the University of Wisconsin-Milwaukee whose research interests include urban political economy, race, racialization, racial capitalism, carceral and abolition geographies, and the geographies of white supremacy in the United States. She is an editor of *Urban Geography* and past chair of the Urban Geography Specialty Group of the Association of American Geographers. Bonds received the 2022 American Association of Geographer's Ruby and Wilbur Miller Award. Together with Derek Handley, she directs a project mapping all racially restrictive covenants filed in Milwaukee County—and Black resistance to them—between the years of 1910 and 1960.

LINSAY M. CRAMER (she/her/hers) is an associate professor in the Department of Communication, Media, & Culture at Coastal Carolina University. Her research focuses on critical intercultural and rhetorical analysis of whiteness, race, and masculinity in popular film, television, and sports media. Much of her research unearths how power is established, perpetuated, and resisted in popular culture and sport via mediated narratives, representations, and constructions. Her research can be found in *Critical Studies in Media Communication, Rhetoric Society Quarterly, Communication & Sport, Communication Studies, Howard Journal of Communications, Southern Communication Journal*, and others as well as edited volumes.

DEREK G. HANDLEY (he/him) is an assistant professor in the English Department, affiliated faculty in African and African Diaspora Studies Department, and affiliated faculty in the Urban Studies Program at the University of Wisconsin-Milwaukee. He is codirector of the Mapping Racism and Resistance in Milwaukee County (MRR-MKE) project, which comprehensively maps racial covenants and uncovers Black resistance to such discrimination. His forthcoming book, *Struggle for the City: Citizenship and Resistance during the Black Freedom Movement*, examines the rhetorical strategies used by African American communities in Milwaukee, Pittsburgh, and St. Paul to resist urban renewal in the 1950s and 1960s.

V. JO HSU (they/them) is an assistant professor of rhetoric and writing at the University of Texas at Austin and the author of *Constellating Home: Trans and Queer Asian American Rhetorics*. They study storytelling as political strategy, and their current research examines anti-trans rhetorics, contested illnesses, and the politics of diagnoses. Most of their work can be found at www.vjohsu.com.

KELLY JENSEN (she/her) is an assistant professor of communication at the University of Wisconsin Whitewater at Rock County. She conducts research at the intersection of critical whiteness studies and the rhetoric of K–12 education. Her most recent work documents how white progressive parents influence unequal systems of privilege through their school choice discourse. She has published essays in the *Quarterly Journal of Speech* and *Communication and the Public*. Jensen's research is informed by her experience as a former K–12 public school teacher and her commitment as a white academic to deconstructing the rhetorical circulation of white supremacist logics.

CASEY RYAN KELLY (he/him) is a professor of rhetoric and public culture in the Department of Communication Studies at the University of Nebraska. He is the author of five books, including *Caught on Tape: White Masculinity and Obscene Enjoyment* (Oxford University Press, 2023). He is the recipient of numerous awards from the National Communication Association, including the Karl R. Wallace Memorial Award and the Franklyn S. Haiman Award for Distinguished Scholarship in Freedom of Expression.

KYLE R. LARSON (he/him) is a PhD candidate at Miami University and English professor at St. Clair County Community College. He researches community organizing and social movement rhetorics with specific emphases on counterpublics and parasitic publics. His published writing appears in *Rhetoric Society Quarterly, Peitho,* and the *Journal of Contemporary Rhetoric*. He has received several local and national awards for research, teaching, and service—including receipt of the 2020 Outstanding Article Award from the Critical/Cultural Studies Division of the National Communication Association for his coauthored essay (with Guy McHendry) "Parasitic Publics." He can best be contacted via krlarson@sc4.edu.

GEORGE (GUY) F. McHENDRY JR. (he/him/his) is an associate professor of communication studies and the Timms Endowed Professor and Director of the Magis Core Curriculum at Creighton University in Omaha, Nebraska. He researches in the areas of rhetoric theory and criticism, privacy and surveillance, argumentation theory, and extremist rhetoric. McHendry earned his PhD in communication from the University of Utah. McHendry is the lead author of *The Rhetoric of Western Thought* (11th ed.). He teaches a variety of courses including "Rhetoric and Public Culture," "Gender Communication," "Resisting the Politics of Everyday Life," and "Communication and Community."

THOMAS K. NAKAYAMA (he/him/his) is a professor of communication studies at Northeastern University. He is coauthor of *Intercultural Communication in Contexts, Experiencing Intercultural Communication,* and *Human Communication in Society*. He is coeditor of *Whiteness: The Communication of Social Identity* and *The Handbook of Critical Intercultural Communication*. He is the founding editor of the *Journal of International and Intercultural Communication* and the cofounding editor of *QED:*

A Journal in GLBTQ Worldmaking. He was a Fulbrighter at the Université de Mons (Belgium). He is a Western States Communication Association distinguished scholar, an Eastern Communication Association distinguished research fellow, and a National Communication Association distinguished scholar.

ADEDOYIN OGUNFEYIMI (he/him) is an assistant professor of English and Black rhetorics at the University of Pittsburgh. He holds a PhD in English from the University of Wisconsin–Madison. Ogunfeyimi, who is on the editorial board of the *Quarterly Journal of Speech*, received the CEA Robert Hacke Teacher-Scholar Award and the NCTE Early Career Educator of Color Award in 2022. He also contributed to a special issue of the *Review of Communication* on (Re)theorizing Communication Studies from African Perspectives, which won the NCA Distinguished Edited Journal Award in Philosophy of Communication and the Ethnography Division Best Special Issue Award in 2023.

RICO SELF (he/him) (PhD, Louisiana State University) is a native of the Mississippi Delta and an assistant professor in the Department of Communication and an affiliate faculty member in the Women's, Gender and Sexuality Studies program at North Carolina State University at Raleigh. Self's research explores the intersections of communication, race, sexuality, and media. Self has published in such journals as *QED: A Journal in GLBTQ Worldmaking, Women's Studies in Communication,* and *Communication and Critical/Cultural Studies*. Self's scholarship was recognized with the 2021 Gerald R. Miller Outstanding Doctoral Dissertation Award from the National Communication Association.

STACEY K. SOWARDS (she/her) holds the Mark L. Knapp Professorship in the Department of Communication Studies at the University of Texas at Austin. She is the editor of the *Quarterly Journal of Speech* (2023–25) and the author of numerous journal articles and book chapters, as well as the 2019 book, *¡Sí, ella puede! The Rhetorical Legacy of Dolores Huerta and the United Farm Workers,* published by the University of Texas Press.

CORINNE MITSUYE SUGINO (she/they) is an assistant professor of English and Asian American Studies at The Ohio State University. Drawing on interdisciplinary scholarship in Asian American studies, cultural studies, rhetorical theory, and media studies, Sugino's research explores the interplay between narrative, Asian Americans, and the racialized construction of the human. For more information, please visit www.corinnesugino.com.

INDEX

AAPI (Asian American and Pacific Islander) peoples: advocates for, 26, 145–46, 148–50, 157–61, 166–67; and Black people, 147, 152–54; violence against, 150–51. *See also* Asian Americans

Abbott, Greg, 193, 202

ability, and race issues, 34, 38, 107, 116

ableism, 205, 216

abortion, 196, 200. See also *Roe v. Wade*

ACA (Affordable Care Act), 220

affect and affects, 12–14, 171–75, 191

affective economies, 12–14, 169–75, 178, 181, 182, 186, 187–88, 192

affirmative action, 33, 34–35, 40, 41, 43

Affordable Care Act, 220

African Students Association, 114

agency, 15–18, 118, 144, 159, 166–67

Ahmed, Sara, 12, 82, 172, 173, 181

Alabama, laws of, 207

Alcoff, Linda Martín, 82

Allende, Salvador, 119

Amaya, Hector, 101, 105, 110, 111, 114, 115; *Citizenship Excess*, 103

ambiguity, in white identity, 84–88

American Academy of Pediatrics, 205n47

American College of Pediatricians, 205

American Magnitude (Olson), 102

Angelou, Maya: "Still I Rise," 49–50

anti-Blackness, 8, 34, 45–46, 49, 50, 64, 66–69, 154

anti-CRT rhetoric, 168–70, 201; context of, 173; and emotions, 186–91; as frontlash, 175, 184, 186, 191; and manufactured crises, 180–81, 186; methods used in, 181–84; targets of, 176, 177

Anya, Uju, 124–25

Arbery, Ahmaud, 179

Arison, Micky, 162

articulations: alternative, 182–84; of identity, 159; parasitic, 176, 181, 185–86, 192; of race, 55, 147–48; rhetorical, 174–75, 180–82, 190

ASA (African Students Association), 114

Asian Americans, 26, 38–42, 50, 145–46, 148, 151, 155, 165. *See also* AAPI (Asian American and Pacific Islander) peoples

Asians, 104, 131

229

230 • INDEX

assemblages, 169–70, 171, 173–74, 180–81, 186–88. *See also* discursive assemblages
assimilation, 99, 103–4, 111, 129, 143, 183, 184
Athanasopoulos, Charles, 24–25, 36
attention, 22, 106–7, 155–56, 188–89, 215

Bahrainwala, Lamiyah, 22
Bakke, Allan, 34–35
Barbee, Lloyd, 60
Berlant, Lauren, 101, 104, 115–16, 117–18
Beverly Hills neighborhood (Wauwatosa, WI), 69–70
Bezos, Jeff, 124
Biden, Joe, 24, 29–30, 32–33, 34, 35–37, 38–39, 45–46
BIPOC (Black, Indigenous, and People of Color), 163
"Black Belt," 59
Black Lives Matter Global Network, 35
Black Lives Matter movement, 148, 151, 153–54
Black Looks (hooks), 139
Black people: and AAPI peoples, 145–46, 152–54; and Asian Americans, 41–44; and CPS, 202–3; disadvantages for, 5–6, 9; as domestic laborers, 184–85; and housing, 8, 58–63; and integration, 136; and political expediency, 35–38; as property, 72–73; and property ownership, 8; social death of, 125–26, 130, 139–40, 143; and violence, 137. *See also* women, Black
Blackness: and identity, 19–20; and masculinity, 183–84; and nihilism, 129–32; and populism, 14; and property ownership, 73; and violence, 137–38, 140–41; and white supremacy, 13; whiteness affecting, 136–37; whiteness served by, 30–31, 35–37, 38, 62, 71, 125–26, 143–44. *See also* anti-Blackness
BLM (Black Lives Matter) movement, 148, 151, 153–54
Bonds, Anne, 25
Bonilla-Silva, Eduardo, 3, 171
Booker, Cory, 41
Brown, Wendy, 2
Brown v. Board of Education, 34
Browning, Kellen, 153
Buchanan v. Warley, 58

Burleigh, Billy, 206

Campbell, Karlyn Kohrs, 15
Camus, Renaud, 219
capitalism: market-based, 8–9; meritocracy in, 116; and neoliberalism, 121, 124–25; and property, 55–56; racial, 10, 45, 62, 69, 76–77, 185
Capitalism and Freedom (Friedman and Friedman), 18–19
Carlson, Tucker, 33, 37–38, 204
Carrillo Rowe, Aimee, 197
Caucasians. *See* whites
CDC (Center for Disease Control), 208–9
Chaput, Catherine, 174–75, 181
Charlamagne tha God, 36
Chauvin, Derek, 123
Chávez, Karma R., 82, 112, 148, 160
Chen, Brian X., 153
Cheng, Hsin-I, 102, 103
Child Protective Services, 193, 202–3
children: conspiracy theories about, 200–201; and CPS, 202; and gender variance, 193, 205–6, 210, 213–14; manipulative uses of, 169, 191; race affecting education of, 20–21, 75, 87–88, 96
Chile, 119
China, 147, 161–67
Chinese Americans, 41, 42. *See also* Asian Americans
Chinese Basketball Association, 149
Chinese Exclusion Act, 42, 220
Chronicle of Higher Education, 98–99
cisnormativity: premises of, 204–7; presumptions of, 195, 196, 213–14; as rhetorical economy, 198–204; and whiteness, 197–98, 215
citizenship: and anti-CRT beliefs, 180, 182, 183, 184–85, 186–87; difficulty in obtaining, 100–101; and higher education, 26, 120–21; inconsistency in allowing, 42, 101–5; and power, 105–6; and property ownership, 72, 112–13; and sexual issues, 112, 114; and whiteness, 110–11, 113, 114–15, 119–20
citizenship excess, 101, 103–6, 110–12, 115, 120–21

INDEX • 231

Citizenship Excess (Amaya), 103
Clinton, Hillary, 36–37
Clyburn, Jim, 33, 35
coalition building, 147–49, 152, 160
Collins, Patricia Hill, 132
colorblindness, racial, 3, 4–6, 16, 19–20, 39, 42, 129, 183
Colpean, Michelle, 147–48
Columbia Savings and Loan, 59
communication, 14, 19, 20, 126–32, 193, 197. *See also* rhetoric
Connolly, Nathan, 8
conservatives and conservativism: anti-CRT rhetoric of, 168–69, 180, 189; and populism, 14; rhetoric used by, 46; and SCOTUS nominations, 32, 34, 35, 36–39, 49; and transgender issues, 196, 199–201, 211, 213–14; and white supremacy, 147
Copland, James, 188
Cornyn, John, 49
counterpublics, 170, 171, 177, 182
counterstories, 148, 154, 157, 167
covenants, racial, 25, 55–58; beginnings of, 52–55; language used in, 64–69, 71–73; legacy of, 73–74; resistance to, 58–59, 60; on servants, 69–71; and whiteness, 61–64
COVID-19: changing impacts of, 218–19, 222–23; comparisons with, 208–9; and minority groups, 26, 122–23, 150–51, 193–94, 211, 216–17; relief efforts for, 149; and whiteness, 220–21, 222
CPS (Child Protective Services), 193, 202–3
Cramer, Linsay, 26
Crenshaw, Kimberlé, 5–6, 19–20
critical race theory: actions against, 27, 143, 168–70, 176, 207–8; mischaracterization of, 180–82, 184, 187, 189–90, 200–201; purpose of, 19, 148, 168; and Supreme Court nominations, 48–49. *See also* anti-CRT rhetoric
Cruz, Ted, 40–41, 48–49

Dane County, WI, 78–79, 80
Davis, Angela, 176
Day, Iyko, 61
death, 117–18, 125–26, 130, 139–40, 143

DEI (diversity, equity, and inclusion) policy, 123–25, 176–77, 178–79, 184
Democrats, 36, 38
denizens and denizenship, 101, 104, 111, 115
DeSantis, Ron, 143–44
diasporic listening, 101, 120
differential belonging, 148, 160–61
Dingo, Rebecca, 147–48
discourses, 27–28, 173, 174, 178–79; on gender issues, 174; on racial issues, 3–4, 5–6, 9, 21–22, 147–48, 160–61, 167, 169–73, 178, 186–87; research methods on, 78, 83–84; on school choice, 85, 87, 92–93, 95, 96–97; and SCOTUS nominations, 30, 32. *See also* communication
discursive assemblages, 169–70, 174, 177–78, 181, 187, 190, 192
diversity: and ability, 38; and anti-CRT rhetoric, 176, 184; as commodity, 16; gender, 204, 213, 215; in higher education, 98, 121, 123; and inclusion, 46; and meritocracy, 33, 35, 39; racial, 30–31, 35; in schools, 88–89, 95
diversity, equity, and inclusion policy, 123–25, 176–77, 178–79, 184
Dolmage, Jay, 110, 193, 197
dominant publics, 16, 23, 169–70, 171, 177, 180–83, 185–87, 192
drag, and drag shows, 213–14
Du Bois, W. E. B., 11, 62
Dying of Whiteness (Metzl), 220

economies, affective. *See* affective economies
economies, rhetorical. *See* rhetorical economies
elections, presidential, 32–33, 35, 36–37, 45–46, 80
Elizabeth II (queen), 124
Ellison, Ralph: *Invisible Man*, 71
enthymemes, 204–5, 207
ESPN, 158, 162
exchange: identity in, 18–20, 26; media presentations of, 125–26; in rhetorical economies, 7–8, 10–12, 13, 14–15, 16–17, 18–19
exclusion, 74; activism against, 58–59; of Black people, 130–31; in citizenship, 101–2, 103–4, 115, 120, 182; and diversity, 46;

factors affecting, 174; in gender issues, 197; inclusion affected by, 31; language supporting, 65–66; media presentations of, 133, 137–38; among minority groups, 41–42; and neoliberalism, 177; in property ownership, 30, 34–35, 55–56, 73; in racial issues, 183–84, 188, 197; and spatialization, 62

Fainaru, Steve, 162, 165
Fainaru-Waida, Mark, 162, 165
Fanon, Frantz, 30–31, 44–46
femininity, 195, 212
feminists and feminism, 132, 136, 170, 195, 197
Fertitta, Tilman, 161, 162
fetishism, 30–31, 44–47, 51
Flores, Lisa, 6, 83, 104, 156
Florida, 143–44, 207–8
Floyd, George, 27, 122–23, 179
foster care, 202
Friedman, Milton, 18–19; *Capitalism and Freedom*, 18–19
Friedman, Rose, 18–19; *Capitalism and Freedom*, 18–19
frontlash, 175–76, 180, 181, 184, 186, 191

Gallagher, Charles, 170
Garden City movement, 53
gaze, oppositional, 138–39
Georgetown University, 122
Geter, Keshia Chanel, 211
Ghorayshi, Azeen, 210
Gill-Peterson, Jules, 195
Glaude, Eddie, Jr., 54–55
Global South, 99, 101, 105
Gonda, Jeffrey, 58–59
Gosar, Paul, 211
Gover, Angela R., 150–51
Grant, Madison: *The Passing of the Great Race*, 220
Great Migration, 60
Great Replacement Theory, 204, 210, 219–20
Greenfield (Milwaukee, WI), 71
Grossberg, Lawrence, 7

guilt, 187–91

Hall, Stuart, 3, 13, 174
Halyard, Ardie, 59
Halyard, Wilbur, 59
Handley, Derek, 25
Harden, James, 161
Harlan, John Marshall, 42
Harper, Shannon B., 150–51
Harris, Cheryl: on legal cases, 34–35, 42; on whiteness as advantage, 21, 62; on whiteness as property, 2, 11, 18, 30, 56, 82
Harris, Joshua, 162
Harris, Kamala, 29–30, 46, 47
Harvard University, 40n36
hate, racial, 155, 157, 159, 161
hate and love, 12–13
hate crimes, 145, 151, 153–54
Hayek, F. A.: *The Road to Serfdom*, 21
Hedva, Johanna, 194
hegemony, white, 20, 46, 76–77, 126–27, 144
Hill, Anita, 37
Hong Kong, 161–63
hooks, bell, 141, 184–85, 194; *Black Looks*, 139
HRT (hormone replacement therapy), 205–6
Hsu, V. Jo, 27, 101, 120
Hyler, Zeddie Quitman, 60

identity: in economic exchange, 18–21; in legal issues, 40; racial, 11, 84–87, 88–89, 91, 94; in rhetorical economies, 25; in school choice, 75, 77–78, 79–80; social, 82–84; whiteness as, 56
immigrants, 120–21; actions against, 30, 102–3, 104; child, 202n39; discourse against, 4, 22; in history, 219–20; personal narratives of, 106–10, 111–15, 116–17, 119–20; and sexuality, 114
Immigration Acts, 102, 104
Impossible Subjects (Ngai), 102–3
inclusion: in citizenship, 101–4; and diversity, 45–47; factors affecting, 174; in gender issues, 212; in higher education, 123; media presentations of, 125; among minority groups, 42; political pressure

INDEX • 233

for, 35, 48; in racial issues, 6n22, 26, 39, 176, 177, 183–85, 188; whiteness served by, 31–32, 36–38, 50–51. *See also* DEI (diversity, equity, and inclusion) policy
Indian Americans, 38–39
Indigenous peoples, 52–53, 72–73, 221–22
innocence, cisgender, 197–98, 206–7
Institute for Neuro-immune Medicine, 208
institutionalization, affective, 175, 186–87, 188, 189, 191–92
intersectionality, 19–20, 86, 86n29, 215–17
invisibility, 184–85
Invisible Man (Ellison), 71
Irreversible Damage (Shrier), 201n32

Jackson, Ketanji Brown, 24–25, 30–32, 34–36, 37, 39–41, 40n36, 43–44, 46–50
Jackson, Matthew, 204–5
Jackson, Ronald L., II, 126
Jackson, Sarah, 23
Jacobs, Paul, 163
James, Joy, 136
Jensen, Kelly, 25
Jeremy Lin Foundation, 146, 149
Jim Crow, 63, 68–69, 73, 74, 132
Johnson, Brazil, 211
Johnson, Hillary, 208
Johnson, Paul Elliott, 14, 190–91
Johnson-Reed Immigration Act, 102, 104
Jordan, Michael, 163

Kinefuchi, Etsuke, 156
King, Steve, 219
Kreiss, Daniel, 23
Krizek, Robert L., 82–83, 127–28, 152, 197

Ladson-Billings, Gloria, 16, 17
Langton, Lynn, 150–51
Larson, Kyle, 27
Latinos, 8, 43–44
legislation, on gender issues, 196, 206
legislation, on racial issues, 42, 104, 143–44, 169, 173, 180, 187–90

liberals and liberalism, 31, 32, 36–38, 39–40, 79, 131, 177
Lin, Jeremy, 26–27, 145–49; activism by, 149–50, 151, 154–61, 167; ethnic identity of, 163–67; sports career of, 149–50
LingoAce, 146, 149, 165–66
Lipsitz, George, 11, 82
Lopenzina, Drew, 197
love and hate, 12–13

Madison, WI, 80–81
Madison Metropolitan School District, 81
Maizland, Lindsay, 164
Marriott, David, 44
Martin, Michelle, 155, 157, 159–60
Martin, Trayvon, 203
Marxism, 44–46, 130, 184
masculinity, 14, 146, 183–84, 190–91, 195
mass shootings, 150, 151, 210, 211
Master (film), 26, 125–26, 143–44; and Black assimilation, 132–37; violence in, 138–43; and whiteness, 126, 131–32
McCune, Jeffrey, 139–40, 144
McHendry, Guy, 27
ME (myalgic encephalomyelitis), 208–9, 216
men and masculinity. *See* masculinity
meritocracy, 6n22, 7, 33, 34–35, 39–40, 116
Metzl, Jonathan, 220–21, 222, 223; *Dying of Whiteness*, 220
Miller, Stephen, 200
Milwaukee, WI, 25, 52–55, 53n4, 62–63, 64–67, 71–73
Milwaukee County, WI, 53n4, 54–55, 57–60, 66, 69–70, 73–74
misogynoir, 126, 137
MMSD (Madison Metropolitan School District), 81
model minority myth, 39, 120, 146, 152–53
Moon, Dreama G., 6, 83, 126–27
Moreton-Robinson, Aileen, 68; *The White Possessive*, 61–62, 113
Morey, Daryl, 147, 161
Mott, Shani, 8
Movement for Black Lives, 179, 181

234 • INDEX

multiculturalism, 29–30, 50–51, 176–77, 184
myalgic encephalomyelitis, 208–9, 216

NAACP (National Association for the Advancement of Colored People), 57–60
Nakayama, Thomas, 27–28, 82–83, 126–28, 152, 197
NAREB (National Association of Real Estate Boards), 69, 70
NBA (National Basketball Association), 26, 145–46, 147, 149, 161–65, 167
NBA China, 162
NBA G-League, 145, 155, 157, 163
neoliberalism, 2–3; consequences of, 4–6; and gender issues, 32; in higher education, 98–99, 101, 104, 110, 120–21, 124–26; and individualism, 14–15; media presentations of, 134–35, 136, 140, 143–44; in multiculturalism, 176–77; and publics, 21, 22–23; and racial issues, 6n22, 9, 16–17, 32, 76–77, 128–29, 148, 161, 166; and school choice, 90, 92, 97; terms used in, 8
New Deal, 134
New York Times, 179, 210
Ngai, Mae, 104; *Impossible Subjects*, 102–3
Ngo, Andy, 213–14
nihilism, 129–32, 137, 140, 141, 143–44

Obama, Barack, 39, 125
Olmstead, Frederick Law, 53n4
Olson, Christa: *American Magnitude*, 102
"Oppression Olympics," 147, 151, 152–53
OPT (Optional Training Program), 100, 116–17
optimism, cruel, 101, 104, 115–18
Orbe, Mark P., 156
Ore, Ersula, 183
Other, the, 83, 104, 139, 177, 183, 184, 187, 190, 221–22
Owens, Candace, 211

Pabst, Frederick, 52–53
parasitic movement, 169, 171–72, 175, 181, 191, 192
parasitic publics, 27, 169–72, 185–86, 192

parks, 53, 53n4
Passing of the Great Race, The (Grant), 220
Paxton, Ken, 193, 205–6
pedagogy, emotional, 175, 186–87, 189, 191
Pera, Robert, 162
Peterson, Ky, 203
Plessy v. Ferguson, 5, 34, 42, 49
positionality, black, 31
positionality, white, 86, 87, 90–91, 93–94, 95, 163
power: communicative, 127–29, 131–32, 197; institutional, 187, 189; and publics, 22–23, 170; technology of, 15–16, 109–10; and whiteness, 86–87
progressives, 25, 76–78, 79, 80, 94–95
publics, 16, 21–23, 168–72, 177, 181–83, 184, 186–87, 191–92. See also dominant publics; parasitic publics

racial identity, white, 75–78, 82, 83, 84–85, 88–89
racialization, 10, 12–13, 31–32, 61, 74, 88–89
Ramírez, Catherine, 103–4, 111
Ramos, Salvador, 211
rape, 20, 203
Regents of the University of California v. Bakke, 34–35
Republicans, 38, 201n32, 206, 214
rhetoric, 1–2, 13; anti-trans, 199; of guilt, 190; harmful, 150–51; nominalist, 82–83, 97; as obstruction, 196, 198, 215; purpose of, 63; scholarship in, 6–7, 15–16; of whiteness, 218, 221–22. See also communication
rhetoric, activist: anti-CRT, 168–70, 176, 180–84, 186–91; in ethnic issues, 146–49, 154, 155–58, 161, 164–65, 166, 167
rhetoric, counterpublic, 177, 182
Rhetoric Society Quarterly, 170, 193, 198
rhetorical economies, 1–4, 6–7; and cisnormativity, 198–201; and communication, 15–16, 17, 18–19, 20, 21–22; as exchange, 7–8, 10–12, 13–15, 16–17, 18–19; and immigrants, 106–8; media presentations of, 137–38; as resources, 10–11, 14, 17–18, 20–21, 22; and scholarship, 15–16, 23; as value, 7–9, 10–12, 13, 14–15, 17–18, 22–23; and whiteness, 31, 60, 161–67, 175, 191

Richmond, Martasia, 211
Road to Serfdom, The (Hayek), 21
Roberts, Dorothy, 202
Robinson, Cedric, 9–10, 45
Roe v. Wade, 196, 211
Roediger, David, 11
Roosevelt, Franklin Delano, 134
Rufo, Chris, 168, 180, 181–82, 184, 189, 201
ruptures, affective, 176, 178, 179, 181, 185–86

"SAFE" Act, 206
Sanders, Bernie, 32–33
school choice, 25, 75–78, 81, 97; options in, 81n19; political views influencing, 94; privilege in, 92–93; racial diversity influencing, 88–89; and white flight, 94–95; and whiteness, 89–90, 91
SCOTUS (Supreme Court of the United States): confirmation hearings for, 48–49; nominations to, 29, 30, 33; opinions of, 207–8; overturning by, 211; and racial issues, 5, 23, 39–40, 43, 46–47; recusals in, 40n36
segregation: acknowledgement of, 122; and anti-CRT rhetoric, 186, 191; laws affecting, 23, 34, 42, 58; legacy of, 28; and property ownership, 56, 62–64, 69, 70, 73–74; in schools, 20, 76, 78, 191; in urban areas, 80–81; white supremacy supporting, 68
Self, Rico, 26
self-reflexivity, 25, 77–78; levels of, 83–84; and school spaces, 88–92; and whites, 84–88, 92–96
Semenya, Caster, 206
September 11, 2001, attacks, 113–14
servants, Black, 54, 64–65, 69–71, 72, 132–33, 138–39
Shapiro, Ilya, 38–40, 41
Shelley v. Kramer, 58–59
shootings, 150, 151, 210, 211
Shrier, Abigail, 200–201; *Irreversible Damage,* 201n32
Sick Woman Theory, 194
silence, rhetorical, 83, 84–85, 197–98
1619 Project, The, 143, 177–79

slavery: abolition of, 42; acknowledgement of, 122; allusions to, 49–50; associations with, 14; and Black ontology, 130–31; and Blackness, 136; and citizenship, 102; comparisons with, 41–42; exploitation in, 132; and gaze, 139; legacy of, 34, 38, 43, 63, 129–30, 138, 177–78; and property ownership, 61, 72; reactions to, 181–82; in rhetoric, 46
"slow death," 117–18
Sotomayor, Sonia, 43–44, 46–47
South Dakota, laws of, 207
Spencer, Richard, 219
sports, 26–27, 166, 214
Srinivasan, Sri, 31, 38–40
Stand Your Ground laws, 203
standpoints, 148, 156–61
"Still I Rise" (Angelou), 49–50
Stop Asian Hate Movement, 147, 148, 151, 153–54, 155, 167
Stop WOKE Act, 143
storytelling, 16, 27, 194–95
students, international, 25–26, 98–101, 103–4, 113–14, 119, 121
Students for Fair Admissions, 40
Students for Fair Admissions vs. Harvard, 33
Sugino, Corinne, 24–25
suicide, 143, 209
Supreme Court of the United States. *See* SCOTUS (Supreme Court of the United States)
SYG (Stand Your Ground) laws, 203

Taiwan, 164–65, 166
Taiwanese Americans, 26, 145, 147, 148, 149, 159, 163–67
Tan, Anson, 99
Taylor, Breonna, 179
temporal existence, 101, 105–11
Texas, 193–94, 198, 211
Thomas, Clarence, 37
time, 105–11
transgender people: actions against, 27, 173–74, 193–95, 211–15; detransitions by, 206–7, 210; media presentations of, 203–4; misconceptions about, 199–201, 201n32,

205–7; as overlooked minority, 197–98; and racial issues, 196, 203–4
transphobia, 195–96, 198–99, 204–5, 210
tropes, 12, 13, 39, 42, 44, 50, 135, 144, 147, 191
Trump, Donald, 22, 29–30, 50–51, 150–51, 221, 222

"Unite the Right," 219
University of Minnesota, 113
US Supreme Court. *See* SCOTUS (Supreme Court of the United States)
USCIS (United States Citizenship and Immigration Services), 106–7

Vargas, João Costa, 136
Vats, Anjali, 3–4
violence: coalition building against, 157, 160–61; gendered, 37; iconography influencing, 36; and inclusion, 32, 37; institutionalized, 30; and invisibility, 184–85; legal language obscuring, 64–65; media presentations of, 126, 136–38, 139–40, 141, 142, 143; among minority groups, 153–54, 155–56; normalization of, 183; and property ownership, 70, 73; rhetoric encouraging, 150–51; and whiteness, 34, 44–45, 50, 131–32
visas, and visa system, 99–101, 106–9, 110, 112–15, 116–17
voice, in agency, 15–16

Warren, Calvin, 14n51, 130, 140
Washington Boulevard (Milwaukee, WI), 53
Washington Highlands (Milwaukee, WI), covenants of, 53–55, 70
Watts, Eric King, 13, 15–16, 183–84
Wauwatosa, WI, 52–53, 55, 60, 66, 69–70
Weaver, Vesla M., 175, 180
white flight, 94–95
white nationalism, 17, 30, 170–71, 219–20
White Possessive, The (Moreton-Robinson), 61–62, 113
"White Reconstruction," 169, 191
white supremacy, 2–3, 177; in anti-CRT rhetoric, 168; associations with, 13; challenges to, 157; enthymeme for, 204–5; forms of, 5; in higher education, 103, 104; media presentations of, 123, 141, 143; murders encouraged by, 153, 210–11; and publics, 21–23; in racial covenants, 54–56, 61, 64, 67, 69–74; and servants, 69–71; in sports, 147, 152, 155–56; validation of, 16–17; and whiteness, 185; and women's issues, 196, 199–200

Whitefish Bay (Milwaukee, WI), 66–67, 68
whiteness, 1–2, 50–51, 218; activism counteracting, 156–57, 159–60, 161; and agency, 16–18; and anti-CRT rhetoric, 168–70, 178, 181–82, 184–88; in communication, 126–32; and economics, 9–15, 24–28; and fetishism, 44–47; in higher education, 101, 104, 110–12, 113, 114, 115, 118, 120–21, 124–25; and identity, 20–21, 77–78, 82–83, 84–90, 91–92, 96–97; in international relations, 164; language supporting, 64–66, 71–73; and migrant children, 202n39; and neoliberalism, 3–7; as property, 33–34, 54–57, 73–74; property as, 61–64; and publics, 22–23; and racial minorities, 39–40, 41–42, 66–69; as self-serving, 6n22, 30–32, 34–38; and servanthood, 69–71; and sexuality, 197–98, 200–201, 213, 215; in sports, 146–49, 152–54, 163, 167; stereotypes about, 8; threats to, 219–25
whiteness, in media: and Black labor, 132–37; and higher education, 125–26, 143–44; and violence, 137–43
whiteness, rhetorical economy of, 167; and competitive suffering, 146–47, 152–54, 159–61; globality of, 147–49, 161–67; political neutrality in, 166–67; resistance to, 155–57
whites: advantages for, 20–21; and education, 75–78, 88–92; and guilt, 189–90; and male dominance, 183; and masculinity, 190–91; and property, 3, 33–34, 58, 61–64, 73–74; racial habitus of, 171; racial identity of, 84–88, 92–96; reactions of, to violence, 179–80; social identity of, 82–84

Whitnall, Charles, 53n4
Wilderson, Frank B., 130–31, 138
Williams, Raymond, 172–73
women, AAPI, 150, 151
women, Black: and intersectionality, 86n29; media presentations of, 26, 125–26, 131–36, 138–43; in positions of power, 29–30;

as SCOTUS nominees, 29–35, 38–41, 43–44, 48, 50; stereotypes about, 195–96
women, cisgender, 195–96, 208, 212
women, Latina, 43–44
women, transgender, 211–12
women, white, 86, 87, 140–43, 199–200, 212

Yam, Shui-yin Sharon, 180–81, 182, 186–87

Zimmerman, George, 203

www.ingramcontent.com/pod-product-compliance
Lightning Source LLC
Chambersburg PA
CBHW020123240426
43673CB00038B/576